# Literacy Links

### Practical Strategies to Develop the
### Emergent Literacy At-Risk Children Need

## Laura Robb

Foreword by Bobbi Fisher

Preface by Steven Kellogg

HEINEMANN
Portsmouth, NH

KH

**Heinemann**
A division of Reed Elsevier Inc.
361 Hanover Street
Portsmouth, NH 03801-3912
www.heinemann.com

*Offices and agents throughout the world*

© 2003 by Laura Robb

The author and publisher wish to thank those who have generously given permission to reprint borrowed material:

"Alphabet Recognition Sheet" and "Student Alphabet Chart" are reprinted from *Guided Reading: Making It Work* by Mary Schulman and Carleen Payne. Reprinted by permission of Scholastic Professional Books.

**Library of Congress Cataloging-in-Publication Data**
Robb, Laura.
    Literacy links : practical strategies to develop the emergent literacy
at-risk children need / Laura Robb ; foreword by Bobbi Fisher ; preface
by Steven Kellogg.
        p. cm.
Includes bibliographical references and index.
ISBN 0-325-00442-0 (alk. paper)
1. Children with social disabilities—Education (Preschool)—United
States.   2. Language arts (Preschool)—United States.   I. Title.

LC4085.R63 2003
372.6—dc21                                                    2002155231

EDITOR: *Danny Miller*
PRODUCTION SERVICE: *Denise Botelho*
PRODUCTION COORDINATOR: *Vicki Kasabian*
COVER DESIGN: *Catherine Hawkes, Cat & Mouse*
COVER PHOTOGRAPH: *Bonnie Forstrum Jacobs*
TYPESETTER: *TechBooks, Inc.*
MANUFACTURING: *Steve Bernier*

Printed in the United States of America on acid-free paper
07   06   05   04          RRD          2   3   4   5

11/22/04

With the greatest respect for five women of courage
who built programs that met the needs of all
children and reached all learners:

Terri Auckland
Jane Rea Gaidos
Connie Fauber
Nancy Reedy
Lisa Tusing

# Contents

# Foreword

Bobbi Fisher

I first got to know Laura Robb when she responded to an email I sent out asking teachers how they balance their personal and professional lives. In response to the question, "When are the times that you feel the most joy in our teaching?" Laura wrote:

> When I'm with the children and I've turned the reading and writing over to them and I'm circulating and having on-the-run conferences—then I feel great joy! The joy comes from prethinking and preparing and watching and listening to my students. I also experience great joy when I team-teach. The planning and the fugue-like interchange of two people in a room is exhilarating and satisfying.

In *Literacy Links* Laura invites us into several pre-kindergarten and kindergarten classrooms and describes in detail ways to create an exhilarating and satisfying reading and writing program. We can imagine Laura and the team of teachers with whom she collaborated, preparing, watching, listening, circulating, and teaching.

When my first grandchild was born, my son-in-law commented on how lucky Colin was to be born into a family that would read thousands of stories to him before he started kindergarten. Due to the current standards and testing frenzy, all children are expected to perform at the same literacy rate after a very short time at school. Colin would have an advantage over children who hadn't been read to, and would be able to take the literacy activities in stride, while many of his peers, without the benefits of years of hearing bedtime stories in a relaxed home environment, would be struggling to catch up.

Those of you reading this book come from literate environments and have surely read to your children, grandchildren, nieces, nephews, and the children of your friends. Together you have probably engaged in rich conversations, played word games, participated in writing and drawing experiences, gone to museums, explored historical sites, and taken family field trips to local places of interest. You know how important early literacy experiences are for success in school, and yet many of the students you teach have not had the literacy-building experiences that are the foundation for learning to read and write.

In *Literacy Links: Practical Strategies to Develop the Emergent Literacy At-Risk Children Need* Laura addresses the gap between children who come to school with a strong literacy set and those who do not. Concerned that proponents of high-stakes testing require that every child must reach the same benchmark at the end of kindergarten, and that every child learn at the same rate from a standardized, systematic set of lessons, Laura offers "a program that reconstructs the early literacy experiences children lack."

What really delights me about this book is that it describes emergent literacy practice that is appropriate for *all* children. Laura positions "family storybook reading, the conversations with adults about books, and the everyday experiences that develop children's knowledge of their world" at the center of any pre-kindergarten or kindergarten program. *Literacy Links* is a thoroughly comprehensive and practical book about literacy for young children, offering strategy after strategy to help young learners in their literacy development. Laura always addresses the best practice but never shies away from controversial topics such as standards and testing, systematic phonics, letter of the week, and writing as "a process, not a prompt."

I have chosen to highlight each chapter because I want teachers and administrators to appreciate the depth and breadth that makes this book an essential resource for emergent literacy in pre-kindergarten and kindergarten classrooms.

In Chapter 1, Laura describes the Literacy Links program that she, in collaboration with administrators and classroom teachers, developed to meet the needs of their school population. For example, they collectively decided on the following components for a Literacy Links kindergarten: simulating family storybook reading, shared writing, writing workshop, conversations, everyday experiences, shared reading, play, word walls, word study, and centers, each of which are described in this chapter and discussed in detail throughout the book.

Teachers and administrators of young children need to have a firm theoretical understanding of emergent literacy if they are serious about advocating for and providing developmentally appropriate practice. Chapter 2, "An Overview of Emergent Literacy," discusses the theories of researchers such as Clay, Graves, Heath, Holdaway, Teale and Sulzby, Wells, and Vygotsky, and weaves them together with stories of current practice of Laura's collaborating teachers. This gem of a chapter I plan to share with every teacher I know, and I heartily suggest that teachers and administrators get it into the hands of colleagues, parents, and policy-makers.

Chapter 3, "Planning for and Organizing the Year," offers practical recommendations for individual teachers as they start the new school year, and describes ways to set up a Literacy Links program. In addressing half- and full-day schedules and room arrangement, Laura relates her suggestions to the goal of providing optimal opportunities for emergent readers.

Suggestions for choosing children for an early intervention program are the topic for discussion in Chapter 4. Included is a comprehensive array of formal and informal assessment strategies that would be useful for assessing the emergent literacy of children in any pre-kindergarten or kindergarten classroom. Anecdotal models and check sheets are provided for the formal and informal assessment of book knowledge, concepts of print, oral language fluency, letter knowledge, and letter/sound knowledge. There is also a chart of activities that students can work on independently to strengthen these skills—welcome help for any teacher as he or she starts the year.

In Chapter 5, "Constructing a Balanced Read-Aloud Program," Laura places reading aloud at the center, solidifying the case for family storybook reading at school. She advocates four or five read-aloud sessions a day for small groups of children as a way for them to make significant gains in letter/sound relationships, sight words, book knowledge, vocabulary development, and comprehension. She details ways to conduct interactive read-alouds, and provides focused strategies, such as inferring with pictures, and rereading to recall details. Drawing on the work of Don Holdaway, Laura presents suggestions for shared reading and reading aloud with big books.

Chapter 6 is a handbook for teachers interested in developing an authentic, illuminating, and vigorous writing program to support children's literacy development. Laura supports the notion that reading and writing go hand-in-hand and should be learned in concert.

In Chapter 7, "Word Play, Pretend Play, and Centers," Laura shows how these strategies enrich the reading and writing that we have read about in the previous chapters. Word play is not a prerequisite to reading and writing, but it develops out of the experiences of hearing and discussing stories and of participating in the process of authentic and meaningful writing. Pretend play, often referred to as the "children's work," enhances the imagination, oral language, and reading and writing development of young children. It is the place where, according to Don Holdaway, children practice or role-play what they have learned from the demonstrations of adults, thus making the learning their own. Centers, which often include pretend play, also consist of areas such as writing, book making, listening, science, math, and thematic play. This chapter shows how literacy comes alive throughout the classroom.

Laura knows it can be a challenge to involve families and community members in authentic literacy development for young children, and in Chapter 8 she offers a wide choice of practical approaches for connecting teachers and families and the community and the school.

A sensible and workable evaluation process for early literacy programs as well as for individual children is presented in Chapter 9, "Evaluation and Beyond." Laura Robb advocates for an array of evaluation tools, such as observational notes, reflections on student writing, and checklists, all of which can be used to help teachers continue to work with their students, and to help the team make changes and improvements in the program. In addition, Laura relates the authentic evaluation to her state standards and guidelines.

*Literacy Links* is a hopeful book. Laura shows us ways to create a literacy program for pre-kindergarten and kindergarten children, which builds upon the foundation of family reading. She advocates for all the children in our classroom, those who come to school with a rich literacy set and those who arrive eager to enter a world of reading and writing and to hear their first story.

# Preface
## Building Creative Partnerships
### Steven Kellogg

In a celebrated poem by Robert Frost called "A Tuft of Flowers," a worker mentally sends a message to a colleague who has labored earlier that day on the same task with which the narrator is concerned, and he says: "Men work together, I told him from the heart, whether they work together or apart." And that's the way we work, as librarians and teachers of reading on the one hand, and authors and illustrators on the other. We are colleagues, co-conspirators who put our energies separately, but together, into the very important and exciting work of turning kids onto books, giving them a passion for their written and spoken language, and opening them up to its vast communicative and artistic range.

As creative partners, we depend on each other to do our work with care and sensitivity. You rightfully expect authors and illustrators to put into your hands books whose words and images can be effective tools for teaching, inspiring, and moving the children in your care. Happily, that expectation is being validated by the continuing surge of interest in literature-based reading programs throughout the country. It seems to be fueled by the conviction that children *do* become excited about stories and pictures that capture their imaginations. Like all of us, they are drawn to works that communicate in the language of feeling, which is the way that elusive thing called art so effectively reaches us. And the communicative power of art, as it is utilized in its varied means of creative expression (from architecture to painting to literature to drama), has been a compelling outlet for every culture and civilization since man's beginnings.

Storytelling is perhaps the oldest art form. Early storytellers used their imaginative powers and their skill as communicators to demystify natural phenomena by incorporating them into ballads and myths. These stories became part of an oral tradition that fostered individual confidence and promoted trust and cooperation within the group. Elders used these traditional stories to inform young people and to establish a bond and a continuity between the generations. Many of these ancient stories from myriad of different cultures have survived and made their way into print. Today they continue to fascinate us with their beauty, their profound insight, and their dramatic richness.

Access to stories in books encouraged a tradition of reading aloud within families that flourished until recently when it was threatened by the introduction of television and other electronic media into our culture. However, it has since become clear that these sources for stories do not generate the benefits that are derived from the reading experience when an adult shares a book with a child.

I recall, with deep gratitude, the relatives who were sensitive and generous enough to give me books as gifts when I was a child, and to share both the books and themselves in magical read-aloud sessions. At such times the book acts as a bridge between two laps, uniting the reader and the audience. The reading adult's voice unlocks the magic of the story, inviting the child to enter the lives of characters and to explore the landscapes that are delineated in the illustrations. There is a special warm and personal quality to the participation in that shared experience that is not duplicated while seated passively in front of a television set in a darkened room. And it is important for all of us who love children and books to continually emphasize the benefits of reading aloud. Fortunately, today many parents are aware of these benefits, and they incorporate the time for sharing books with their preschool children into the daily family schedule. Their children arrive in kindergarten with a well-developed enthusiasm for books and eager to share stories of their own. Skilled teachers channel that eagerness into an introduction to the writing process, confirming for the children that they are *authors* just like the writers who create the books they enjoy. Then teachers proceed to give them the tools they need to communicate their stories with eloquence, accuracy, and confidence.

Of great concern are those children who reach school without having had the experience of being read to in a warm and cuddly setting. They do not bring to the classroom a well-established, loving relationship with books that the teacher can build on. It is a challenge to make up for this, and the teacher must summon auxiliary resources of creativity, enthusiasm, expertise, and love! The teacher must bring the children and books together with a sensitive understanding of each child and with a knowledge of, and a quality of excitement about each individual book.

If the book is recommended, shared, and read aloud as if the teacher were presenting it as a treasured gift, then the chances are much greater that the child will respond to that generosity and attention, and to the book itself. Long afterward, the teacher will be gratefully remembered as being part of the creative vitality of that book as surely as if his or her name were printed on the cover as a colleague, a co-conspirator, and a creative partner of the author.

As an illustrator and an author of children's books, I fervently hope that I will be fortunate enough to have such enlightened and dedicated teachers sharing my books with their students. Indeed, I wish the same for all authors, which presents a challenge for teachers who must preside over a smorgasbord of books that deal

with many facets of the human experience. The books should present the opportunity to explore a great range of emotions exposing children to stories and images
that inspire laughter, tears, shivery-spooky feelings, flashes of glowing, loving
warmth, fascinating information, and poignant insight. Young readers would be
acquainted with the creative approaches of many different authors and illustrators
so that each can find the ones that speak to him or her with particular clarity,
illuminating the pathways toward the truth and fulfillment that they are seeking.

# Acknowledgments

It's interesting that one question posed to me by Nancy Lee, principal of Quarles Elementary School, turned my attention from middle school reading to early literacy. Questions are powerful because they stimulate inquiry, thought, reflection, and ultimately collaboration. Questions raised about children as they learned and played helped me and teachers recognize that one program can not meet the needs of individual children. We turned our reflective energy to walking alternate pathways.

And our inquiries led to the development of a program called Literacy Links—a program that offers hope to children, teachers, and families for developing emergent literacy among all children. The teachers, teaching assistants, and administrators who helped me develop Literacy Links were risk-takers whose primary goal was to construct a responsive and evolving program that would continually meet the needs of every child.

My thanks to Nancy Lee, the kindergarten teachers, and teaching assistants at Quarles Elementary School in Winchester, Virginia. Their support and continual communication were the key to helping young children learn. I owe countless thanks to Nancy Reedy, teaching assistant and reading tutor at Quarles Elementary. Her deep belief in Literacy Links resulted in an outstanding summer program which she headed.

How I appreciate the imagination and innovative thinking of Jane Rea Gaidos who made the dream of two all-day Literacy Links kindergartens and a transition first grade at Robinson Elementary School in Woodstock, Virginia a reality. Her honest philosophical belief became the program's beacon: If what we are doing is not working for a group of children or one child, then we must find anouther way to support learning.

Many thanks to Connie Fauber, who became principel of Robinson after Jane retired Connie's endless hard work and dedication to finding ways to obtain the ongoing study teachers needed enabled us all to grow as professionals and learners. For their risk-taking, for their belief that every child is unique, for their role in developing the Literacy Links program, my deepest thanks go to Terri Auckland and Lisa Tusing. Thanks also go to Maryann Sherry and Pamela Bradfield, Bright Star teachers at Robinson.

To Deena Baker, my gratitude for inviting me into her classroom at Virginia Avenue/Charlotte DeHart School in Winchester, Virginia. From that invitation emerged a Literacy Links program for small numbers of at-risk children in heterogeneously grouped classes. Thanks as well go to Deena's principal, Diane Carpenter, who had the vision to make positive changes at her school. My work at Virginia Avenue was continually enhanced by conversations and collaborations with reading specialist, Betty S. Wymer, and lead teacher, Kathy Wetsel.

I am grateful to Danielle Waters, Head Start teacher at Keister Elementary School in Harrisonburg, Virginia, for sharing her classroom with me for five years. How much we learned as we journeyed together and with the children.

Special thanks go to Danny Miller, my editor at Heinemann. Always there for me, Danny fielded many telephone calls and quickly responded to my email queries. His great sense of humor as well as his guidance and expert feedback has shaped this book.

Finally, I want to thank my husband, Lloyd, who patiently read my chapters from raw, first drafts to final drafts. His comments and questions were invaluable.

# Introduction

It's August; one week before school begins. On a rug in a kindergarten classroom is a basket filled with picture books—classic favorites such as *The Three Little Pigs*, *The House That Jack Built*, and *The Gingerbread Man*. Sitting on the rug with me is five-year-old Richard (pseudonym). I invite Richard to choose a book. He stares at the rug and does nothing. I wait. No reaction. Then I pick a book, open it, slowly turn the pages, and say: "Wow! Look at the gingerbread man running away. I wonder if he'll get caught." I hand the open book to Richard. Without looking, he tosses the book onto the rug, turns his back, and crawls toward a crate of toy trucks and cars.

Two weeks later, Richard and twenty-three other kindergartners sit on a rug listening to their teacher read aloud *Over in the Meadow* by Leo Lionni. Richard, legs crossed, rocks back and forth. Next, Richard pokes the head of a boy until the child complains, "Richard's poking me." After two warnings from the teacher, Richard sits in the time-out chair, far from the shared reading rug. Again and again, Richard disrupts shared reading. Repeated visits to the time-out chair don't improve Richard's listening behavior. In fact, according to his teacher, Richard's behavior worsens. He insists, "I don't want to sit on the rug." He pushes in line; he refuses to write during writing workshop; he continually talks out of turn; he has angry outbursts when his teacher insists Richard join an activity.

All over our country, students like Richard arrive at school prepared and wanting to learn (Clay 1998), yet unprepared to learn from state-mandated curricula that assume children have a literacy background that includes family storybook reading, countless opportunities to write and talk to an adult or caregiver about books and play, and experiences that build basic background knowledge such as shopping for groceries, baking cookies, setting the table, depositing money at the bank, and mailing letters at the post office. Put four to eight Richards in a kindergarten class, and one teacher with a group of twenty-four students experiences frustration daily. Punishments are ineffective and only help Richard reinforce and build a negative image of his ability to learn and cooperate in a small group or with the entire class. Unable to work quietly and focus on a task independently while the teacher meets with others, Richard's group continually needs teacher support and learning experiences that meet their unique needs. However, that kind of support is not available in this class setting.

Developing emergent literacy is important for all children. When our society reaches this goal, children will arrive at school with a background of rich conversations with adults, with varied experiences at home and in the community, having heard thousands of books and oral stories, and having played word games that develop their ability to hear letter/sound relationships. However, when children have been deprived of literacy-building experiences, is it fair to ask children to start school learning the same way as those with a rich reading and writing background?

This book responds to that question by introducing a program called Literacy Links, a program that reconstructs the early literacy experiences children lack. The goal of the Literacy Links program is to provide the background knowledge at-risk children and all children need to succeed at learning in classrooms where a required curriculum that emphasizes explicit phonics, oral language games that develop phonemic awareness, and memorizing the Dolch High-Frequency Sight Word List dominates instruction. A primary goal of mandated curricula is for students to pass high-stakes testing.

The expectations of high-stakes testing is that every child will reach a specific benchmark by the end of kindergarten—a benchmark that indicates that the child is ready for first grade. Based on the belief that all children arrive at school with rich literacy backgrounds, high-stakes testing also assumes that all children learn at the same rate from a standardized set of lessons.

The research of Allington (2000), Clay (1998), and Wells (1986), supports an opposing view: children's experiences, the knowledge they bring to school, and their ability to learn from specific lessons differs widely. For these reasons, high-stakes testing punishes children, teachers, and schools, especially when state departments of education use these tests to deny a school accreditation or to fire principals and teachers.

# 1

# Changing the Landscape for Literacy-Deprived Learners

*Reading problems are very difficult to fix but very easy to prevent.*
Mem Fox, *Reading Magic* (2001, 13)

The day Nancy Lee, principal of Quarles Elementary School in Winchester, Virginia, invited me into her office to discuss her kindergarten population, my thinking about helping young children deprived of rich literacy experiences changed. I traveled from believing class groupings should always be heterogeneous to considering short-term homogeneous grouping for children who cannot keep up and experience success within a prescribed curriculum.

At that point in the school year, I was in my second week of facilitating a study group with kindergarten and first grade teachers at Quarles. During and after our meetings, I heard rumblings from teachers:

"More than half my class doesn't know the alphabet."
"I have four children who can't write their names!"
"Some of my students won't sit still when I read stories."
"All I get is angry scrawls on paper during writing workshop."

1

Nancy invited me into her office and pulled up a chair next to mine. "What do we do, Laura," Nancy asked, "with children who don't know what a book is?"

"How did you determine that?"

"When a teacher handed a child a book, the youngster didn't know what to do with it. Some held the book upside down, others tossed it onto the floor, and some flipped through pages, then put the book aside. When invited, these children were unable to show the front cover of a book, to point to the part that tells the story, to point to a word, or a space between words. In class these children can't sit still. They're restless and talk or crawl away from the group during storybook reading and shared reading. Some might have emotional problems or attention difficulties," continued Nancy. "We'll sort that out. The bottom line is that most of these children need more than our kindergarten program can deliver."

The next day, I visited three kindergarten classes. Again and again, the same boys and girls disrupted the class with behaviors such as talking out of turn, pushing another child, taking a toy from a classmate during free play time, throwing a doll across the room, talking loudly when the teacher read a book. Even though teachers' voices were kind and gentle, saying things such as, "Please listen. We need your help," and "Let me show you how to hold that doll," I felt uneasy. What troubled me deeply was the daily attention to negative behaviors these children received from teachers who obviously were frustrated coping with twenty-four kindergarten children with widely diverse needs. Often, the instructional assistant would take a child aside.

Nancy Reedy, instructional assistant, sits on a chair with a child who has punched a classmate and interrupted shared reading three times with these questions and statements: "Know what my daddy did last night? I'm thirsty. I want a drink. I got in trouble on the bus." Here's the conversation that I noted on my visit.

NR: Is something bothering you that you can tell me?
CHILD: [No answer.]
NR: Can you tell me why you hit Kenny?
CHILD: [Shrugs shoulders and bends head down.]
NR: Do you want to tell me what happened on the bus?
CHILD: I got up and walked.
NR: You could get hurt if the bus stopped suddenly.
CHILD: Don't care.
NR: Let's sit together and listen to the rest of the story. [Nancy takes his hand, the child reluctantly walks with Nancy and both sit on the rug.]

When Nancy Reedy and I talk during recess, she astutely observes, "It's so hard for these kids who don't know much about books and listening to talk to me about their behavior. They had few experiences with sitting and listening to draw upon. In the children's minds, their behavior seems fine, so they become silent and sullen. They all need me to sit with them and help them. How can I?"

On my way out of Quarles that day, I poke my head in Nancy Lee's office and say, "Give me a few days to think about this and do some research." As I drive home, ideas and phrases of Gordon Wells (1986), Denny Taylor and Dorothy Strickland (1986) and Bernice Cullinan (1992) zoom and zigzag around my mind. Their research would back up part of the solution I would offer: reconstruct family storybook reading, the conversations with adults about books, and the everyday experiences that develop children's knowledge of their world.

## What Research Says About Reading, Talking, and Writing

According to the longitudinal "Children Learning to Read" project in Bristol, England, directed by Gordon Wells, success in reading and writing at school depends on children's home literacy experiences (1986). Wells and his researchers observed children from shortly after their first birthday until they were ten years old. By placing a microphone and a radio transmitter on each child, researchers, at random times each day, tuned into the interactions between adults and children, children and siblings, and children and friends. Wells discovered that success in school did not depend on children's socioeconomic status, but on the number of stories parents read aloud, the amount of oral storytelling, and the meaningful conversations between adult and child. Wells concludes from the data collected that "the single most important factor in accounting for the differences between children in their subsequent achievement was how much they understood about literacy on entry to school" (165). Other factors that contributed to children's success in school were the amount of help parents gave with homework, studying for tests, and encouraging reading, as well as parents modeling literate behaviors that clearly showed they valued reading, writing, and conversation.

Denny Taylor and Dorothy Strickland (1986) in *Family Storybook Reading* support Wells' emphasis on sharing stories at home by stressing the importance of reading aloud to a young child's literacy development. By offering written transcriptions of parents reading aloud to their children, the authors show that family storybook reading is much more than the child listening to a story. From hearing and interacting with thousands of books, children come to understand the structure of narrative, nonfiction, and poetry and build their knowledge of these genres. Children use the stories they've heard to create their own oral texts, by dramatizing favorite parts and imagining they have become beloved characters (Coles 1989, Heath 1983). In addition, children enlarge their vocabulary, discuss pictures and text, make predictions, raise questions, and have countless opportunities to hear the language patterns in fine literature—patterns that differ widely from conversations with peers, siblings, and adults as well as talk on the television.

Bernice Cullinan, in her book *Read to Me: Raising Kids Who Love to Read* (1992, 2000), addresses the affective nature of reading aloud and storytelling. Cuddled under a parent's loving arms, a child becomes the focus of the parent's attention and receives these emotional messages:

- ❏ You're important to me.
- ❏ I love spending time with you.
- ❏ It's great to read aloud because we're together.
- ❏ I love showing you what's important to me.
- ❏ I want to hear what you have to say about the book.
- ❏ I want to give you wonderful memories to share with others.

These moments are magical and forever imprinted in children's memories (Fox 2001). When my brother Gene's first grandson was two, Gene called me on the telephone and said, "Remember when dad told us the story about the lions in Africa? Well, I just told it to Jake. When I told it," my brother said, "I felt so close to dad—like he was there coaching me. Jake loved being the chief lion photographer and asked me to tell it again and again."

That telephone call reclaimed treasured memories of Sunday mornings in a tiny three-room apartment in New York City. My parents slept in the living room. On Sundays, my brother and I played "sailing the ocean" in his bed, waiting for our father to shout, "You can come in now!" While mom fixed breakfast in the cramped kitchen, my brother and I each curled next to daddy and listened to him tell stories about his life in Poland, how he left home when he was nine years old to become an apprentice to a shoemaker in Crakow, and his ride to America in the bowels of a steamship.

However, the story my brother and I repeatedly asked for, the one my brother so clearly recalled, was about searching for lions in Africa. Though parts of the plot continually changed, the constant story element was that my brother and I were the chief lion photographers. It became our favorite because we were the protagonists living and learning about an exotic country far away from the Bronx. Equally memorable were the cuddles and assuring pats that my father generously dished out.

## Stories Define Our Humanity

Family stories and storybook reading are the legacy that bind us to our past, enable us to understand the present, and support predicting the future. Mexican poet, Alberto Blanco in *The Desert Mermaid* (1992), an original folk tale expresses his belief that without stories, people can not survive. The mermaid, who lives on an oasis in the Sonora Desert, learns that her people are disappearing because they have forgotten the songs and stories of their ancestors. The lonely mermaid embarks on an epic journey in search of these lost songs and stories. The discovery of her people's melodies and tales returns the mermaid to the roots of her people and leads her to the sea where she finds thousands of other mermaids. There, in the ocean, stories help her discover who she is and where she belongs.

Like the mermaid, stories help children survive and make sense of their world. Books read aloud allow children to experience the world and the universe at home or in school. Children who arrive at school, story and conversation deprived, don't develop the listening-and-sitting-still-stamina that read-alouds build (Campbell 2001, Fox 2001, Santman 2002). Asked to participate in listening, talking, and writing experiences that are not part of their background knowledge frustrates children and often results in disruptive behaviors that teachers continually correct. The result? Children's self-confidence plummets. Frustration and anxiety increase when children have no experiences that let them connect to the teacher's lessons.

Take five-year-old Justin who is in the all-day Head Start program at Keister Elementary in Harrisonburg, Virginia. Each month I meet with Justin's teacher, Danielle Waters, to observe the children and discuss their progress. Five-year-old Justin is part of a group of 10 four- and five-year-olds. With my support, Danielle abandoned skills sheets, coloring pictures, and memorizing the alphabet. Instead, Danielle and her assistant took turns reading aloud several times a day. Cuddled on each side of an adult were two children, for the goal was to simulate family storybook reading. Each day children also engaged in writing workshop.

At first Justin, like several others, did not want to write during workshop; Danielle never made them write. Like Justin, several throw their marker pens and crayons and crumple their paper. Before workshop, Danielle patiently models talking about what she might write. Then, on chart paper, she draws a picture and writes a few words about it. Justin's first attempts at writing have no form. Intensely, Justin presses crayon to paper and quickly scrawls (Figure 1–1). Random scrawling continues until December when Justin dictates his first sentence for a drawing (Figure 1–2): "What could you do when you are afraid?" By the end of the year, Justin's writing imitates the print in books he now pretend-reads during sustained silent reading (Figure 1–3).

In Danielle's class, Justin had the gift of time without the pressure of learning the alphabet, matching letters to sounds, learning sight words, and listening to whole-group read-alouds, playing phonemic awareness games—literate experiences that did not match the background Justin brought to school. It took a year and for some children two years, to develop the literacy knowledge needed to make meaning in a classroom where the curriculum assumed children had a rich literacy background.

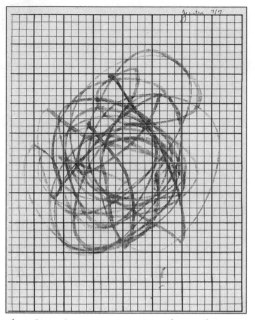

**Figure 1–1.** In September, Justin's writing consists of scrawls.

**Figure 1–2.** By December, Justin dictates his first sentence.

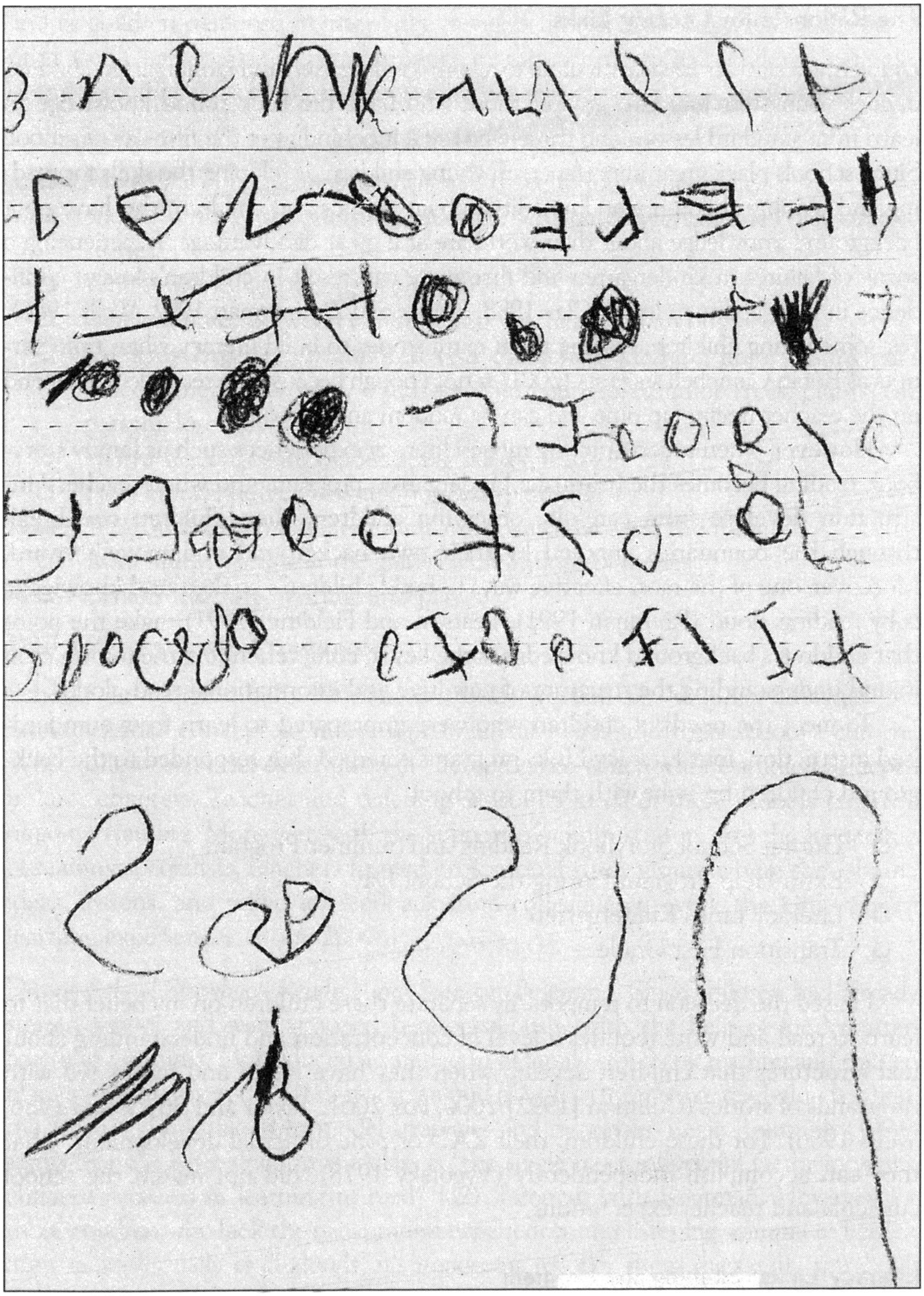

**Figure 1–3.** Justin's writing imitates print he observes in books.

the year, these children heard 20 stories a week and more than 600 stories during the year. In addition, the Winchester School Board set aside funds for summer school. At the end of kindergarten, for 6 weeks, thirty to forty children spent their summer mornings listening to stories, writing their own stories and books in writing workshop, engaging in shared writing and reading, and talking. More than 85 percent of these children were able to move on to first grade; a small group repeated kindergarten and moved into first grade the following year.

*Extra Help Program During the School Day*  Reading specialists at Virginia Avenue/Charlotte DeHart School in Winchester, Virginia, Kathy Wetsel and Betty Wymer brainstormed with me to develop a program for high-risk kindergarteners within their regular classroom. In addition to the family storybook reading that teaching assistants completed, the classroom teacher worked with groups of five to eight children 3 to 5 times a week while the teaching assistant supported the other children. One-hour sessions offered children, who rarely had a chance to answer or work through a problem because classmates immediately responded, opportunities to develop prereading, phonics, and writing skills.

*Literacy Links Kindergarten*  When Jane Rea Gaidos, principal of Robinson Elementary School in Woodstock, Virginia, heard about the Quarles program she was anxious to develop a literacy-building program for young children. Already in place at Robinson, was a program for three- to five-year-olds who needed extra support to develop emergent literacy skills. Besides working with these teachers to adjust their program, Jane created two kindergarten classes that would not follow the traditional curriculum. Instead, teachers would build children's literacy with a program that centered around family storybook reading, writing workshop, conversations, oral word games, and learning about the world. Each kindergarten would have no more than ten to twelve children. Staff included a certified kindergarten teacher and a half-time teaching assistant. Adjacent to each other, these classes were on the first grade corridor, to avoid any comparisons with other kindergartens.

*Transition First Grade*  After the first year of Literacy Links at Robinson Elementary, Jane Rea Gaidos, Lisa Tusing and Terri Auckland, and I met to discuss the four children who were not ready to succeed in first grade. Jane had a list of a dozen students from other kindergartens whose scores on the Virginia PALS test remained low. Besides the Phonological Awareness Literacy Screening (PALS) tests, we also studied children's writing and met with their teachers to hear the reasons why these boys and girls had been recommended for a transitional first grade. Here's what these children were unable to do at the end of kindergarten:

❑ Match letters to sounds by stretching words.
❑ Segment words into onset and rime.

❏ Put words together when the teacher pronounced the onset and rime.
❏ Voice-to-print match.
❏ Hear rhyming words.
❏ Use ear spelling to write about the pictures they drew in workshop.

We believed that this small group of children wasn't ready to succeed in first grade. We felt that four children from the Literacy Links program and six children from regular classrooms would benefit from instruction that matched their needs. Their teacher, Melissa Foltz, an expert reading specialist, and Melissa's half-day teaching assistant had a reasonable goal. Children would be able to enter second grade because the program would take them where they were, offer experiences that would build on what the children could do, and eventually prepare them for second grade. And that's exactly what occurred—ten children entered heterogeneously grouped second grades ready to learn with their peers.

## Closing Reflections

In *The Meaning Makers: Children Learning Language and Using Language to Learn* (1986) Gordon Wells draws this conclusion from his Bristol, England study:

> We are the meaning makers—every one of us: children, parents, and teachers. To try to make sense, to construct stories, and to share them with others in speech and in writing is an essential part of being human. For those of us who are more knowledgeable and more mature—parents and teachers—the responsibility is clear: to interact with those in our care in such a way as to foster and enrich *their* meaning making. (222)

In the preface, Steven Kellogg expresses grave concern over those children who come to school never having listened to books or oral stories. Kellogg calls upon teachers to use their "creativity, enthusiasm, expertise, and love" to bring books and children together. When high-stakes testing seeps down to kindergarten and when the federal government and states mandate that teachers use scripted programs that assume every child has the same background and learns at the same rate, we lose sight of children's diverse literacy backgrounds and their unique learning needs (Clay 1991, 1998).

The Literacy Links program builds on the belief that some children require different kinds of learning and curricula. When these youngsters arrive at school with levels of competencies and background knowledge that continually place them in a frustration zone (Vygotsky 1978), progress and learning are greatly diminished. Instead of dwelling on what children can't do when they arrive at school, the Literacy Links program accepts and meets children where they are and offers experiences that develop the emergent literacy behaviors children need to read, write, speak, and think.

# 2

# An Overview of Emergent Literacy

*Going hand in hand with the practice of reading-like behaviour is an
equally spontaneous involvement in writing-like behaviour. Both activities
are message or meaning-oriented and support each other, especially after
the stage when precise attention to print detail becomes appropriate.*

Don Holdaway, *The Foundations of Literacy* (1979, 61)

It's mid-October. I'm observing children during free choice time which occurs the
first twenty to thirty minutes of class in Robin Northrup's kindergarten at
Powhatan. Powhatan, nestled in the Blue Ridge Mountains of Virginia is the independent school where I teach three days a week. Robin's nineteen kindergarten
children come from single parent or traditional families that place a high value on
literacy.

Today, in the reading loft, four children "pretend read books," telling the story
in their own words. Matthew and Supreeti, pointers in hand, read poems about the
wind that Robin has printed on large charts. Often, their pointers run ahead of the
text, but the pair joyfully read the poems to one another again and again. At the
science table a group of boys and girls look at leaves with magnifying glasses and
talk about the colors and veins. In a corner, two write shopping lists. "We're going

to buy stuff at our grocery store," they tell me. Several build skyscrapers with blocks, a few sit at a table and draw, while two children try to read yesterday's morning message. Engaged in emergent literate behaviors, these children began their literacy journey early in life at home. Observed free choice behaviors reflect children's experiences with reading and writing and their ability to link their backgrounds to school learning events. Based on her observations of children actively learning, Robin continually plans and adjusts experiences that build on what the children can do with Robin's support.

## What Is Emergent Literacy?

The concept of emergent literacy describes the process children naturally experience at home and in their community as early as the first few months of life. Emergent literate behaviors develop when children are frequently read to at home, when adults engage them in and extend meaningful conversations about books and their environment, and when parents encourage young children to use writing in ways adults write. A literacy-rich environment tunes children's ears to the sounds of language. Listening to books read aloud, pleading for favorites to be read again and again, enables young children to figure out the structure of narrative and nonfiction (Clay 1998, Gillet and Temple 2000, Teale and Sulzby 1989).

According to Teale and Sulzby, "Literacy is not regarded as simply a cognitive skill to be learned, but a complex sociopsycholinguistic activity" (2). This belief emerges from a change in literacy research that studies children outside of their environment to researchers observing young children's interactions in their homes and communities—much as Wells and his team worked in the Bristol study. Equally as important is that researchers of emergent literacy observe the development of literate behaviors from the child's point of view. The goal of their observations and conversations with young children is to get inside the child's head, see and experience the world as the child does, then deepen teachers' insights on how young children become literate. The following are some points research invites teachers, caretakers, and parents to consider. Instead of adults imposing on children a system of learning that does not match ways children naturally explore their world, these points show us the ways children learn about language and use language to learn (Clay 1998, Taylor and Strickland 1986, Teale 1986).

❑ Literacy is functional and develops from authentic, meaningful activities such as family storybook reading and observing adults read, from reading environmental print, using recipes to cook, reading directions for building a playhouse, and writing notes, letters, invitations, and checks.
❑ Reading, speaking, and writing are interrelated. Children and adults write to communicate to readers and read to make meaning and learn more about

writing (Calkins and Harwayne 1991, Graves 1983). Carol Chomsky's research (1971) shows that children write before they read and use writing to enlarge their knowledge of letter/sound relationships and how print works. In addition, strong oral language development also supports literacy learning (Pflaum 1986, Wells 1986).

❏ Children learn best when engaged in hands-on active experiences that emphasize the *doing*. Wells calls this *"the guided reinvention of knowledge"* (220). The responsibility of adults is to offer children countless opportunities to *do*, such as drawing texts and writing about them by saying and stretching words to match sounds with letters or retelling a story heard dozens of times in their own words or playing with letters to learn the alphabet and construct words.

## Other Perspectives on Early Literacy Development

The emergent literacy perspective is a departure from three philosophies about children's literacy development—philosophies that have affected how educators invited children to learn at school in the past. Included is a brief historical overview because by reflecting on the ideas and practices that preceded emergent literacy research, we can more clearly recognize the importance of offering children rich and varied literacy building experiences long before they enter kindergarten.

These theories have resulted in school environments that do not consider how children learn during the first four to five years of their lives. Instead, these educators ignored the accomplishments of early childhood when children learn to speak and use language, gain insights into syntax and grammar, and come to understand how books work from listening to read-alouds—accomplishments that clearly show how children learn about and use their language.

### Reading Readiness: Waiting for That Ideal Moment

In the 1930s, the research of Arnold Gesell developed the belief among educators that children had to mature until they reached the point where they were ready to learn to read. Gesell and Frances Ilg (1949), along with their followers, believed that before children reached "reading readiness," it was pointless to provide instruction that could move them toward readiness. No doubt physical and mental growth and maturation contribute to a child's readiness to learn to read.

Although Gesell believed maturation was the only measure of readiness, research today supports the belief that immersing children in literacy-rich environments stimulates curiosity and motivation to learn (Cambourne 1988, Holdaway 1979). Moreover, teachers who strictly follow Gesell's theory may deprive children of important prereading experiences such as learning the alphabet, playing with rhymes, and letter/sound games.

## Isolating and Teaching Skills

In the middle of the twentieth century, educators, influenced by behaviorist psychologists, believed that preparation for and learning how to read could be accomplished by teaching skills isolated from these everyday, authentic literacy experiences: meaningful conversations, storybook reading, and sights and experiences that enlarge children's background knowledge of their home, community, and the world. Programs for young children broke learning down into sets of skills and drilling skills which became the centerpiece of prereading and early reading instruction. Children practiced discriminating between shapes such as circles from squares, straight from curved lines, then learned to see the differences between the shapes of letters in the alphabet. Skill-and-drill lessons also included telling the differences between sounds such as a ringing bell and a cat's meow because it was believed that such practice would transfer to discriminating between the sounds letters make and eventually help children say whole words. Advocates of this isolated skill-practice believed that eventually, children would connect the drills and apply them to reading.

This approach placed the responsibility of linking skill-and-drill practice to reading and comprehending real books on young children. It reminds me of the piano instruction I received in the Bronx while attending P. S. 105. I sat in a large auditorium along with more than a hundred children in grades 3, 4, and 5. On every lap was a cardboard replica of a piano keyboard. A man, standing on the stage, used an oversized keyboard model to teach us the names of the notes, which we dutifully "pressed." We even played simple songs but never heard them. The skill-and-drill educators sent me directly back to this experience. Those of us who did not have access to a real piano never connected the names of notes to making musical sounds; we never understood that the way one touched a note on a real piano affected the tone and dynamics produced. Forget the pedals, we didn't have any. The only sounds that filled that auditorium were the raps of fingers on fake keys. Like learning to play the piano on a cardboard keyboard instead of on a real piano doesn't create accomplished pianists, practicing isolated skills divorced from books, dialogue, and environmental print doesn't develop readers.

Even more disheartening was the fact that the skills young children practiced came from what a curriculum developer believed was logical, not from research. This adult-centered approach did not consider the initiative of children as they learn to walk, talk, feed, and dress themselves; nor did learning environments immerse children in print or provide them with reading and writing models they could use to build the background needed for reading.

## Developmentally Appropriate Instruction

It's also important to celebrate the research, done by psycholinguist Noam Chomsky and those who followed him. Chomsky believed that adults were models, not teachers (1968). Psycholinguists, like Chomsky, explained that children learned to talk and understand language, a major accomplishment, without practicing skills. By interacting with adults, children hear, discover and experiment with the sounds and patterns in words and sentences. So adults are not only models, Bruner, a psychologist, argued, but they are also partners in children's learning process (1985).

Psychologists and linguists like Jean Piaget (1976), Lev Vygotsky (1978), and Michael Halliday (1975) emphasized that learning language and solving problems are social and active, and that learners comprehend how language works through discovery and always with the children leading the way.

There are teachers who latch on to the notion of children discovering literacy when they are developmentally ready, and they create a controversial issue that I've observed in programs for four-year-olds and kindergarten programs. In these classrooms, teachers do not introduce the alphabet to children until the children show an interest in learning letters by writing some independently. Once children's actions demonstrate that they have discovered the letters, teachers conclude that they are developmentally ready for instruction. In one class, the teacher would not play rhyming and other word games with a group who had not shown they could pick out rhyming words or find other words that began with the same consonant as the word the teacher said. When the developmental approach becomes inflexible, there's a downside: it favors children with rich literacy backgrounds, and continues to deprive dependent, at-risk learners from the modeling and direct instruction they require to move forward (Delpit 1986, Wilhelm 1997).

While facilitating a class on emergent literacy and guided reading at Quarles Elementary school in Winchester, Virginia, I invited teachers to read "Theory Becomes Practice at the Point of Intersection" by Fielding and Roller (1998). This article uses Vygotsky's research to explain that children who have some knowledge of or related to a topic, but not enough to work independently, can learn with the assistance and support of more competent adults and peers.

The group consisted of four kindergarten, four first grade, four second grade, two special education teachers, and one reading resource teacher. Using jigsaw, a team-learning strategy that helps partners or small groups comprehend material by becoming an expert on and teaching one part of an article or chapter, I organized three groups of teachers. Next, I divided the article into three parts and asked each group to discuss, then present the key points of their section. As I circulated around the room, I noticed several disengaged teachers who were not communicating with other group members. One outspoken kindergarten teacher quickly informed me of the problem: "We're developmentalists. We don't believe in this stuff [points to article]." In fact, five teachers never read beyond the second page of the article.

Working hard to conceal my emotions, I gently replied, "Sometimes it's helpful to read information that you disagree with, for it can help you confirm your belief or challenge you to rethink ideas." Paradigm shifts among three of the five strict developmentalists occurred toward the end of the year, after they completed many observations of colleagues and me working with children from deprived or limited literacy backgrounds. The idea that provoked change was the notion that teachers were holding back those who really needed modeling and direct instruction.

## Lev Vygotsky and Emergent Literacy

Sir Isaac Newton said, "If we see further today, it is simply because we stand on the shoulders of giants." Russian psychologist, Lev Vygotsky, is one of the giants who has deepened our understanding of ways to support children's learning by describing three zones of development.

1. *Independence—The Zone of Actual Development (ZAD)*. Uvaldo, a kindergarten student in Deena Baker's class at Virginia Avenue/Charlotte DeHart School in Winchester, can recognize all of his alphabet letters. Regarding identifying the 26 letters in the alphabet, Uvaldo is functioning in his zone of actual development because he can complete this task independently. Continuing to drill Uvaldo on letter recognition is not a good use of this child's learning time, for Uvaldo can successfully and repeatedly complete this task. Instead, Uvaldo needs to practice matching sounds and letters and segmenting words into onset and rime.

   No teaching occurs in the ZAD since this zone represents what children can do on their own. Yet in primary classrooms I visit in Virginia and other states, I observe time devoted to teaching tasks that all or most of the children can do independently. This kind of repetition can build self-confidence and automaticity, but to nudge a child forward means teaching within each child's zone of proximal development.

2. *Support from an Expert—The Zone of Proximal Development (ZPD)*. When you teach new information and tasks by supporting children and helping them use what they already know to understand new ideas, children are learning. It is in the zone of proximal development that teaching and learning occurs. In this zone, children can experience success with a new task as long as they receive support. Gradually, with continual assistance, children can learn the task and do it independently.

By January, in Danielle Water's Head Start class at Keister Elementary School, five-year-old Tyler's writing shows that he has moved from squiggles and lines (Figure 2–1) to writing letters, drawing pictures, and telling what his story means. In the fall, Tyler could say his alphabet and recognize 15 letters. By listening to and observing Danielle write a daily "Morning Message," by working side-by-side with Danielle to hear the beginning sounds of words when Tyler was writing, and by watching classmates share their writing, Tyler was learning about what writing looks like and how writing can communicate ideas and feelings. Danielle was helping Tyler learn within his ZPD. By January, Tyler draws a picture of his teacher and is able to write the first letter of several words in his message: My teacher likes ABC (see Figure 2–2).

3. *Tasks Beyond the Child—The Frustration Zone.* Tasks that are too difficult for a child even with the teacher's strong support cause frustration and can not be learned. Inviting children to learn tasks they do not have the background to understand can cause anxiety, a loss of self-confidence, and destroy young children's natural curiosity and motivation to learn (Turner 1997). Poor learning habits such as guessing and tuning out develop because children don't have enough knowledge to reason through a problem, to listen to a whole class read-aloud, or to follow directions. Children working at their frustration level often misbehave; they shout out of turn, shove peers, and refuse to try the task.

4. *Learning in the Frustration Zone.* It's mid-November. I'm observing a culturally diverse kindergarten of twenty-four that includes Hispanic, African

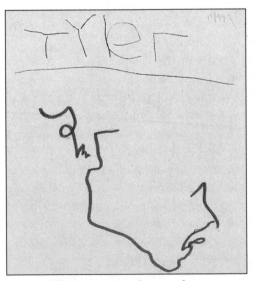

**Figure 2–1.** In November, Tyler's writing is lines with no message.

**Figure 2–2.** In January, Tyler can write the first letter of many words.

American, Asian American, and Caucasian children. While the teacher gives out pencils and paper, children sit at their tables chatting quietly. After the children print their names on the paper, the teacher says a letter, makes its sound, then asks children to write it. At one table, four children enthusiastically write each letter, whispering or mouthing the letter's sound as they write. In contrast, two girls make circles and lines all over their paper. One crawls under the table and draws there. The other child puts her head down.

Later, their teacher tells me that in September, both girls could not write their names. I also learn that there are seven other children who have a weak knowledge of the alphabet and don't seem to be able to match letters and sounds. In defense of this teacher, she is delivering the month-by-month curriculum spelled out by her school district for kindergarten children. Based on my work with four- and five-year-olds, I would argue that children can learn from a standardized curriculum only after we fill in the background knowledge gaps. When learning tasks can be accomplished with the assistance of the teacher, children move forward at a faster and more successful rate than when we force them to accomplish learning that they lack the experiences to connect to and receive (Clay 1998, Neuman 1998).

Participating in this dictation activity is not only frustrating, but it continually reminds these children that they are less capable than their classmates. One boy summed up this group's problems when he whispered to me, "They can't do school." Knowledge of Vygotsky's zones, combined with systematically observing children, enables teachers to plan instruction that builds on each child's background knowledge and experiences.

## How Vygotsky's Findings Affect Teaching

Here's what we learn about teaching when we apply Vygotsky's principals of learning to four-year-old programs and kindergartens:

1. It's crucial to match learning experiences with children's background knowledge, offering them activities that allow children to use what they know to construct new understandings about books, spoken and written language, and phonics.
2. It's our responsibility to use *front loading* (Wilhelm 2000), a strategy that asks the teacher to enlarge children's background knowledge before they plunge into an activity. Front loading prepares youngsters to develop the emergent literate behaviors necessary for success in reading and writing throughout their education.
3. It's appropriate to vary whole class teaching with small group and one-on-one teaching so you provide opportunities for children to learn with your support, slowly nudging them to independence.

4. It's helpful to think aloud and show children how a task works, and what you expect them to do. If a child has difficulty, then step in and give that support or scaffolding that enables her to learn new tasks. For example, I use drama to build children's knowledge of *trotting, shepherding,* and *protecting,* words from *Bashi, Baby Elephant* by Theresa Radcliffe (1997). Uvlado plays Bashi who trots away from the herd. Instead of trotting, Uvaldo charges forward with three giant leaps. I affirm his ability to leap, explain that leap is the opposite of trot, then take Uvaldo's hand and together we trot across the room while the group watches. I invite others to trot, so again and again, the children *do* and *observe* the meaning of this word. The minidrama enables them to talk about the word and recall what they did when I bring it up the next day.

5. It's beneficial to offer interactive read-alouds where you name and model comprehension strategies good readers use. Interactive read-alouds can build children's vocabulary, knowledge of text structure and how readers respond to and think about texts. Repeated interactive read-alouds build children's background knowledge of reading comprehension and fix-it strategies.

## Developing Emergent Literacy at School

I'm spending the morning in a kindergarten class observing a teacher who I will be coaching. Groups of children have just made jello and put bowls filled with lime, grape, orange, cherry, and strawberry-flavored liquid into the refrigerator in the school's kitchen. Their teacher plans to ask these kindergartners to write about making the jello, then after lunch write about eating it. Each child receives a piece of paper with the same message typed across the top: *Today we made yummy jello.* With their teacher, the children choral read the sentence. Next, the teacher invites the class to draw what they remember about making jello. To observe the children working, the teacher and I circulate around different tables.

When I hear, "I want you to draw a picture. The words are on the paper," I quickly walk to the other table to hear the rest of this exchange. On the piece of paper, the youngster had written his own sentence: *I sr t jl* (I stir the jello.). Ignoring the child's answer, "But I like my words better," the teacher again requests a drawing, repeating that words were already on paper. Standing next to the child, the teacher waits until he begins illustrating what his group did.

Flashback! I was in kindergarten, writing my own words on paper. The teacher had told my mother that I was uncooperative because I refused to draw pictures about *her* sentences. My mother tried to drill the teacher's message into my stubborn head: *You can write when you can spell.* But my desire to write my ideas continued, even though I lost recesses and sat in a time-out chair for being "totally intractable."

21

The research of Carol Chomsky (1971), Ann Haas Dyson (1982), and Donald Graves (1983) all point to the fact that children feel empowered to write before they are able to read. Young children's writing includes drawing pictures and writing squiggles, random letters, and eventually matching the sounds they hear to letters. We can look at the boy's sentence about making jello, *I sr t jl,* and celebrate how much this youngster knows about language, instead of trying to impede his experimentation and risk-taking. He writes "I" correctly; he hears the first and last consonant sounds of "stir" and "jello"; he uses the first letter of "the" to represent that word. Pretty terrific for a five-year-old at the end of September.

In fact, research shows that writing words by stretching their sounds and using spelling inventions heightens phonemic awareness and deepens children's knowledge of letter/sound relationships (Bear et al. 2000; Casbergue 1998; Cunningham 1995; McCarrier, Pinnell, and Fountas 2000). Moreover, teachers can use children's writing to understand how much it's possible to move them beyond what they are hearing and writing. For example, Holly is able to hear and write the initial consonants of words. Sitting side-by-side, during independent writing, I help Holly stretch words and invite her to hear and write final consonants. By scaffolding instruction for Holly within her zone of proximal development, I model what I want Holly to do when she writes.

Since children's writing informs us about what they can do, you can build on these strengths to introduce word families, onset and rime games, picture sorting for initial consonants, rhyming words, or stretching words to hear all of the sounds.

When I work with teachers to plan a curriculum that fosters the development of emergent literacy, we include authentic reading, writing, speaking, and listening. As you plan your curriculum, keep in mind too, that children learn about how literary, oral, and written language work by actively using and experiencing language to learn (Clay 1979, 1998; Fountas and Pinnell 1996; Holdaway 1979; Strickland 1986; Wells 1986).

## Building a Balanced Emergent Literacy Program

Two of Webster's definitions of *balance* apply to shaping a curriculum: (1) to bring or keep in equilibrium; (2) to have equal value. Like a juggler keeping several balls in continual motion or five acrobats using their bodies to create and hold a complex and artistic formation, maintaining the balance among various key elements of an emergent literacy program requires knowledge of the task, training with experts, practicing to improve and progress, and concentration that allows you to monitor yourself and others. So, when applying these four elements to developing learning experiences for young children, teachers need:

❑  A knowledge of how young children learn.
❑  Training or ongoing professional study with colleagues, experts, and by reading professional books, journals, and children's literature.

❏ Time to practice the art of teaching by supporting and observing young children playing and learning.

❏ Opportunities to concentrate on how their students learn as well as time to evaluate their teaching practices.

For a juggler, acrobats, and educators, all four are recursive and work in concert as you develop, adjust, refine, and continually strive to balance the elements of your program.

For children who arrive at school with rich literacy experiences, a balanced emergent literacy program immerses children in oral, written, and spoken language. Such a program includes reading, writing, conversation and discussion, phonics, language games that develop phonemic awareness, knowledge of the alphabet, and the sounds letters make. In addition, these programs develop children's concept of word, encourage them to memorize texts and point to each recited word, and offer problem-solving experiences that grow out of the children's inquiries. The program you develop can support four-year-olds, kindergartners, and first-graders as long as what you invite children to do builds on what the children already know.

As you read on, you'll review a brief summary of the key components of an emergent literacy program—components that you will study in depth in chapters that follow. Balancing the elements of your program means keeping some experiences, such as reading aloud and independent writing, constant, while continually rotating and integrating other experiences such as dance, painting, drama, phonics, and word study activities.

## Varied Reading Experiences

Immersing children in varied book experiences offers them multiple opportunities to use pictures and text to build book knowledge, comprehension, recall of information, listening skills, an understanding of fiction, nonfiction, and poetic structures, enlarge vocabulary, and continually tune children's ears to the rhythms and sounds of literary texts (Cambourne 1988, Campbell 2001, Fisher 1998, Holdaway 1979, Routman 1991).

I've included independent and interactive writing under reading experiences because these support young learners by asking them to read what they wrote, tell the story about their picture, and listen for the sounds in words, then write them. Children read to learn to write and write to read to themselves and communicate to an audience. The following are reading building blocks that develop a literacy foundation.

*Read-Alouds*   These occur several times each day and include fiction, nonfiction, letters, diary entries, news articles, songs, and poetry. Reading aloud is the ideal way to start and end the day and transition to new learning experiences because books and poems and songs can change the emotional climate in a classroom.

*Shared Reading*   Teachers read aloud from big books and songs and poems printed on large charts. Shared reading simulates family storybook reading because an entire class can feel close to the pictures and words of an oversized text.

*Interactive Read-Alouds*   The teacher reads aloud and makes visible the strategies being applied by thinking aloud (Robb 2000c, Wilhelm 2000). These strategies include: thinking about a word's meaning, linking the meaning of two to three sentences, and summarizing short passages.

*Interactive Writing*   Children help teachers compose a wide variety of texts. Some are the morning message, retellings of stories, graphs that explore favorite foods, original stories, and letters. Again and again, children read back these texts and play games with them such as putting the events of a retelling in sequence or finding words that start with the same letter as their names. Collaborative texts help you nudge children forward. For example, when they use a compound word or contraction, it's the ideal moment to teach more about these.

*Choral Reading*   Groups or the entire class chant a song, read a poem or passage from a big book, a retelling, or the morning message.

*Independent Reading*   Every day, for five to ten minutes, children "read" books they choose from baskets or crates and engage in and practice the appropriate behaviors of an authentic reading experience. During independent reading, the teacher can observe and record children's behaviors and their book knowledge.

*Independent Writing*   Set up a writing workshop and invite the children to compose their own stories every day (Calkins [1986] 1994, Graves 1983, Fisher 1998, Routman 1991). Children's writing and sharing in author's chair enable you to monitor their knowledge of genres and their ability to apply what they are learning about words and letters and sounds.

## Other Key Learning Experiences

*A Rich Word Study Program*   Surround children with words by building an alphabet word wall and mini-word walls with theme words. Invite the children to help you label and read the room, create word banks so children continually improve their thinking, speaking, and sight-word vocabulary. Play phonemic awareness games, teach letter/sound relationships, build charts of word families, and engage them in picture sorts, making sure you integrate these activities into authentic learning events such as shared reading and writing.

*Inquiry Experiences*   Invite children and the teacher to pose questions about what they are studying in math, science, and social studies (Strickland 1986). The emphasis is always on solving a problem through active investigations. You can encourage inquiry by setting up a problem that needs solving, such as, "Do all apples have the same number of seeds?" Inquiries can also come from displaying items such as a rusty nail, a plant with brown leaves, or different kinds of nuts. Sometimes children will generate questions from a demonstration of ice melting, water boiling, or seeds sprouting.

*Play*   Include free play where children can make choices and freely use and develop their imagination, directed play that allows you to plan games and dramas where you scaffold and guide them, helping children do with you what they could not do alone (Vygotsky 1978). Through play, young children learn to cooperate and converse while actively doing and working with peers on activities such as banking, shopping, or a board game (Fisher 1998).

*Meaningful Discussions*   Discussions among students and teacher or among and between students can deepen children's understanding of their environment inside and outside of school, their comprehension of books, inquiry investigations, the writing process, playing, and during share time. Hearing and interacting with many speaking models build children's background knowledge, vocabulary, and improve sentence structure. Moreover, Wells points out that for those children who "lack facility with written language, . . . oral language could perhaps provide a viable route towards the goal of effective thinking and symbol manipulation" (1986, 189).

*Fine Arts*   Integrate painting, drama, music, and dance into each day, for the fine arts stimulate the imagination, foster connections to self and others, and help children comprehend and recall new information.

While the school environment should always nurture and cultivate emergent literate behaviors, the development of these behaviors starts in the home. Since children's home environments are so diverse, children who arrive at school have a wide range of literacy experiences from few to an overwhelming abundance.

## Developing Emergent Literacy at Home

A child's literacy development begins at birth when parents coo and talk in sweet and soft singsong voices, responding to and interpreting their babies babble, movements, and cries. Interactive talk is crucial to a child's development of oral language—that's how all of us learn the most complex task—speech.

The value parents place on literacy in the home—books for adults and children, frequently reading aloud to children, adults reading books, magazines, and newspaper, enlisting children's help with writing tasks—plays a large part in children's success with learning to read and write. One reason for this success is that these skills are the centerpiece in the one-size-fits-all programs schools deliver (Ohanian 1999). Unfortunately, these same programs initiate the cycle of failure for children who enter kindergarten lacking a rich literacy background.

The four-, five-, and six-year-olds I teach all want to learn and succeed. And they can if teachers meet them where they are and help them develop the skills and strategies they will need to enter the literacy club Frank Smith discusses in *Joining the Literacy Club* (1988).

### *Educating Parents*

The intent of this book is not to blame those parents whose children come to school with limited literacy experiences or to celebrate those who do. The point is to adjust school programs so they meet all children's needs and allocate state and federal funds to create programs for three- and four-year-olds that provide rich play, talk, painting, writing, and read-aloud experiences.

In addition, it's the responsibility of teachers, school administrators, obstetricians/gynecologists, nurses, and pediatricians to help parents understand the relationship of reading and writing to success in our society. Schools and hospitals and clinics need parent centers stocked with videos and materials that model effective read-alouds, storytelling, and language play and games. When schools sponsor programs for families that focus on family storybook reading and sharing stories, schools can help adults feel confidence and pleasure when reading aloud to their babies, toddlers, and older children.

In our society, books are available to all and can be easily checked out of public and/or school libraries. Telling this to parents is not enough. Bringing librarians and bookmobiles to parent programs at school, then inviting parents to obtain library cards and check out books can bring about positive change. Adults who themselves had limited literacy experiences as well as negative associations with education and school, need all the support and nurturing we can give to enable them to feel comfortable reading to their children and choosing to read themselves.

## Balancing Acts: Literacy Programs for At-Risk Children

As you read on you'll explore how some schools have adjusted existing four-year-old, kindergarten, and first-grade programs to meet the needs of children who come to school to learn but lack the literacy experiences to connect to the school's standardized curricula. Random support just isn't enough to build, in one or two years, the background knowledge these children need to learn to read and write and experience success in school.

Leading literate lives not only enriches our personal life, but it also enables us to work in professions closed to those who can't read or write. All children deserve the opportunity to live literate lives.

By making a conscious effort to support instead of blame, to individualize pre-k and kindergarten programs and discover successful ways to scaffold children's learning, it's possible to help delayed learners and all children achieve and defy negative predictions. To accomplish this, teachers need time to discover the methods and strategies that open children's ability to learn to read and write. Scores won't rise immediately, but given the gift of one to two years, scores eventually will show the progress individual children have made. Those who have worked with me on the Literacy Links programs have discovered that children can do amazing things and defy the gloomy predictions that accompany them when they enter school.

## Closing Reflections

To prepare young children for state and federal high-stakes tests, schools have developed programs for kindergarten and first-grade children that have resurrected the old skill-and-drill philosophy. Taking the cue from the past, tutors drill the names of letters and sounds, have children practice rhyming words, and ask them to write a sentence from a given prompt—all this with children who have never had stories read aloud to them or held books.

My intention is not to teach preschool and kindergarten children how to read, but to show how to develop these emergent literacy behaviors that enable them to become successful readers as they continue their education. They are

- ❏ A knowledge of why we read and write.
- ❏ Phonological awareness.

- ❏ Concepts about print.
- ❏ Sight-word vocabulary.
- ❏ Alphabet knowledge and the sounds letters make.
- ❏ Writing with spelling inventions.
- ❏ Imaginative play.
- ❏ Knowledge of the structure of fiction, nonfiction, and poetry.
- ❏ Meaningful discussions about books, environment, and daily experiences.

Kindergarten teacher Deena Baker's comment sums up my feelings and present teachers and administrators with ideas to reflect on: "You can teach these kids to pass the Virginia PALS test or any other standardized test for this age group, but they still will not be able to learn to read." Why? Because they don't have a deeply embedded concept of word, a hefty sight vocabulary, and experiences with books and oral and written language that construct the background children need to become successful readers and writers in our society.

# 3

# Planning for and
# Organizing the Year

*What happens at the beginning of the school year lays
the foundation for the rest of the year.*

Jane Perlmutter and Louise Burrell, *The First Weeks of School:
Laying a Quality Foundation* (2001, 9)

Thinking about the beginning of school always activates my five senses. I smell composition notebooks, feel my fingers brushing the smooth, blank sheets of paper, and picture words marching across the lines as my pen records observations of children at work. New books, crisp and clean as garden lettuce sparkling with morning dew, drum rhythms as I drop them from desk to desk. Feelings of excitement and anticipation mingle with a churning, tight stomach at the start of a new school year. I return to the child in me, wondering if she'll have friends, please the teacher, and do well. That's fine, I think, for I'm pleased I'm able to reclaim those feelings, so I can empathize with my students' anxieties. Now, as teacher, I've added another layer of emotions: Will I be able to help every child? Will students and I build community and trust quickly? Will my class be overcrowded? Will students respond to a reading-writing workshop? Do I have a range of books in my classroom library that will meet every child's recreational reading level?

It's the middle of August, and I'm dealing with these myriad questions as I drive down Route 81 to Robinson Elementary School in Woodstock, Virginia. My mind is a maelstrom of questions that I will pose to the Literacy Links teachers and their assistants. Questions, that I hope will enable us to sketch some plans for the opening day and first few weeks of school.

## Preparations for the Literacy Links Kindergarten

Jane Rea Gaidos, principal of Robinson, has asked all the kindergarten teachers, their teaching assistants, teachers in the Bright Star program, and two reading specialists to attend the training for family storybook reading. Including all kindergarten teachers, Jane believed, would keep them abreast of the content and goals of the Literacy Links program while investing all teachers in part of the planning. Moreover, practicing and modeling the benefits of family storybook reading and interactive read-alouds could benefit everyone.

## Training for Family Storybook Reading

My first goal was to build background knowledge. I divided twenty teachers into groups of four and gave them articles and sections from professional books on family storybook reading. I introduced jigsaw, a strategy that invites learners to work cooperatively, read assigned material, then collaborate to plan a presentation. First, each group thoroughly read their articles, discussed key points, then chose a spokesperson to share salient information with everyone. Each time a group presented, I opened the floor for questions and discussion. Teachers completed the process in one and a half hours. Next, I asked groups to generate questions about family storybook reading. Here are some of the teachers' queries and discussions. I've included the group's conclusions in italics.

Q: *Will small groups of children listening to stories be distracted by what others are doing?*
A: This will definitely occur. Perhaps, if we explain to the children that everyone will be read to three to four times a day, that will relieve their concerns about receiving a turn. Once children understand and have experienced the routine of small group work, distractibility should lessen.
Q: *Can we bridge gaps in emergent literacy that took years to build?*
A: We won't know until we try the program. What we've done in the past has not supported these delayed learners during kindergarten. By the end of a year in our regular kindergarten, many lose the self-confidence they had when they arrived at school, and they continue to struggle with reading in later grades.

Q: *Do we have enough books to sustain the program?*
A: Lisa and Terri definitely need larger classroom libraries. Their colleagues agreed that both could use the school library and borrow books from other kindergarten teachers. The PTO also set aside funds for them to purchase new books.

Q: *Can we really fit in family storybook reading three to four times a day?*
A: With ten to twelve children in a class, Terri and Lisa felt confident this would occur, especially if they made it a priority. Everyone agreed that Literacy Links would not always look like the traditional Robinson kindergarten program.

Next, teachers and I discussed establishing a loose set of guidelines for the readers, keeping in mind that the students had few experiences with listening to stories at home. Here's the list I gathered on chart paper:

- ❏ Keep groups to a maximum of six children. Four is ideal so two can sit on either side of the reader and see the book.
- ❏ Maintain the spirit of invitation. If a child does not want to join a group, invite her to sit on the sidelines and observe what's happening. Hopefully, the child will conclude that the experience is enjoyable and soon join the group.
- ❏ Think aloud, so that discussion, at first, comes from the adult reader. However, once a child chimes in with a comment or question, listen carefully, be responsive, and offer praise. Positive and enthusiastic reactions from the adult reader can eventually encourage all the children to participate.
- ❏ Focus on thinking aloud to develop book knowledge, respond to the story and pictures, raise questions, and make predictions.
- ❏ Record, on a special sheet, the books read each day.

Using these guidelines, pairs of teachers practiced family storybook reading, alternating the roles of reader and listener. Practice builds confidence and comfort in the process. And, teachers loved getting acquainted with the newly published picture books that I brought and let them borrow. The group agreed that simulations also raised their own awareness of the benefits, for all children, of thinking aloud about book structure (see Chapter 5) while reading aloud. "Sometimes, we take this knowledge for granted and omit it during read-alouds," several pointed out. "It's important to include so all children deepen their knowledge of how books work."

At Robinson, teachers in the same grade level have one common planning period a day. I encouraged grade level teams to meet two to three times a week to discuss their read-aloud program, share ideas and successes, and support one another when a teacher asked for feedback on a reading experience that didn't work well.

On the afternoon of that first day at Robinson, and during the following two days, I collaborated with Lisa Tusing, Terri Auckland, and their teaching assistants to create the scheduling framework for their full day Literacy Links kindergartens. We also discuss room arrangement and the first two weeks of school.

## Planning Schedules

At the start of the meeting, we all agreed that whatever framework we developed would need tweaking and adjusting throughout the year. The schedules in Figures 3–1 and 3–2 are a blend of six schedules that several teachers developed for a whole-day and half-day kindergarten. Reflect on them and adapt them to the needs of the population you teach. Lunch will vary from school to school, and subject blocks can be shifted.

It's interesting to note that the Head Start program at Keister Elementary in Harrisonburg and the Bright Star program at Robinson were both a full day. With a rest period, full-day programs can better develop emergent literacy through play, read-alouds, and writing in a relaxed environment that permits time for reflection and reading aloud frequently. Moreover, the language arts block in a full-day program is 1 hour 45 minutes compared to 50 minutes in a half-day program.

| | |
|---|---|
| 8:00 | Free play. Choose from: One-on-one instruction for those who arrive early; Family storybook reading; breakfast; bathroom. |
| 8:20 | Announcements. Moment of silence. Pledge. |
| 8:30 | Calendar. Morning message. Possible small groups: Name activities; Family storybook reading; Counting. |
| 9:10 | Recess. Bathroom. |
| 9:30 | Language Arts Block. Whole group gathering; family storybook reading; shared reading; language games; word wall work; picture sorts; phonemic awareness games, alphabet activities; centers. |
| 11:15 | Snack. Read aloud. Bathroom. |
| 11:30 | Specials: Day 1–Music; Day 2–Art; Day 3–Library; Day 4–Computer; Day 5–Family storybook reading. |
| 12:00 | Physical education. |
| 12:30 | Lunch. Bathroom. |
| 1:00 | Writing workshop/Journals. |
| 1:30 | Rest. Groups for family storybook reading. Bathroom. |
| 2:00 | Math activities. |
| 2:20 | Centers. |
| 3:00 | Clean up. Pack up. Bathroom. |
| 3:10 | Dismissal. |

**Figure 3–1.** Whole-Day Kindergarten Schedule

| 8:00 | Free play. Choose from: One-on-one instruction for those who arrive early; Family storybook reading; breakfast; bathroom. |
|---|---|
| 8:20 | Announcements. Moment of silence. Pledge. |
| 8:30 | Calendar. Morning message. Name activities. |
| 9:00 | Language Arts Block. Family storybook reading (dominates during first two to three months); shared reading; language games; word study; interactive read-alouds. |
| 9:50 | Recess. Snack. Bathroom. Read aloud. |
| 10:10 | Math activities. |
| 10:30 | Writing workshop and centers. |
| 11:15 | Clean up. Pack up. Bathroom. |
| 11:25 | Dismissal. |

**Figure 3–2.** Half-Day Kindergarten Schedule

*The Language Arts Block in a Full-Day Kindergarten*   At the start of the year in Robinson's Literacy Links kindergarten, the language arts block focuses on family storybook reading. Two adults, the teacher and teaching assistant, always plan and work together during this long block of time. First, at a gathering, the teacher explains what students will do that morning. With ten or twelve students in a class, both Terri and her assistant can read to two groups simultaneously while the rest of the children draw or play. The following is a sample agenda for the first month of school. (Times are merely suggestions; always respond to students' needs and adjust times accordingly.)

❑ Gathering. Explain experiences for the day. Show-and-tell or name games. (15 min.)
❑ Two family storybook reading groups. One group plays. (20 min.)
❑ Song or poem and language play with whole group alternates with learning how to use centers. (15 min.)
❑ Two groups work on name activities; one group has family storybook reading. (20 min.)
❑ Two family storybook reading groups. One group plays. (20 min.)
❑ One group works on name activities; the rest of the class listens to a story. (20 min.)

By the second month, when children understand how to use centers and are comfortable with daily routines, you can add shared reading three times a week to the schedule. As the year progresses, other language play replaces name activities— playing with rhyming words, picture sorts, syllable claps, and constructing mini-word walls. When children have gained book knowledge and can listen to stories, transform small sections of read-alouds into interactive read-alouds where you show the children how you use strategies to make meaning (see Chapter 5).

In heterogeneous classes, where there might be four to six at-risk children, set aside one hour of the language arts block to support this group. Small group sessions gives them opportunities to participate without more confident classmates dominating discussions. The teacher and teaching assistant can take turns working with the small, at-risk group and the rest of the class. Family storybook reading is a constant. Select from other suggested learning experiences when children show they are ready. Here is a menu of what you might include in that one hour block.

❑ Family storybook reading. (20 min.)
❑ Shared reading with a poem or song. As the year progresses, alternate these with big books. (20 min.)
❑ Dramatize part of a story or a word, build vocabulary, or write about reading. (20 min.)
❑ Name activities. (10 to 15 min.)
❑ Mini-word wall. (10 to 15 min.)
❑ Rhyming words, picture sorts, and word families. (20 min.)

In four- or five-year-old programs, working with small groups allows you to closely observe students and better support their individual needs. For example, when I support Uvaldo, Channing, Timea, and Holly, I notice that Holly is reluctant to stretch words that invite her to segment a word's sounds so she can write the word, matching letters to sounds she hears. On the next day, I'm sitting side-by-side Holly inviting her to stretch a word after hearing me do it. During writing workshop, Holly's teacher, Deena Baker, makes sure she spends time each day helping Holly stretch words. Continual practice over several weeks, along with positive feedback from adults, eventually enables Holly to match letters to sounds she stretches.

The half-day kindergarten schedule in Figure 3–2 offers fewer opportunities for family storybook reading. Teachers can provide those children who need to hear stories in small groups with extra experiences during writing workshop and center time.

### Transition First Grade

Near the end of my first year at Robinson Elementary, I met with principal Jane Rea Gaidos to review the performance assessments of the children and the state PALS testing results. Six children from the regular kindergarten classes and four from Lisa and Terri's classes were not ready for first grade. "Repeating kindergarten," Terri and Lisa explained, "was not a good decision because the children would be bored most of the year. Repeating definitely won't meet their needs."

We all agreed that a transition first grade was the ideal way to support this group. With small numbers and a half-day teaching assistant, their teacher would continue to read aloud several times a day, have shared reading every day to strengthen children's understanding of the concepts about print, writing conventions, alphabet and book knowledge, and the structure of fiction and nonfiction. In addition to playing phonemic awareness games, the children would practice making lists of words with word families. Picture sorts and word study notebooks would enable the children to build a solid foundation of letter/sound relationships which they could apply to their own writing.

Robinson's principal called for first-grade teachers to apply for the transition first-grade position. Using the same standards established for selecting the two Literacy Links kindergarten teachers, the administration chose Melissa Foltz. A few classes away from earning her reading specialist Masters from the University of Virginia, Melissa had the expertise and empathy that these children needed. At the end of Melissa's first year, every child was reading and promoted to second grade. Now, the transition first grade would be part of Robinson's class offerings as long as there were children who could benefit from it. Adapt, to your needs, the daily schedule for the transition first grade (see Figure 3–3).

| | |
|---|---|
| 8:00 | Free play. Choose from: One-on-one instruction for those who arrive early; breakfast; bathroom. |
| 8:20 | Announcements. Moment of silence. Pledge. |
| 8:30 | Calendar. Morning message. Name activities. Counting. Picture sorting with pocket chart. |
| 9:10 | Recess. Bathroom. |
| 9:30 | Language Arts Block. Whole group gathering, read aloud or warm-up with poem or song; shared reading; language games; word wall work; picture sorts and word study notebooks; phonemic awareness games, alphabet activities; centers. |
| 11:15 | Snack. Read aloud. Bathroom. |
| 11:30 | Specials: Day 1–Music; Day 2–Art; Day 3–Library; Day 4–Computer; Day 5–Interactive writing. |
| 12:00 | Physical education. |
| 12:30 | Lunch. Bathroom. |
| 1:00 | Writing workshop/Journals; Word study. |
| 1:40 | Bathroom. |
| 1:50 | Math activities. |
| 2:20 | First half of year: read-alouds, making books, word study, hands-on experiences that relate to Science or Social. Studies. |
| 3:00 | Clean up. Pack up. Bathroom. |
| 3:10 | Dismissal. |

**Figure 3–3.** Transition First-Grade Schedule

## Room Arrangement

Both Terri Auckland and Lisa Tusing have smaller rooms than other kindergarten teachers because their classrooms are on the first-grade corridor. Danielle Waters held her Head Start program in a trailer and always had to find creative ways to use space and places to store materials. In contrast, Robinson Elementary housed their Bright Star program in a very large space.

The shape and size of your room and the funds available for creating special learning places always vary. Instead of offering a diagram of one particular room plan, I will suggest some furnishings and items for facilitating specific learning experiences in your classroom. Money for these can come from the school's budget and/or dollars that your PTO raises.

*Family Storybook Reading*   For seating in small rooms, try beanbags and oversized pillows. These can be stacked in a corner when not in use and made available in the classroom and in the hallway outside of the classroom during the day. Two teachers had the luxury of a sofa in their rooms donated by parents. Each sofa held a reader and four children.

*Shared Reading*   This area needs a rug for children to sit on and an easel to display the big book. In a classroom with limited space, one table for six children was on the rug for writing workshop, name activities, and so on. To recoup this space for shared reading, the teacher moved the table and the children stacked their chairs.

*The Morning Message*   The same easel that's used during shared reading also works for the morning message. I prefer a 24 × 16 inch chart pad for composing morning messages. However, Nancy Reedy did not have funds to purchase charts, so she used pieces of construction paper that she hung with magnets on the chalkboard. Every week, Nancy clipped her morning message charts on skirt or trouser hangers and stored these in a closet.

*Writing Workshop Demonstrations*   Most teachers use large chart paper to record their minilessons (see Chapter 6). I prefer having a chart pad, because it's easy to locate the lessons you want children to revisit and review. Some teachers had to use sturdy pieces of lined construction paper, then clipped several lessons together on skirt hangers.

*Tables and Chairs*   These are standard preschool and kindergarten furnishings. Teachers fortunate enough to have an extra table use it for special projects and working with clay and paint.

*Small Desks or Tables*   Two to three of these are ideal for those children who want to work alone. They provide enough space so a child and a tutor or teacher or a pair of children can work together. You can also place a fish tank or an animal in a cage on one of these.

*Shelves*   Built-in bookshelves are ideal. However, if cost is an issue, purchase wood planks and cinder blocks to create shelf space. Place classroom libraries, games, literacy centers, word study materials, and writing workshop folders on shelves.

*Plastic Crates and/or Cardboard Boxes*   Fill with books for the children to choose from during independent reading and/or with games and literacy center materials. Smaller plastic containers help you and the children organize crayons, pencils, markers, scissors, and glue. Because crates are easy to stack, these are terrific space savers.

*Book Display Areas*   Use the tops of shelves to display books. You can also lean books against the chalkboard or the wall underneath the chalkboard. By keeping them in constant view, it's a great way to immerse children in print and pictures and continually transmit the message that books are important.

*Conversation Area*   Two chairs placed side-by-side create an ideal space for pairs to discuss books or a problem. Having the space to talk about a child unwilling to share materials, or not letting a peer play enables children to confront and take ownership of everyday issues that arise during the year. Once children have agreed to a compromise or solution, they share it with the teacher and move on.

*Metal and Plastic Hooks*   I encourage teachers to have lots of these around the room. They hold children's painting smocks, charts, a basket of materials, center hats, word rings, and so on.

At Robinson Elementary, parents register their children in kindergarten a few days before school officially starts. Terri and Lisa carefully plan this half-day event, for they both recognize how crucial it is for parents and children to depart feeling positive about their programs.

### Parent Workshop on Registration Day

"Registration day is extremely important," Lisa remarks. "That day and the two scheduled conference days are usually the only times we see parents." During the year, communication about the program and a child's progress is through telephone conferences, letters, progress reports, and work sent home with the child.

Lisa and Terri invite groups of five to six parents and children to arrive at separate times on registration morning. While the teachers talk to parents, the teaching assistants supervise the children who color and play with blocks and a carton of toys. After a tour of the room when each teacher explains centers and materials, parents listen to Terri or Lisa explain the goals of Literacy Links. Parents learn that three times a week, journals go home and must come back to school the next day. Teachers explain that children write by drawing and that parents should encourage their children to tell the story that goes with a picture. They also give parents a list of ten things they can do at home to facilitate their children's literacy development.

### Ten Ways to Have Fun with Your Child

1.  Join the public library. Each week take your child to the library, let him or her browse through picture books, and choose several to check out and take home.
2.  Read to your child every day. Then, invite your child to use the illustrations to tell you the book's story after several rereadings.
3.  Talk to your child and explain how and why you do things such as water plants, wash and iron clothes.
4.  Encourage your child to help at home with:
    - ❏ setting and clearing the table
    - ❏ dusting and mopping
    - ❏ folding laundry
    - ❏ putting toys away
    - ❏ caring for pets and farm animals
    - ❏ unpacking and putting groceries away

    While working together, talk to your child about the activity. Include in your discussion the "how-to" and importance of each activity. Avoid multiple directions such as, "put the cereal in the closet then fold the bag and put it under the sink then put the canned soup on the shelf." These details confuse young children and can transform home learning experiences into negative, frustrating situations.

    Always weave positive statements into your conversations—statements that celebrate the way your child completes a task and express your appreciation for working together. When your child feels satisfaction from helping you and the family, he or she will want to repeat the experience again and again.
5.  Take your child with you when you go to the bank, post office, grocery store, and so on, etc. Explain the purpose of your trips and encourage questions.
6.  Look out the window and talk about the weather. Predict whether the day will be sunny, cloudy, warm, cold, or rainy. Then discuss the kind of clothing you need for specific kinds of weather.

7. Walk around the neighborhood together and talk about the sounds you hear and the flowers, birds, insects, and animals you see.

8. Keep a small notepad and pencil in the kitchen. Have your child help you pretend to write the grocery list and take telephone messages.

9. Read together road and restaurant signs and the names of cereals and favorite packaged and canned foods and drinks.

10. Make paper and crayons available and encourage your child to write by drawing pictures.

Before families depart, the teachers photograph each child. Parents learn that the photo will be placed next to the children's names on a large construction paper chart. "It's a great way to help children learn one another's names quickly," both teachers point out.

## The First Day of School

"We're all nervous—me and the kids—on the first day," Lisa tells me. "I have to build trust the minute they cross the threshold of my room." What happens the first day can set the tone for the upcoming weeks. Because there are so many school procedures for the children to learn, it's helpful to introduce them slowly, over the first two weeks. On the first day, work on procedures the children must have to experience success that day, then enjoy learning together. We'll visit Lisa Tusing's and Terri Auckland's classrooms and observe what they do to build a friendly, caring, nurturing environment.

As children check in on the first day of school, Lisa invites them to play at a table with puzzles, books, and a tub of counting chips. "I make the choices as active and hands-on as possible to maintain high interest. So while some play, I can help each child who arrives put their things in a cubby." Next, Lisa reads one or two short books such as *Come Out and Play, Little Mouse* by Robert Kraus (1987) and *McDuff Goes to School* by Rosemary Wells (2001). Between practicing and learning some procedures, Lisa and the children sing songs or Lisa rereads one of the books that opened the day.

Next, Lisa and her students get acquainted with one another. She starts by telling them her name and favorite thing to do which is working in her garden. Then, one-by-one, the children point to their name and photograph on the attendance chart and tell one thing they like to do. This is voluntary. Some children are shy and reluctant to stand in front of the group. Each day of the first week, Lisa invites the children to share a favorite food, game, place to play, relative, and friend. By the end of the week, most are sharing because their observations have shown them that in this room, sharing is safe. Lisa also sprinkles several play recesses throughout the first day. "I continue these for the first few weeks," she says. "It's hard for them to sit still and focus on learning all day."

In the morning Lisa has the children practice lining up before traveling outside of the classroom. After a bathroom break and review of hand-washing rules, one-by-one, the children wash their hands with soap and water, then tour important places in the building: the cafeteria, library, gymnasium, school offices, and the outdoor playground.

Back in the classroom the children learn to sit cross-legged on the shared reading rug and discuss their tour. Before lunch, the children role play going through the cafeteria line to pick up food using a tray, paper plates, and plastic cutlery. They bring trays to their assigned table, and pretend to eat and chat in quiet voices.

After lunch, the children relax on mats in their assigned resting spaces. Lisa reads a story, then plays an audiocassette of nursery rhymes or other songs. The last activity of the first day is writing workshop. First, Lisa explains the materials in the writing center and asks the children to keep pencils, crayons, and markers in separate containers. Then, Lisa presents her first minilesson. The day closes with everyone sitting in a circle on the rug. The children hear Lisa praise them as a group, saying things such as: "I liked the way you walked quietly to the cafeteria. I noticed that many said 'thank-you' when receiving a plate of food. You put all the writing materials back so well." As the children line up to leave, Lisa stops each one, makes eye contact, and celebrates one thing she noticed so that "every child departs feeling really good about the first day."

Much of Terri's first day mirrors Lisa's. However, Terri starts the day off with the morning message followed by looking at and talking about the pictures in a big book. "I do this until the children ask if there's a story to read." This usually occurs soon after the first week, when they've participated in several family storybook reading sessions.

In addition to constructing an attendance chart with the children's names and photographs, Terri makes name hats for each child; they wear these during the opening weeks and use them to learn each other's names. During writing workshop, Terri explains that each month the children will write about kindergarten in a memory book. The first day of school, children receive blank books. On the cover is a photocopy of the picture Terri took and the child's name. The first page is a self-portrait. On chart paper, Terri demonstrates how she draws a portrait of herself, then the children complete theirs. Near the end of each new month, Terri has the children complete another page by drawing a favorite activity or experience. "In June, you'll take home a book of kindergarten memories to look at and share with your parents," Terri tells the class.

Praising everything that worked as children interact, practice, and learn daily routines is one way to build community as well as enlarge children's self-esteem. Terri and Lisa point out that they have no time agenda for children absorbing routines. "It depends on the group," both explain. "We practice lining up, walking in the halls, how to use glue, center materials, share games, clean up, and talk as long as it takes for the children to gain independence."

## Building Community

The first weeks of school are crucial for building a community of learners. In addition to helping the children learn the routines of centers, the language arts block, and so on, it's important to build in experiences that create a supportive community of learners. Both Terri and Lisa read books about kindergarten and books about school that address the anxieties children have about school life and making friends. They also introduce counting concepts with 100-day books (see Figure 3–4).

---

Here is a list of books that young children will relate to and enjoy discussing.

### Books About School

- ❏ *Annabelle Swift, Kindergartner* by Amy Schwartz, Orchard, 1998.
- ❏ *Chrysanthemum* by Kevin Henkes, Greenwillow, 1991.
- ❏ *Edward Unready For School* by Rosemary Wells, Dial, 1995.
- ❏ *Fox at School* by Edward Marshall, pictures by James Marshall, Dial, 1983.
- ❏ *Lilly's Purple Plastic Purse* by Kevin Henkes, Greenwillow, 1996.
- ❏ *Never Spit on Your Shoes* by Denys Cazet, Orchard, 1990.
- ❏ *Oliver Pig At School* by Jean Van Leeuwen, pictures by Ann Schweninger, Dial, 1990.
- ❏ *Timothy Goes to School* by Rosemary Wells, Dial, 1981.
- ❏ *Wemberly Worried* by Kevin Henkes, Greenwillow, 2000.

*Books by Joseph Slate and illustrated by Ashley Wolff*

- ❏ *Miss Bindergarten Gets Ready for Kindergarten*, Dutton, 1996.
- ❏ *Miss Bindergarten Stays Home From Kindergarten*, Dutton, 2000.
- ❏ *Miss Bindergarten Takes a Field Trip With Kindergarten*, Dutton, 2001.

### Books About Friendship

- ❏ *Amanda Pig and Her Best Friend Lollipop*, by Jean Van Leeuwen, pictures by Ann Schweninger, Dial, 1998.
- ❏ *Amos and Boris* by William Steig, Puffin, 1977.
- ❏ *Best Friends* by Steven Kellogg, Dial, 1986.
- ❏ *Edward's Overwhelming Overnight* by Rosemary Wells, Dial, 1995.
- ❏ *Little blue and little yellow* by Leo Leoni, Mulberry Books, 1995.
- ❏ *My Best Friend* by Pat Hutchins, Greenwillow, 1993.

### Books About Number Concepts

- ❏ *Emily's First 100 Days of School* by Rosemary Wells, Hyperion, 2000.
- ❏ *Miss Bindergarten Celebrates the 100th Day of Kindergarten* by Joseph Slate, illustrated by Ashley Wolff, Dutton, 1998.

**Figure 3–4.** Break-the-Ice Books for the Opening Weeks of School

Connections to these topics are quick, for they are part of the children's experiences. Children listen to these books during family storybook reading and when the teachers read aloud to everyone.

What teachers and children do all year can strengthen or weaken the bonds of community forged during the first weeks of school. Here are some small- and whole-group activities that can continue to build community in your classroom. The important thing is to enjoy everyday life with your students.

❑ Make snacks such as jello, popcorn, trail mix, and cookies.
❑ Collaborate and write dictated stories about field trips, a class pet, and a visitor. Write invitations and thank-you notes.
❑ Survey, then graph on chart paper students' preferences: mitten or gloves, red or yellow apples, plain or chocolate milk, and so on.
❑ Share independent writing and teach the children to respond positively to one another's work.
❑ Have administrators visit to observe and praise children's progress.
❑ Continue learning about each other throughout the year.
❑ Develop a system of helpers so students support you and each other.
❑ Decorate the room with children's work instead of ready-made materials.
❑ Praise what children do well so they can build on these behaviors.
❑ Use poems, songs, chants, and big books for shared reading experiences.
❑ Play whole-group games such as *Simple Simon* and the *Hokey-Pokey*.
❑ Continue to read and discuss books to small groups and the entire class.
❑ Rotate class jobs and celebrate the importance of helping.
❑ Lead sing alongs.
❑ Invite visitors and community helpers into your classroom to model that community extends beyond the school's walls.

*Outside Helpers*

Though two adults seems like a superb ratio to ten to twelve children, there were days that Terri and Lisa wished they had a third hand to help a child during writing workshop or to repeat picture sorts or practice rhyming words. After a brainstorming session with Jane Rea Gaidos and Connie Fauber, principal and assistant principal of Robinson, Lisa and Terri explored two possibilities.

1. Telephone area churches and senior citizen's organizations to see if any retired men and women were willing to volunteer.
2. Contact the high school and speak to the teacher who leads the family living class. Lisa and Terri hoped that the teacher would add volunteering in Literacy Links kindergartens to her curriculum.

Gene Geatry, a retired senior citizen who lives near Robinson volunteered two afternoons a week, spending one with Lisa's group and the other with Terri's class. Because Gene was sensitive, kind, and a top-notch listener, every child wanted to work with her. Gene's afternoons were packed; she and children played name games with plastic letters, reviewed word sorts that needed extra practice, or reread a favorite book. She also helped out during center time.

One day, Kali, Shana, and Samantha were in the "School Center" with Gene who held a whiteboard and marker pen. She was astute enough to let the girls lead the play. "I'm Miss Kali," and "I'm Miss Shana," said the girls. "Samantha, you be the student," offered Kali, obviously the master organizer of the script.

Pointing to Gene, Kali said, "You are the helper. You do what we say." Meeting the girls' requests meant Gene had to correctly spell words they asked for on the whiteboard. Their notes on playing school (Figure 3–5) tell what they will be doing—"reading about school." Kali also writes that Samantha likes her mom and dad and that she likes Samantha. When I asked Kali why she wrote "I like Samantha," she quickly replied, "I have to make her feel great to help her learn." In addition to enlarging children's knowledge base, Terri and Gene were also educating the children's affective domain by raising their awareness of the relationship between self-esteem and achievement.

In the spring, high school students volunteered twice a week for six weeks in both Literacy Links kindergarten classrooms. Because Terri and Lisa met with the teacher in the fall, students arrived prepared to support the children. They read to small groups, worked on picture sorts, helped during center time and writing workshop. Their exit comments revealed how much volunteering taught them about the importance of reading books to children and letting them choose topics for independent writing.

## Dealing with Behavior Problems

Behavior problems occur in all classes. They include shoving a peer, refusing to share or try an activity, hurting someone's feelings, getting in front of a peer while lining up, eating someone's snack without obtaining permission, shouting, and fist-fighting. When children fight and/or physically hurt each other, teacher intervention and consequences are necessary. If the hurtful behavior continues, contact the parents. You might also recommend that the child work with the school's guidance counselor on anger management.

Like Terri and Lisa, I believe that most problems can be solved by the children, placing the responsibility for mending hurt feelings on them. In each class there is a "Time Out Corner" with materials from a program called *It's Your Choice!*, 1994, Rhinestone Press, P.O. Box 30, Winchester, OR, 97495-0030.

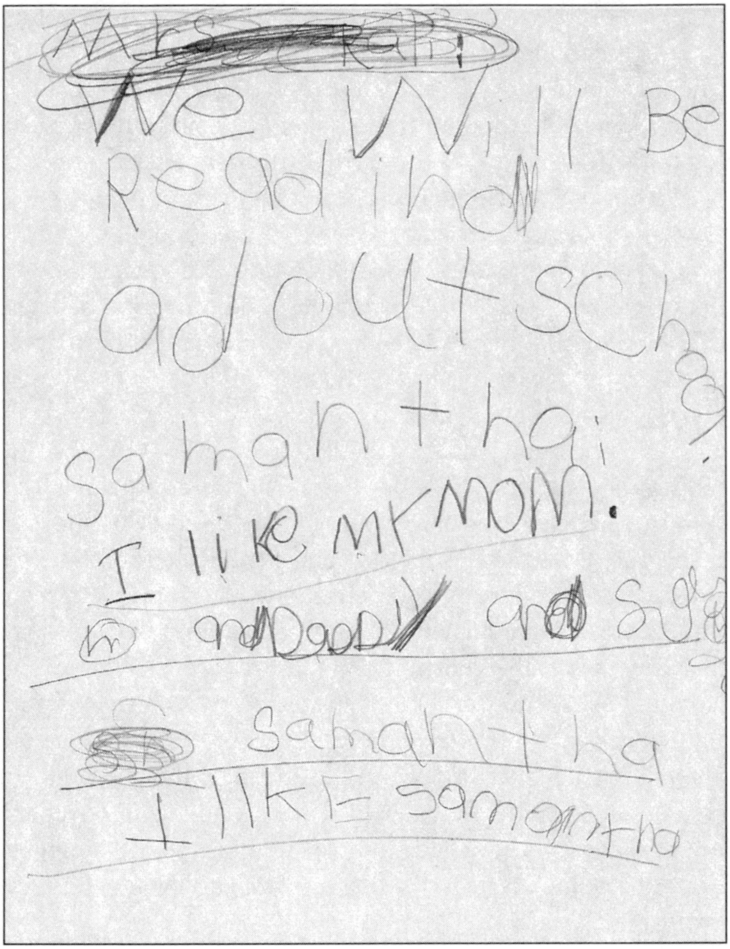

**Figure 3–5.** Kali's notes "playing school"

The program encourages children to think for themselves. First the teacher asks, "What can you do about it?" Then the teacher reads the list of possible solutions until the children choose one or two (Figure 3–6). The list, written on chart paper, includes some of the suggestions in this program.

"It takes time for the process to be absorbed," Lisa and Terri explain. "Offering ideas that can help them resolve differences is what makes this program work." The teacher is there, but the children make the decisions and carry them out. A system that encourages and teaches children to own and solve their problems raises their awareness of how their actions and words affect others. The goal is to prevent unproductive behaviors by encouraging the children to pause and think before acting impulsively and breaking a class rule. A time out corner that invites the children to problem solve works well during the year and in summer school programs.

**Try one or two of these ideas:**
- ❑ Take a deep breath and try to cool off.
- ❑ Go to another game.
- ❑ Ask to move to another center.
- ❑ Talk it out with the person.
- ❑ Walk away and play with another classmate.
- ❑ Ignore it and continue the activity.
- ❑ Tell them politely, "Please stop."
- ❑ Apologize.
- ❑ Explain how you are feeling.
- ❑ Make a deal.
- ❑ Take a time out to think about ways to solve the problem.
- ❑ Ask your teacher for help.

**Figure 3–6.** Having a Small Problem?

## Summer School Schedule at Quarles Elementary School

In Winchester, summer school runs for six weeks. The schedule (see Figure 3–7) reflects the main focus of this post-kindergarten program: reading, writing, and word study. When planning the curriculum for the program, Nancy Reedy, three additional teaching assistants, and I met with the kindergarten staff to gather their recommendations. We studied the children's performance on assessments that measured book and alphabet knowledge, concepts about print, and children's ability to match sounds to letters (see Chapter 4). Depending on children's needs, the emphasis of a post-kindergarten program will differ annually.

| | |
|---|---|
| 8:00 | Warm-up with a song or poem. Morning message. |
| 8:30 | Shared reading of a big book or poem printed on a large chart. |
| 9:20 | Word study: letters, sounds, word families, rhyming, and sight words. |
| 9:45 | Snack/Recess/Family storybook reading. |
| 10:15 | Writing workshop. |
| 11:10 | Read aloud and family storybook reading. |
| 11:30 | Dismissal. |

**Figure 3–7.** Literacy Links Summer School Schedule

*Student Helpers for the Summer School Program*    In order to provide the four teaching assistants with extra help during summer school, I asked them, "How do you feel about having rising ninth grade student helpers?" Reactions, at first, were mixed. Some felt that it might work; others felt that since there was no money to offer students a stipend, their attendance would be erratic. By the end of the discussions, there was consensus to pilot student helpers during the first year of summer school. However, teachers wanted students to commit to participating during at least four of the six weeks. We composed the following list of things student helpers would do, and I shared it during interviews.

- Bring children from buses to their classrooms.
- Prepare the morning snack of peanut butter, crackers, and juice.
- Read aloud to small groups.
- Help monitor recess.
- Prepare materials for lessons.
- Support teachers during lessons.

The first year, two rising ninth graders, Alicia and Jaime, made a commitment to the program. Both girls were in my eighth grade reading-writing workshop, at Powhatan School in Boyce, Virginia. Grounded in reading and writing workshop, I believed the girls could offer excellent support to young children because they had completed hours of community service in area day care centers. Moreover, since fifth grade, Alicia and Jaime had worked with primary grade children at Powhatan and other area schools.

Training the student assistants included meeting the four teaching assistants as well as gaining background knowledge through reading and hands-on experiences with the morning message and shared reading. We all agreed that if a child disrupted the group, instead of the traditional time-out-to-think consequence, one of the girls would quickly name the behavior, discuss with the child ways to change it, then read a story to diminish the escalation of frustration and anger. The girls attended two of the teacher prep meetings held prior to the arrival of the children. Their day, like the teachers, started thirty minutes prior to the buses arriving so they could listen to teachers discuss the children and prepare materials.

During the second year, a third young adult, Rebekah DeHaven, joined the student assistants. The girls rotated among the four classes, supporting all the teachers. They had perfect attendance records, and continued with the program throughout high school.

Nancy Reedy had the girls keep journals of their experiences which she read daily. Alicia's journal chronicled daily work, her feelings toward the children, and their enthusiasm for participating (Figures 3–8 and 3–9).

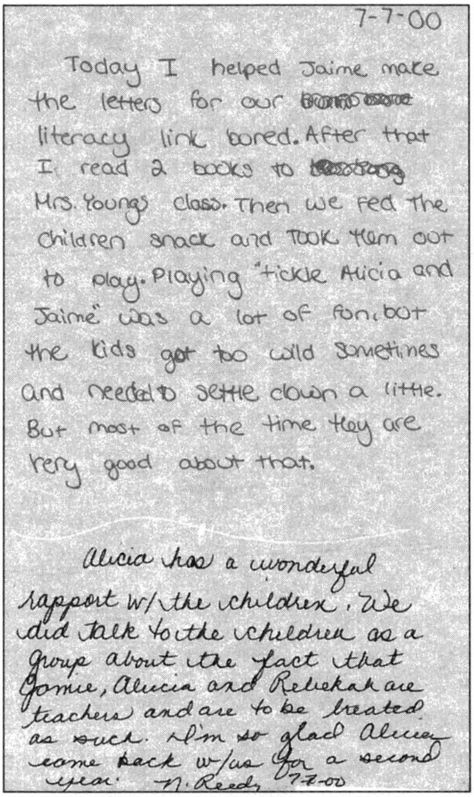
7-7-00

Today I helped Jaime make the letters for our [illegible] literacy link bored. After that I read 2 books to [illegible] Mrs. Youngs class. Then we fed the children snack and TOOK them out to play. Playing "tickle Alicia and Jaime" was a lot of fon, bot the kids got too wild sometimes and needed to settle down a little. But most of the time they are very good about that.

Alicia has a wonderful rapport w/ the children. We did talk to the children as a group about the fact that Jamie, Alicia and Rebekah are teachers and are to be treated as such. I'm so glad Alicia came back w/us for a second year. N. Reedy 7-7-00

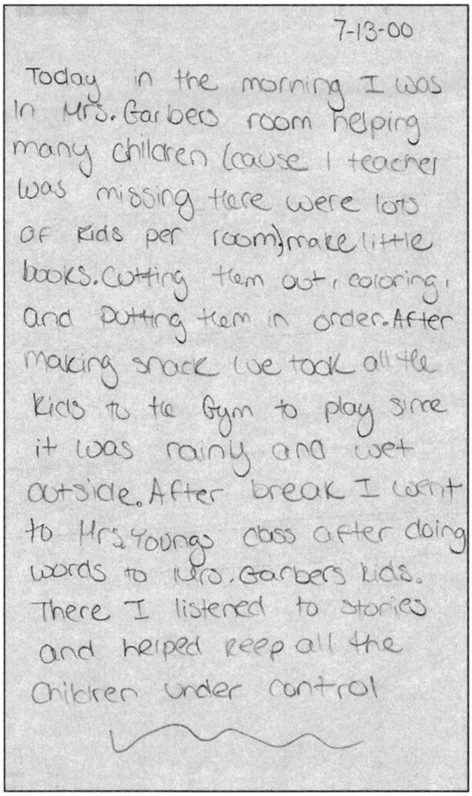
7-13-00

Today in the morning I was in Mrs. Garbers room helping many children (cause 1 teacher was missing there were lots of kids per room) make little books. Cutting tem out, coloring, and putting tem in order. After making snack we took all the kids to the Gym to play since it was rainy and wet outside. After break I went to Mrs. Youngs class after doing words to Mrs. Garbers kids. There I listened to stories and helped keep all the children under control

**Figures 3–8 and 3–9.** Alicia's journal records some of the things she does while helping with the summer program.

Rebekah asked if she could learn how to observe a child and log what she noticed in her journal. When she handed me her journal to read, Rebekah said, "Young children who struggle really need one-on-one help, Mrs. Robb. It helps them see they can concentrate." Then she wistfully added, "I wish every young child could have tons of individual attention at school. Some don't even get it at home because their parents have to work two or three jobs." Rebekah's journal reveals her insights into Katie's behaviors and her empathy and sensitivity to this youngster's needs (Figures 3–10 and 3–11).

After each summer school session ends, I meet with the student helpers to discuss what they have learned. Jaime's comments are ones I will always remember: "I really learned how to read to little children and get them involved with the book. I think this will really help me when I have children. It showed me that reading to little kids is what they need to learn later on."

> I have decided to write about Katie and monitor her progress in my journal.
>
> Friday, July 13
>
> Katie is a very sweet little girl, but she seems very unhappy. She is slow to respond, and Mrs. Reedy told me that the decision to pass or retain her has not been made yet. Katie has a hard time listening to directions, and then applying the directions to an activity. Simple directions seem to confuse her. When she doesn't understand, she sucks her thumb or on her hair, instead of asking questions to try to understand. I have seen some progress with Katie in the past week. She answers questions about letters and words more easily than she did at the beginning. I'm not sure if that is because she recognizes and has learned more, or if she is simply more comfortable with the class now that she knows everyone. Despite being slow, Katie could do much better if she had more attention and one on one interaction.
>
> Monday, July 16
>
> Katie continues to be slow in responding. She was the happiest I had ever seen her when she played with chalk at recess today. She and many of the other kids were unsure about what a sentence was during writing workshop.
>
> Friday, July 20
>
> Katie was excited because her old teacher was the substitute today. Katie knows much more than she acts like. She asks how to make a letter, but if you tell her that she knows and can do it herself, she figures it out. Katie's biggest problem seems to be that she can't take information she knows, or directions and apply them. If she could get past this roadblock, school would be much easier for her.

**Figures 3–10 and 3–11.** Rebekah, a student helper, records her observations of a student in the summer program.

If high school seniors were required, for graduation, to read to and support young children for a semester, they could use their experiences to understand the relationship between reading aloud and becoming literate. Strong bonds develop between young children and their older tutors during read-aloud sessions (Robb 1993). Stories that touch deeply have transforming powers. Stories that touch deeply form friendship bonds that can enlarge the self-confidence of the child and reader. The high school volunteers at Robinson and the student assistants at Quarles discovered, as Alicia said, "That the kids' favorite thing was to hear stories. The more I read to them, the more they loved books." Armed with knowledge born of such powerful experiences, many of these young men and women changed their view of reading from "boring and for school" to "fun and enjoyable." Hopefully, when they have families, each one will read to their own children, thereby fostering emergent literacy in the next generation.

## Closing Reflections

The schedule you plan and continually adjust as well as what happens during the first weeks of school are an important part of building a community of learners. Children begin a new year at school shaky, frightened, and worried about succeeding in a new environment. With the support and guidance of nurturing teachers, they can end the year with enlarged self-confidence, a willingness to take risks and learn from mistakes, the knowledge that they can learn, an understanding that their ideas and opinions matter, and that they can produce meaningful, high-quality work.

The reflective comments teachers made at end-of-the-year debriefing meetings reveal the growth they observed among students and in their own teaching lives.

> When Titus drew a huge book and wrote, "buks ar grt!" I felt that all the reading aloud truly made a difference.—Terri Auckland

> Sometimes it took almost the entire year for small group and one-on-one support to help children match letters and sounds in their writing. But when it happened, there was no stopping them.—Deena Baker

> I learned to be patient. My goals did not always match where the child could go. For me, watching, listening, and studying their writing helped me respond to the child's needs.—Lisa Tusing

As you read on, consider other learning experiences that you can offer children as the school year unfolds. Study a wide range of assessment suggestions in Chapter 4, the elements of a balanced read-aloud program in Chapter 5, how to develop a writing workshop in Chapter 6, and in Chapter 7, discover ways to play with spoken and written language as well as develop literacy through play centers. Then integrate, into your curriculum, those learning events that your observations indicate can best build each child's emergent literacy foundation.

# 4

# Assessing and Selecting Children for Literacy Links

*A close look at early literacy awareness shapes up an understanding of how diverse the literacy foundations are from child to child, how important interactions between teacher and child become if new kinds of awareness are to emerge and, when we understand where the child is, how easy the next step becomes.*

Marie Clay, *By Different Paths, to Common Outcomes* (1998, 4)

"When I watched the video about the Literacy Links program at Quarles Elementary School in Winchester, a realization kept replaying itself in my mind," Jane Gaidos, principal of Robinson Elementary School in Woodstock, Virginia, told me. This video, taped at our local cable station, was a conversation among me and the teaching assistants of Quarles Elementary School in Winchester, Virginia. The purpose of the video was to raise our community's awareness of a program that reconstructed family storybook reading for those children who entered school with little book knowledge.

"What thoughts did that video trigger?" I asked.

Jane explained her epiphany. "Take those children who arrive at school and are not ready for our kindergarten program. Even if they spend two years in kindergarten, their progress can be minimal and not enough to be successful in first grade. These children repeat in a program that is inappropriate for their needs and gather two years of unsuccessful school experiences. If the first year in kindergarten did not serve them well, how can a repeat of the same program support their specific needs?"

Jane's insights mirrored my own thinking—thoughts that developed as I observed the children in kindergarten at Quarles during family storybook reading and whole-group lessons. In small groups, at-risk learners were more attentive and interested in listening to books. When part of a small or large heterogeneous group, delayed learners rarely answered questions because responses from their more literate peers came faster. Gradually, at-risk children became more and more silent and appeared disengaged during book discussions, phonics lessons, and shared writing experiences. When playing at the block, grocery, or home centers, the children from literacy rich backgrounds often dominated play, offering at-risk boys and girls minor roles or not including them. In need of more time to process, think, and connect information to what they already knew, in need of additional background knowledge about narrative, nonfiction, print, and letter/sound relationships, this group did not interact with the teacher and peers during daily experiences and play that required emergent literacy (Owocki 1998).

Deena Baker, a gentle, observant, and talented kindergarten teacher at Winchester's Virginia Avenue/Charlotte DeHart School, describes what happened to Uvaldo, a delayed learner, during writing workshop. When Uvaldo entered Deena's kindergarten, he could identify three alphabet letters and was unable to match sounds to letters. "I would watch Uvaldo's hand tremble during writing workshop," Deena told me. "He'd see his friends writing letters and words, and Uvaldo felt so anxious and worried about writing—even when I sat with him to support and comfort him. His hand and whole body trembled. To me, it felt like writing, for Uvaldo was torture because he feared that what he wrote was 'no good.'"

In his groundbreaking book, *The Foundations of Literacy* (1979), Don Holdaway points out that children who have not developed emergent reading behaviors do poorly in programs that assume they have a "strong literacy set." Holdaway states, "Without adequately developed strategies for exploring written language, we would expect such children to experience great difficulty and confusion in facing the highly complex and refined processes of relating cues in early reading" (57).

In January 1999, Jane and I began constructing the foundation for a different kind of kindergarten—one that would support those children who lacked emergent literacy. The first hurdle was to find funding for two kindergarten classes with a maximum of twelve to thirteen children, each staffed with a full-time teacher and teaching assistant.

## Funding Two Additional Kindergarten Classes

Knowing that finances were extremely tight, Jane had to think outside of the easy box of asking for state and federal funds—money from neither coffer was available. At Robinson, there are eight kindergarten classes with twenty to twenty-one children in each section. In addition to a certified kindergarten teacher, each class had a half-day teaching assistant. Annually, every kindergarten teacher had two to five students who were unable to learn from the standard kindergarten program and who made little to no progress after one year. Moreover, Jane's observations and conversations with kindergarten teachers revealed a common feeling: We don't have enough time to meet these children's needs and we just don't know how to support this population's learning. So, Jane called a meeting of kindergarten teachers and proposed two adjustments to class numbers and organization.

1. In exchange for giving up two to four delayed learners, six kindergarten teachers would have up to twenty-six children whose testing showed they were ready to learn from Robinson's kindergarten program. The number of kindergarten teachers remained the same, so funding salaries was not an issue.
2. Each of the six kindergarten teachers would have a teaching assistant for half instead of a whole day. This freed two teaching assistants to spend a full day in the two new Literacy Links kindergarten sections.

In the fall, Jane invited her kindergarten staff to meet in large and small groups to discuss and consider this proposal, look at the benefits and drawbacks, and report their decision by the end of February. After several meetings, teachers decided to approve Jane's reorganization plan. This meant that Robinson would have two kindergarten sections, each with no more than thirteen students. Classrooms would be located side-by-side in the first grade corridor to avoid any negative questions or feedback from kindergarten peers in other sections.

Profits from picture money and soda machines and money raised by the school's PTO provided funds for classroom supplies and a rich classroom library. At Robinson, the PTO annually raises $8,000 to $10,000 for school and classroom libraries. Some of the PTO funds help stock the Literacy Links kindergartens with books and materials.

### *Organizing Literacy Links in Small Schools*

Schools with smaller populations than Robinson Elementary can also meet the needs of diverse learners and reconstruct the family storybook reading they lack. Instead of organizing separate kindergarten classes, teaching assistants and parent volunteers can read aloud to four children three to four times a day. During the reading-writing block, teaching assistants can work with one group while the class-room teacher supports children who are at risk for not developing emergent literacy and moving on to first grade. A summer school program like the one at Quarles Elementary can also develop and improve emergent literacy. The important point is to serve these children well so they become literate and productive members of our society.

However, for both Literacy Links kindergartens at Robinson Elementary School to succeed, Jane and I wanted two teachers who were willing to abandon the standard lessons that had not served these children in the past and step into uncharted territory, constructing and adjusting their maps as the year unfolded.

## Choosing Teachers for the Program

When Jane and I chatted about choosing two teachers for the Literacy Links kindergartens at Robinson, we brainstormed a list of desirable qualities in candidates who applied for these positions. We agreed that the following qualities were key to the program's success. We wanted teachers to:

- ❑ Feel as passionate about the program as Jane and I did.
- ❑ Look closely at what children say and do in order to respond appropriately and to plan supportive and meaningful learning experiences.
- ❑ Grow to know and respect what children were able to accomplish throughout the year.
- ❑ Have inner strength of purpose and a belief in the program that would support their taking paths that differed from a standard set of instruction in order to develop emergent literacy.
- ❑ Communicate with one another, with Jane and me, with the guidance counselor, and with both reading recovery teachers to explore and discuss each child's progress and responses to various experiences.
- ❑ Have the flexibility to adjust and/or change tasks so that they can identify what each child can do, build on that strength, and help the child progress.

First, Jane invited teachers from the Bright Star program for four-year-olds and from her kindergarten staff to apply for these positions. Bright Star is a Head Start program for three- to five-year-olds whose families are in poverty and are unable to consistently support their children's literacy development. After several rounds of interviewing, Jane, with the support of her assistant principal, Connie Fauber, chose two teachers with diverse backgrounds: Lisa Tusing and Terri Auckland. Jane and Connie based their decision on the pair's passionate desire to support delayed learners and their willingness to create a program that responded to and focused on children's strengths. Their administrators believed that both women had three qualities that would enable them to tune into children's talk and questions and improve children's social interactions. They had:

- Keen listening skills.
- A positive stance that continually celebrated what children did well.
- The ability to communicate with colleagues and administration.

Lisa had two years of teaching experience. She worked with preschool children ages three to five in Robinson's Bright Star program—an all-day preschool for two groups of ten children who would benefit from play and literacy experiences. More than anything, Lisa wanted to continue to help the children who "needed something different than the standard kindergarten curriculum at Robinson." Terri, a veteran kindergarten teacher with twenty years in the classroom, wanted a chance to help those who "I knew could be successful learners if I had the time and support to work closely with them every day and develop their literacy."

Terri Auckland, Lisa Tusing, and I created a program that builds on what children can do when they arrive at school. We believed that if students experienced success instead of continual frustration, if students lived through experiences designed to promote and not impede their learning, gaps in children's literacy knowledge could and would be bridged. Moreover, I hoped that by immersing the children in literacy experiences they could connect to, their self-confidence and motivation to learn would increase and flourish (Cambourne 1988, Clay 1998).

## An Overview of the Families of Children in Literacy Links

The families of children in the Literacy Links programs of the Virginia schools I worked in came from varied backgrounds. Economically, the group ranged from those who worked but struggled to make ends meet because of low incomes to two parents working with adequate incomes. Jobs ranged from night or day shift work in area factories to working on farms, doing odd jobs, or custodial and office work. Some families experienced short or long bouts of unemployment and received government food stamps and welfare assistance.

Single parents and families with both parents working sent children to area day care facilities from early in the morning until dinnertime. In some families, grandparents, other relatives, or friends cared for the children during the day. For several children, one or two working grandparents were the caretakers.

Most parents were exhausted from working long hours, running a household, and caring for children. Because populations in these rural and small city areas were fairly stable, principals and teachers had taught many of the children's parents. "These parents had unsuccessful school experiences. They were not good readers and writers, and they lacked the personal confidence and background to create strong, literacy-rich environments," Jane Gaidos and Connie Fauber explained. Principals at other schools made the same observations.

There were parents who dropped out before completing high school and parents who could barely read. No parent attended or graduated from a community or four-year college. Some in the group had drinking problems. Some were serving jail sentences. In several homes, the father was absent and the mother lived with one or a series of different boyfriends.

Each year a group of parents did not want their children to participate in the Literacy Links kindergarten. Administrators invited these parents to meet the teachers, learn about the program, and ask questions. Parents received assurance that their children would not be labeled, but would be offered the support needed to experience success at school. When parents did not come to school, teachers made home visits. If resistance did not diminish, we asked parents to give the program a trial run for the first two months of school.

Most of the parents in the Literacy Links programs were pleased that their children were receiving the attention and support they never had as children. These hardworking men and women arrived home physically worn out, had to prepare dinner, go to a laundromat to wash clothes because they couldn't afford a washing machine, clean their trailer or apartment, and so on. Factor in their own discomfort with reading and writing and it's understandable that reading to their children was not high on their daily agendas. I offer this information not to pass judgment on or blame these parents, but to provide a more complete picture of poverty and the daily lives of the children we served.

### Life at the Financial Bottom of Society

In her book, *Nickel and Dimed: On (Not) Getting By in America*, Barbara Ehrenreich (2001) destroys the stereotypes about poverty and families that struggle to make ends meet. Uninformed and therefore unable to step into the shoes of poor families, it's easy for those of us who earn enough to live comfortably to embrace these false generalizations:

- ❑ Poor people are lazy and don't want to work hard.
- ❑ Poor people waste their money purchasing nonessential, luxury items.
- ❑ Poor people don't take pride in keeping their living quarters neatly furnished and clean.
- ❑ Poor parents don't care about developing their children's literacy.
- ❑ Poor people don't know how to manage money efficiently.
- ❑ Poor parents don't use their time to talk and read to their children.
- ❑ Poor people have no knowledge of good nutrition and eat junk food.

In 1998, Barbara Ehrenreich decided to join the millions of Americans who work full-time all year but earn poverty-level wages. Her decision was prompted by the empty rhetoric of welfare reform—rhetoric that preached that any full-time job would build a better life than welfare checks for men, women, and families. In Florida, Maine, and Minnesota, Ehrenreich obtained jobs as a waitress, hotel maid, sales clerk, cleaning woman, and nursing home aide. Her experiences showed that one person working steadily at minimum wage jobs or jobs that paid $7 to $10 per hour was not enough to meet monthly expenses. Even with two parents working full-time, it was impossible for them (or parents with one to two children) to meet basic expenses of rent, food, clothing, medical bills, and transportation costs. Unreasonably high rents for dilapidated, vermin infested living quarters consumed 50 percent or more of workers' low monthly incomes, forcing adults with children to seek additional employment. Employers do not provide minimum wage earners with health insurance. When illness strikes, it quickly depletes any savings. Therefore, family members don't receive adequate medical or dental care because they don't have the money to pay the costs.

Again and again, Ehrenreich reveals how tough it was for her to pay all of her bills. Fortunate because she used her own savings to pay a security deposit on an apartment or a large doctor's bill, Ehrenreich points out that most of her coworkers did not have the luxury of a savings account. Moreover, many families that work full-time in cities end up in homeless shelters because they don't make enough money to pay high rents or security deposits. When parents work twelve to fourteen hours every day and still struggle to survive, it takes chutzpah, nerve, to indict them for not reading aloud, visiting the library, and engaging their children in meaningful conversations.

Education is one way to reverse the cycle of low wages born of a lack of marketable skills and training. As Ehrenreich says, "There seems to be a vicious cycle at work here, making ours not just an economy but a culture of extreme inequality" (212). Instead of pouring millions of federal dollars into more high-stakes tests, the government needs to adopt a multipronged approach, making its primary goal the elimination of poverty so parents have money, time, and energy to build literate home environments. Dollars spent on developing extra tests should go to building affordable housing, developing a nationwide cadre of outstanding teachers, then supplying schools in poverty areas with the finest teachers, books, and materials. In addition, state and local governments should develop community outreach programs that model and encourage literacy for all community members.

Studies completed by Bembry and colleagues (1998) showed that after three years, those students learning in classrooms with high-quality instruction scored 40 percentile ranks higher on standardized reading tests than students learning in classrooms with low-quality instruction. Pressley and coauthors (2000) studied outstanding first-grade teachers. In these classrooms, the lowest-achieving students did as well as the average students. What this means is that excellent instruction, along with appropriate materials, holds the potential of improving the academic performance of all children.

## Extending Our Reach: The Goals of Literacy Links

The purposes and goals of the Literacy Links program are to develop emergent literacy, children's belief in themselves as capable learners, as well as a pride and joy in being literate. Teachers communicate with parents and caretakers through conferences, telephone calls, and by sending journals for children to complete at home. We set high goals, but kept Terri Auckland's cautionary words close to the surface of our minds: "If we push these children too fast, in the long run we lose growth."

Instead of dwelling on the lack of literacy experiences that children brought to school, we emphasized these goals:

❏ To grow literate children who will share their love of reading and writing with one another, their families, and eventually their own children.
❏ To help these children feel comfortable in the school and local library, visit regularly, and check out books.
❏ To develop social skills and children's ability to extend conversation so they can participate as equals in play and learning events with all children.
❏ To enable children to gain the literacy that generates hope in the possibility of gaining an education, instead of the hopelessness born of knowing that your limited literacy skills close door after door.

The dreams of a sixth-grade boy who moved to Clarke County, Virginia, from Jamaica define the hope and determination to succeed that I want for all children. Jack's (pseudonym) mother worked as a maid; his dad did odd jobs on area farms. The family of six lived in a makeshift house in a garage that had no plumbing or running water. They used an outhouse in back of the garage and pumped cold water from a nearby well. For three years, Jack attended an extra reading/writing class I facilitated before the school day started. In sixth, seventh, and eighth grade, teachers required attendance in this class because Jack read two years below grade level and had difficulty learning from content area textbooks. Jack's goal, to go to college, get a good job, and rent a decent house for his family, was the beacon that motivated him to study and complete extra work.

In high school, Jack's work was excellent, and each year he found teachers willing to support him when he struggled with subjects such as chemistry or calculus. Because Jack became a proficient reader and developed solid study habits, he was successful and eventually went to college. However, Jack started his education journey in sixth grade; powerful goals nudged Jack to work diligently and break his failure cycle. Most struggling middle school students are not as fortunate. The 1998 National Assessment of Educational Progress (NAEP), the test that has become our nation's literacy report card, shows little progress in reading scores from 1971 to 1998. In fact, according to the NAEP, only six percent of high schoolers are advanced readers who can infer and critically analyze texts (NAEP 1999). That's why literacy interventions must begin early on.

When children receive support in preschool and kindergarten, launching their literacy journey the moment they arrive at day care centers and school, there is hope that most will develop the emergent literacy to become good to excellent readers and writers. Children benefit from programs that, as Lisa Tusing and Terri Auckland explain, "Don't ask children to walk before they crawl. But meet children where they are."

That's why Literacy Links teachers and I cheer and shout "Hurrah!" every time a child asks, "Will you read that book again?" Those six words inform us that indeed the book and child have connected, the desire to reexperience the story, savor and resavor every part is developing, revealing the first root of the child's emerging literacy.

## Choosing Students for Literacy Links Programs

"How do we choose the children?" "What if we fail to spot a child who would benefit from this program?" All teachers and teaching assistants I worked with agonized over the process of selecting a limited number of students. The principals and I supported them by eliminating specific groups from consideration because schools already offered supportive special services for learning disabled, emotionally disturbed, special education, and ESL.

Choosing children for the Literacy Links kindergartens at Robinson Elementary was the most difficult. Because of the maximum of thirteen children in each class, it was not possible to place every child in the program. Based on a variety of screening instruments, teachers chose the most delayed children. Children, who Lisa, Terri, and others such as the speech therapist and guidance counselor believed would be able to develop emergent literacy were considered. Were their decisions always on target? Of course not. However, 90 to 95 percent of their choices worked because they had a wide range of information about the children.

The family storybook reading and summer program at Quarles, as well as the specialized support program at Virginia Avenue/Charlotte DeHart Schools, could support more children. For example, forty kindergartners at Quarles participated in the family storybook reading program and forty to fifty children attended summer school. At Virginia Avenue/Charlotte DeHart, groups of six to ten children in each of the five kindergarten classes received additional support throughout the year. The Head Start programs at Keister Elementary in Harrisonburg and Robinson Elementary in Woodstock used poverty income and data from area Social Services and day care centers to make admission decisions.

By using several screening instruments and by reviewing the feedback of everyone who assessed the children, schools were able to make informed decisions. In Virginia, I worked in rural or small city schools. Each school developed their own criteria for choosing children, which is appropriate, because of the scheduling variations and the differences in the populations each school served. As you study and reflect on the ways to assess emergent literacy, think of and select the screenings and feedback that help you best assess your school's population. Use the screenings and the thoughtful reflections of teachers to support your decisions.

**Criteria for Admissions into Literacy Links Programs**

*Use the guidelines that follow to help you gather and reflect on information about each child entering kindergarten. I recommend that a team of teachers review and discuss the data.*

❑ *Parents' age.* Young teenage parents still need parenting themselves and have not developed a philosophy of child rearing. Many return to school or work to support their child, forcing them to use inadequate day care.

❑ *Parents' educational level.* Those who dropped out of school because they had difficulty learning to read and write well often pass these feelings about books and learning to their children by not reading aloud. Moreover, many high school dropouts are functionally illiterate and can not read to their children.

❑ *Socioeconomic level.* Parents living in poverty struggle daily to feed and clothe their children and pay rent for housing. Totally exhausted at the end of each day, literacy development is not always high on their list of things to do.

❑ *Family history of learning problems.* Children who inherit learning difficulties benefit from extra support at school.

❑ Additional issues that can result in children arriving at school developmentally delayed.

    ❑ No preschool experience.

    ❑ A child's age.

    ❑ The child's oral language development.

    ❑ The child's school entry standardized testing scores.

    ❑ Anecdotal records compiled by the school entry team.

    ❑ Recommendations by a child's pediatrician.

    ❑ Recommendations by preschool teachers, speech therapists, and/or occupational therapists.

Considering a range of information gathered on each child can assist you in making decisions about where to place those entering kindergarten. Record the notes and comments gathered. Then invite the admissions team to review and discuss these in order to make a placement recommendation.

## Assessments That Describe Emergent Literacy

The assessments that follow will enable you to collect data on different aspects of emergent literacy for all children entering kindergarten (Clay 1991, 2000). Given in the spring, prior to admission into kindergarten, teachers readminister all or parts of these assessments at different points during the year to measure children's progress and to adjust their instructional plans. With these assessments you can look at each child's:

- ❑ Book knowledge
- ❑ Concepts of print
- ❑ Oral language fluency
- ❑ Letter knowledge
- ❑ Letter/sound knowledge

As you read on, consider how each assessment enables you to gain insights into emergent literacy behaviors as well as guidelines for assessment (Clay 1985, 1991, 1998; Fiderer 1998; Gillet and Temple 2000; Hill and Ruptic 1994).

## Assessing Emergent Literacy Behaviors

Gathering information about each child's knowledge of reading and writing before they enter preschool and kindergarten enables you to gain insight into what children can do and develop a program that teaches them within their zone of proximal development (Vygotsky). This is what I call responsive teaching. Responsive teachers observe, listen, and assess what the child does and says. Then, they frame learning experiences that respect and honor where the child is regarding literacy and social development. Responsive teaching is the exact opposite of designing a program to teach a standardized body of information you know that the child does not know.

Throughout the school year, either you or your teaching assistant can repeat assessments to monitor students' progress. In Literacy Links schools, I trained teaching assistants to administer screening tests and to do interactive read-alouds. Once your observations tell you that a child has absorbed and can apply information, reassess to document your hunches. These assessments, combined with your careful observations of children at work and play, will enable you to adjust instruction and learning experiences so you can support the progress and growth of every child.

## Book Knowledge

Not only is it important for children to have heard hundreds of stories read aloud prior to kindergarten, but it's also necessary for children, when they arrive in kindergarten, to know their way around books (Clay 1985, Snow and Griffin 1998). With book knowledge, listening to and discussing pictures and stories become meaningful experiences. Once children have book knowledge, teacher's references to the title, author, top and bottom of a page, and the direction of reading make sense. Matching speech to print, valuing books as sources of pleasure and learning, knowing how to "read" and "write" books, all require that children have a knowledge of how books work.

## Guidelines for Assessing

To assess book knowledge and behaviors, use a favorite picture book. I repeatedly use *The Snowy Day* by Ezra Jack Keats (1962), *Silly Billy!* by Pat Hutchins (1992), and *The Missing Mitten Mystery* by Steven Kellogg (2000). Continue to assess behaviors that the child has not yet developed, so you can plan supportive learning experiences. The following are suggestions for gathering information on children's knowledge of books (Clay [1979] 2000, Gillet and Temple 2000). You can record children's responses using Figure 4–1. If the child does not follow your directions, then make sure you jot down exactly what the child does.

*Book Structure*   With the spine facing the child, give him or her the book. Note how the child holds the book. Next, ask the child to show you the front cover, the title, then the back cover.

*Top and Bottom of Page*   Open the book to a pair of pages that have print and pictures on one page and pictures on the other. Make sure the book you select has these kind of pages. Place your finger in the middle of the page with print and ask the child to point to the top, then the bottom of that page. Repeat the procedure with the illustrated page.

*Print Contains the Message*   Using the same pages, ask the child, "Show me where I begin to read." If the child's pointing is unclear, repeat: "Can you show me the exact place I begin to read?" The child should point to the first letter or word on that page.

*Directionality: How We Read Print*   Continue with the same pages. Invite the child to put a finger on the print. If the child points to print, then ask the child to use her finger to show what you would read next. Continue asking, "What do I read next?" and observe whether the child moves her hand across the page from left to right and drops down to the next line, continuing from left to right. Note exactly what the child does, even if the child removes her finger from the page or jumps to the illustration.

# A Checklist for Assessing and Monitoring Book Behaviors

Name_____

| Behavior and Teacher's Notes | Dates |
|---|---|

Holds book correctly

_____    ____

Knows front and back covers and title

_____    ____

Top and bottom of page with print/pictures

_____    ____

Knows top and bottom of page with pictures

_____    ____

Turns pages right to left

_____    ____

Knows where print starts on a page

_____    ____

Demonstrates line directionality

_____    ____

Demonstrates we read print from left to right

_____    ____

Knows concepts of beginning and end

_____    ____

Knows the next page

_____    ____

Makes meaningful comments about illustrations

_____    ____

Pretend reads, retelling story in own words

_____    ____

Looks at books independently

_____    ____
_____    ____

**Figure 4–1.**   A Checklist for Assessing and Monitoring Book Behaviors

*Knows the Concept of Beginning and End of a Page*   Turn to another page and ask the child to point to the place where the story begins on that page and the place where the story ends on that page.

*Knows the Next Page*   Invite the child to turn to the next page of the story.

*Can Talk About the Pictures*   Help the child take a picture-walk through half of the book, asking him to look at and think about the illustrations. Next, start from the beginning, and pointing to two to three illustrations, ask the child to tell you about the pictures.

## Pointers for Using the Reproducible

Once you have screened a child's book knowledge, you can note her progress by observing the child's book behaviors during independent reading time and when you sit side-by-side and read aloud. You can redo parts of the book knowledge assessment in the middle and at the end of the year to confirm your observations and gather specific information to pass onto the child's next teacher. Moreover, your noted observations make parent-teacher conferences more accurate and add credibility to suggestions you offer to parents regarding what they can do at home to develop their child's book knowledge.

During independent reading, when you invite children to choose a book and "read" silently, you can easily observe when they start "pretend" reading and whether they choose a book during free choice and center times.

## Oral Language Fluency

The data Gordon Wells collected from his Bristol research project placed listening to stories as the key prerequisite for literacy development (1986). Family storybook reading also stimulates rich and varied questions and dialogue between the adult and child. Such conversations offer countless opportunities for developing children's knowledge that what they say can be written with words as they watch an adult point to and speak the words on a page.

Discussions about books build background knowledge and often, the stories children know and love enter their play, thus extending the talk between children and when children play alone. The research of Snow, Burns, and Griffin (1998) points out the relationship between children's oral language fluency and their literacy development. Children who use oral language learn to express ideas with ease and competence. They develop more sophisticated syntax patterns through continual exchanges with adults and peers (Pflaum 1986).

At home, parents can develop oral language based on the children's observations of their environment and children's curiosity and comments about illustrations in storybooks (Pflaum 1986). For example, my neighbor, Ann Havron, waits for the school bus with Sam, her three year old. As the yellow bus nears the corner, Sam points and says, "Mommy. Look. Bus."

Ann's response extends and expands Sam's words: "Yes, the school bus is coming. It will stop at the corner. Look for your sister walking down the aisle and stepping off the bus." By providing her son with an oral language model that expands Sam's three words, Sam, in a wide range of situations, repeatedly hears how he can develop his thoughts (Pflaum 1986). Eventually, Sam will imitate the models his mother offers, and transform his noun-verb-centered utterances into complete and complex sentences. Parents can also extend their children's speech by asking a question that encourages the child to respond with words as well as offering a clear explanation of a child's question.

*Guidelines for Assessing Oral Language Fluency*   It's possible that some children will arrive at school demonstrating that they need to develop book knowledge but also showing well-developed oral language ability. These children have listened to oral stories and engaged in meaningful conversations with family members and other adults. I have found that their knowledge of how oral language works will enable them to link what they know to storybook reading. Therefore, it's important to gain insights into children's oral literacy.

*Assessing Oral Language Fluency Through a Conversation*   As much as possible, use the same introductory question with each child, making sure the question can stimulate a meaningful exchange. I use the phrase "as much as possible" because the follow-up questions that probe deeper into the child's experiences depend on each child's initial answers. Using the same opening statement/question enables you to compare children's responses. Record on paper all follow-up queries, and what you and the child say. What follows is the procedure, which takes about five minutes, and some initiating questions. You can use these or, as a team, create questions that you feel the incoming kindergarten population will enjoy.

### Oral Conversation Procedure

1. Come to the conversation believing that the child will want to participate and will respond.
2. Maintain a sense of equality between yourself and the child. Never talk down to the child.
3. Introduce yourself. Briefly explain what you and the child will do. Let the child know that you will be recording what both of you say. Here's what I say: "Hi! My name is Mrs. Robb. I'm a teacher and a mom with two children. Today, you and I are going to chat for a few minutes, and I will write down what we say."

4. Say out loud the words you are writing. If the child says, "I don't want to talk to you," honor the statement by saying, "So you don't want to talk today. Can you tell me why?" Responses might include: *I don't want to; I don't feel like it; I don't know.*

If you can't gain cooperation within a few minutes, note exactly what has happened. These responses can indicate a need for socialization, a mistrust of adults based on personal experiences, or emotional difficulties. Reviewing other assessments, talking to parents and preschool teachers will enable you to decide whether to refer the child to the school's guidance counselor for additional screening.

5. Here are two introductory statements and the questions I have posed.
   - ❏ I love to ride my bike. What do you do in your free time?
   - ❏ I like to swim in the city pool in the summer? What do you like to do in the summer?

### What to Look for When Evaluating Oral Conversations
   - ❏ Note whether the child speaks in single words, phrases, or sentences.
   - ❏ Note whether the child uses specific nouns for events and objects.
   - ❏ Note the syntax. Is it correct or incorrect?
   - ❏ Note the tone the child used. Did he whisper? Did she hesitate between words? Did she mumble?
   - ❏ Note the rate of speech: clear and distinct, slow, rapid, words run together, pauses that indicate punctuation.

Figures 4–2 and 4–3 are two contrasting records of oral conversations. One shows well-developed oral language fluency, the other reveals limited development. Note the kinds of follow-up questions I ask to maintain the conversation. Avoid questions that can be answered with "yes" or "no" because these don't continue the exchange.

*Concepts of Print: Word, Spaces, Letters, Punctuation*   Marie Clay developed a Concepts About Print Test in 1979 that assesses what children know about words and punctuation on a printed page (1986). Like Clay, many educators believe that specific print knowledge is part of emergent literacy. Knowing that there are spaces between words on a page and where words start and end, and knowing basic writing conventions all support children's learning to read and write.

Though many children entering school have acquired most or all of the concepts of print, assessing incoming kindergarten children will reveal a number of children who do not. Because these concepts are an important part of emergent literacy, knowing what children can do prior to entering kindergarten will enable teachers to plan a program that develops these behaviors in every child.

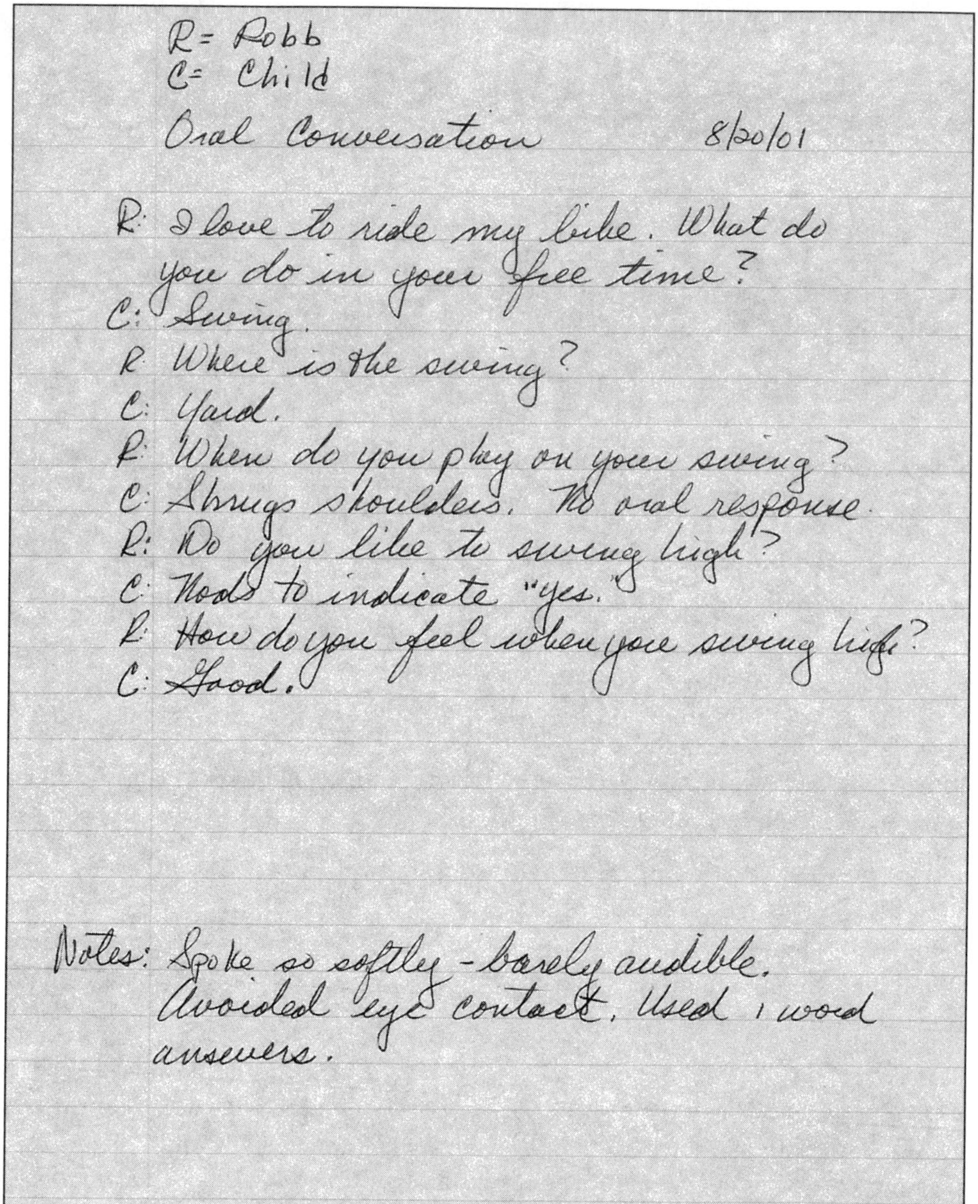

R = Robb
C = Child

Oral Conversation                    8/20/01

R: I love to ride my bike. What do you do in your free time?
C: Swing.
R: Where is the swing?
C: Yard.
R: When do you play on your swing?
C: Shrugs shoulders. No oral response.
R: Do you like to swing high?
C: Nods to indicate "yes."
R: How do you feel when you swing high?
C: Good.

Notes: Spoke so softly - barely audible. Avoided eye contact. Used 1 word answers.

**Figure 4–2.** Oral conversation of a child who has difficulty expressing ideas

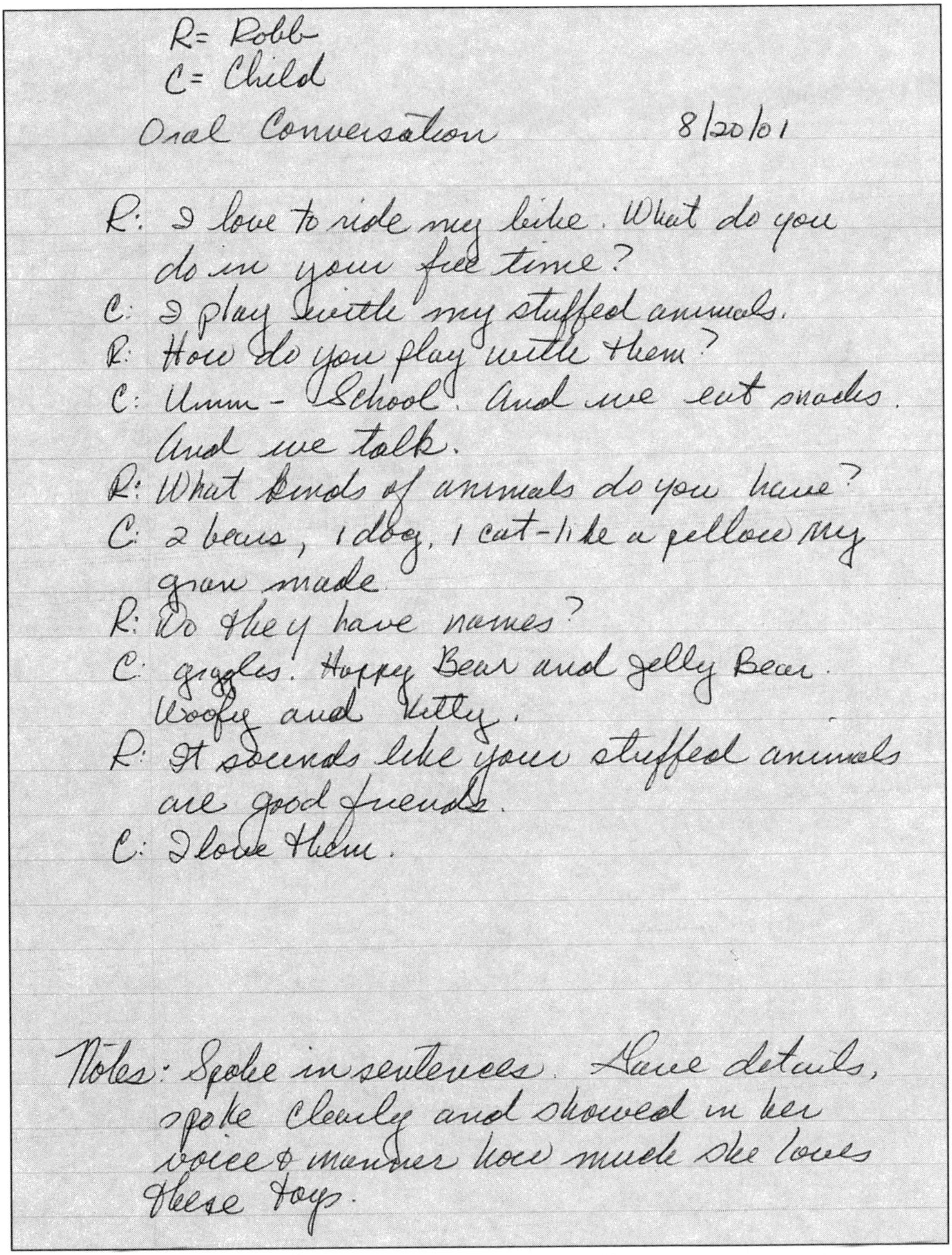

R = Robb
C = Child
Oral Conversation                                8/20/01

R: I love to ride my bike. What do you
   do in your free time?
C: I play with my stuffed animals.
R: How do you play with them?
C: Umm — School. And we eat snacks.
   And we talk.
R: What kinds of animals do you have?
C: 2 bears, 1 dog, 1 cat — like a pillow my
   gran made.
R: Do they have names?
C: giggles. Happy Bear and Jelly Bear.
   Woofy and Kitty.
R: It sounds like your stuffed animals
   are good friends.
C: I love them.


Notes: Spoke in sentences. Gave details,
spoke clearly and showed in her
voice & manner how much she loves
these toys.

**Figure 4–3.** Oral conversation of a child who develops ideas

*Guidelines for Assessing Concepts of Word, Spaces, Letters, and Punctuation*   This assessment is easy to administer. Like Yetta Goodman (1981), I recommend that teachers select a picture book that is culturally relevant to their school's population instead of using Clay's books *Sand* or *Stones*, which she developed for and used with children from New Zealand. Choose a book that the child has not seen. I find it's helpful to have two to three books available, so if a child knows one, we can choose from two other books. Using Figure 4–4, note exactly what the child does and says.

*Words and Spaces Between Words*   Open the book to a page with print. Next, give the child both parts of a 3 × 5 index card that has been cut in half. Ask the child to use both pieces of the index card to show the beginning and end of one word on the page. Then have the child use both pieces to show the space between two words.

*First and Last, Upper- and Lowercase Letters of Words*   Using the same page, ask the child to point to the first letter of a word. Then ask the child to point to the last letter of the same word.

Use the terms *uppercase* or *capital* or *lowercase* or *small letters* for this next assessment. Be consistent so you don't confuse the child. Now, point to an uppercase letter and ask the child to point to a lowercase letter that is the same. Next, point to a lowercase letter and ask the child to find and point to the same uppercase letter. Make sure these letters can be found on the page you've chosen.

*Punctuation*   Open to a page that has a period. Point to the period and ask the child to tell you what it is and what it's used for. Do the same for question mark, comma, and quotation marks.

## Alphabet and Letter/Sound Relationships

"I can say all the letters," Tanisha tells Danielle Waters at the start of the school year. And, indeed, Tanisha proceeds to recite all twenty-six. According to Danielle, Tanisha arrived in Keister's Head Start program knowing her alphabet. At the end of the year, in her observational notes, Danielle writes:

> By the end of this year, she [Tanisha] was sounding out words, building a sight word vocabulary, tracking with voice-to-print match, matching letters and sounds, rhyming and clapping syllables.

Danielle's notes provoke a key idea about teaching children the alphabet—an idea that invites the consideration of our goals. Knowledge of the alphabet is one of the literacy behaviors we want kindergarten children to have. However, when assessment shows that children do not know their alphabet, drilling them with flash cards and games so they can say the letters considers one narrow benefit of learning

## Concepts of Words, Spaces, Letters, and Punctuation

Name_____

                                        **Date**

Points to a letter on the page.       ____ ____ ____

Points to a word.       ____ ____ ____

Points to a space between words.       ____ ____ ____

Points to a complete word.       ____ ____ ____

Points to the first letter of a word.       ____ ____ ____

Points to the last letter of a word.       ____ ____ ____

Points to an uppercase or capital letter.       ____ ____ ____

Points to a lowercase or small letter.       ____ ____ ____

Can name "period" and knows its use.       ____ ____ ____

Can name a "question mark" and knows its use.       ____ ____ ____

Can name a "comma" and knows its use.       ____ ____ ____

Can name "quotation marks" and knows its use.       ____ ____ ____

**Additional Comments:**

**Figure 4–4.** Concepts of Words, Spaces, Letters, and Punctuation
© 2003 by Laura Robb from *Literacy Links*. Portsmouth, NH: Heinemann.
Based on Marie Clay's *Concepts About Print: What Have Children Learned About the Way We Print Language?*
Portsmouth, NH: Heinemann, 2000.

the alphabet. For alphabet knowledge to be considered meaningful, children must understand its purpose (Schickedanz 1998). This means adding games that foster letter/sound relationships. Then, it's the teacher's responsibility to connect the children's knowledge to daily reading and writing and speaking experiences.

### Guidelines for Assessing the Alphabet

1. Give the child the alphabet charts (Figures 4–5 and 4–6).
2. Point to the letters and ask, "What are these?"
3. Point to each letter, moving from left to right across the line. Each time ask, "What is this letter?"
4. Use follow-up prompts to support children who don't answer. "Do you know its name? Can you tell me the sound it makes? Do you know a word that starts with that letter?"
5. Record responses on the record sheet.
6. Score by counting the correct letter names, sounds, or words that start with the letter.
7. Add the total uppercase letters and lowercase letters the child identified.

### *Additional Ways to Assess Emergent Literacy*

In addition to the assessments outlined in this chapter, many schools use other measures to screen children. The more information that is gathered, the better equipped teachers are to plan instruction and to request that a child receive support from a speech therapist and/or guidance counselor.

A wide range of information collected about each child informs teachers whether the entire or parts of a program are developmentally appropriate for that child. Like Nancy Lee's observations of kindergarten children who she believed would not progress in Quarles' standardized program, you can use data about children to decide whether a teaching practice or curricular requirement is appropriate and offers enough support for the child to improve and learn (Schickedanz 1998). Here are thumbnail sketches of extra assessments schools use to evaluate children entering kindergarten.

*State Standardized Tests* States have developed tests that measure some of children's emergent literacy behaviors. I feel compelled, however, to press teachers to use and review a wide range of assessments for standardized tests cannot:

❑ Take into consideration special learning needs, ESL children, and those who are in poverty.
❑ Offer a full portrait of the learner because the child takes the one test at one point in time.

# Alphabet Recognition Sheet

Name_____     Date_____

✔ = correct response for letter name, letter sound or word
● = incorrect response

| | letter | sound | word | | letter | sound | word |
|---|---|---|---|---|---|---|---|
| A | | | | a | | | |
| E | | | | e | | | |
| X | | | | x | | | |
| M | | | | m | | | |
| Q | | | | q | | | |
| U | | | | u | | | |
| G | | | | g | | | |
| B | | | | b | | | |
| F | | | | f | | | |
| J | | | | j | | | |
| T | | | | t | | | |
| R | | | | r | | | |
| V | | | | v | | | |
| N | | | | n | | | |
| C | | | | c | | | |
| Y | | | | y | | | |
| K | | | | k | | | |
| O | | | | o | | | |
| I | | | | i | | | |
| W | | | | w | | | |
| D | | | | d | | | |
| L | | | | l | | | |
| S | | | | s | | | |
| P | | | | p | | | |
| Z | | | | z | | | |
| H | | | | h | | | |
| | | | | a | | | |
| | | | | g | | | |
| Total Correct:_____ | | | | Total Correct:_____ | | | |
| Comments: | | | | | | | |

Adapted from *An Observation Survey* by Marie Clay

*Guided Reading: Making It Work*  Scholastic Professional Books

**Figure 4–5.** Alphabet Recognition Sheet

# Student Alphabet Chart

**Figure 4–6.** Student Alphabet Chart

❏ Prevent the teacher from misunderstanding the process or how the child arrived at an answer.

❏ Provide information open to accurate interpretation. For example, on Virginia's PALS screening text, some students score high in the alphabet, letter recognition part of this test and low in rhyming words, matching sounds to letters, and so on. These high scores can raise the total score, giving the impression that the child has more literacy development than he actually does.

*Draw a Human Figure* At Robinson Elementary, the spring prior to entering kindergarten, teachers invite children to draw a human figure. They look for richness of details such as eyes, eyebrows, nose, mouth, ears, hair, fingers, clothing, and so forth when scoring the drawing. Cheyenne's drawing (Figure 4–7) of her baby brother was one factor that helped teachers decide to place her in the Literacy Links kindergarten. Compare Cheyenne's drawing to five-year-old

**Figure 4–7.** Cheyenne's drawing of her baby brother

Tanisha's drawing of her family (Figure 4–8). Tanisha spent two years in Danielle Water's Head Start program at Keister Elementary School in Harrisonburg, Virginia. Danielle's literacy immersion and parent program developed the reading and writing skills Tanisha needed for a successful year in the school's kindergarten program.

*Sight Words Test.*    In Winchester City schools, children entering kindergarten are given a list of words to read. Every nine weeks, teachers reassess students using the same list (see Figure 4–9).

**Figure 4–8.**  Tanisha's drawing of her family

# Sight Words Test

**Name**_____

| | |
|---|---|
| I | a |
| see | do |
| and | you |
| in | what |
| come | the |
| will | run |
| yes | no |
| is | have |
| it | not |
| can | |

1st nine weeks_____          2nd nine weeks_____

3rd nine weeks_____          4th nine weeks_____

**Figure 4–9.** Sight Words Test

© 2003 by Laura Robb from *Literacy Links*. Portsmouth, NH: Heinemann.

*Speech Therapist and Guidance Counselor*   When children exhibit speech and hearing difficulties and uncooperative behaviors, teachers should refer them to these specialists who provide feedback from additional interactions.

*Social Services*   Local social workers often have current data on children and families because of their interventions and support. Contacting these professionals supplies schools with extra information.

*Preschool/Day Care Teachers*   When the school knows the preschool the children attended, they often contact teachers to collect their data on a child. Sometimes, the preschool is the Head Start program in a school that can provide helpful feedback when making decisions about a child's needs and placement. Miguel, for example, an ESL child at Robinson Elementary, spent mornings with Lisa Tusing in order to receive family storybook reading, writing workshop, and literacy play experiences. In the afternoon, Miguel returned to his kindergarten class. Teachers based their decision to split Miguel's day on feedback from Maryann Sherry, who taught in the Bright Star program (Robinson's Head Start), the PALS test, and other one-on-one assessments.

## Evaluation of One Child's Assessments

We can use assessments to label children as "at-risk" or "struggling" learners. However, categorizing is not the goal here. The purpose of gathering assessments is to interpret the data and plan interventions for children so they can progress with the teacher's support (Robb 2000c, Yaden and Tam 2000).

Tamika (pseudonym) receives free lunch and is from a family that struggles to earn enough money to meet the basic needs of rent, food, clothing, and health care. When Tamika entered kindergarten, she had turned seven years old in July and was about a year-and-a-half older than her classmates. Her late entrance into school was due to the fact that she had not been formally adopted and her parents did not have a social security number or birth records for her. Tamika attended a local day care center before entering kindergarten at Virginia Avenue/Charlotte DeHart Elementary School.

In September, Tamika could not write her name; she recognized uppercase "O," was unable to match any sounds to letters, and had no sight words. Able to identify the front and back covers of a book, Tamika also held the book correctly and said that books had been read to her. She enjoyed talking and could carry on a conversation about playing with her friends.

At school, Tamika took on the role of observer during the morning message and shared reading of a big book. When asked to respond, Tamika would make faces then cover up her face with her hands, for she lacked the self-confidence to interact with classmates during these reading and writing experiences. However, Tamika enjoyed playing during center time.

Tamika's strengths were her ability to dialogue for a short time with an adult, her beginning knowledge of how books worked, and her positive interactions during center times. Based on these strengths, Tamika's teacher and teaching assistant decided that Tamika and four other children would benefit from one-on-one support several times during the day. The goal was to help the children learn their alphabet letters and sounds and develop additional book knowledge. Individually and in a group of five, children were read to, observing the adult point to the words while reading and modeling how to talk about pictures and print. Writing workshop was a natural setting for the teacher and her assistant to circulate and help Tamika and her classmates stretch words to hear the sounds and engage children in discussions about their work.

By the second nine weeks, with continued one-on-one and small group support at school as well as parent support at home, Tamika knew all her upper- and lowercase letters; she recognized nine out of the twenty-one sight words.

Matching sounds to letters developed at the end of the third nine weeks, yet Tamika's writing did not reflect this growth. On her report card, Deena Baker notes: "Tamika has made improvement in letter and sound recognition. She is still struggling to apply these skills when writing."

In February, I met with the school's reading specialists, Betty Wymer and Kathy Wetsel, to discuss ways to develop emergent literacy in children who were not progressing enough in the standard kindergarten program. I suggested two interventions: written conversations (Duffy 1994, Gallagher and Norton 2000) and interactive reading, then writing about the reading with this small group (Heath 1983).

### Written Conversations

Conversing on paper would enable me to closely model writing and help children like Tamika use spelling inventions and spaces between words when writing. During my first one-on-one meeting with Timea she wrote the letter "I" correctly and matched some letters and sounds (Figure 4–10). By the fourth meeting, she was on her way to matching letters to sounds, consistently spacing words, and reading what she wrote to me. Timea punctuated her first sentence after I asked, "What comes at the end of your sentence?" However, she did not apply this writing convention to other sentences (Figure 4–11).

### Interactive Read-Alouds and Writing

Working in a small group gave these children time to process their responses instead of always witnessing classmates' quick answers. By thinking aloud while

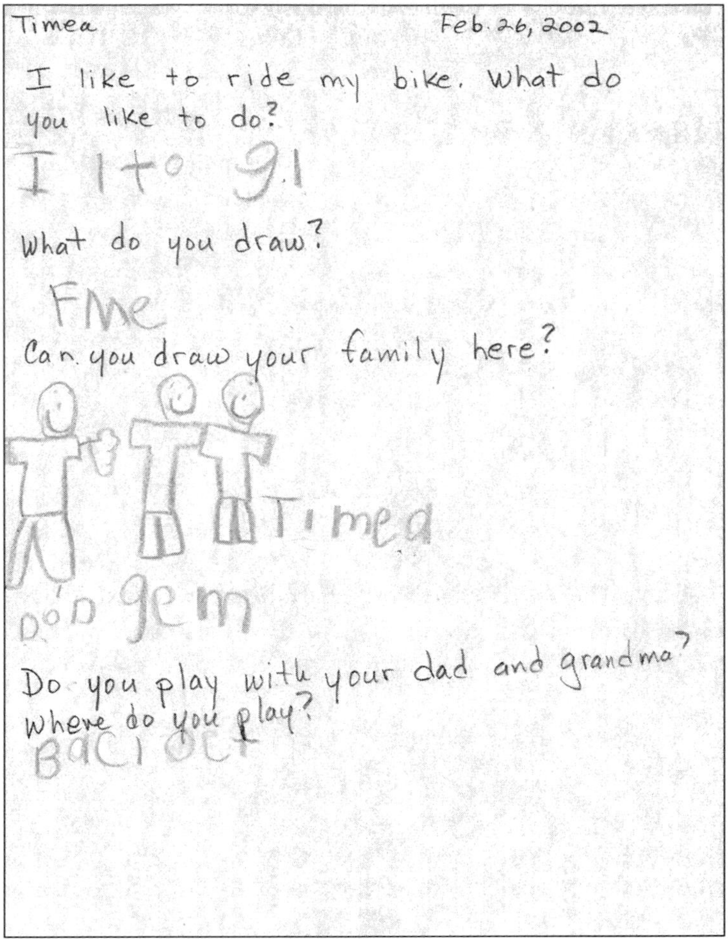

**Figure 4–10.** Timea's first written conversation
*Translation:* 1. I like to draw; 2. A family; 3. Dad, Grandma, Timea; 4. Outside (written last)/Basketball (written first).

reading aloud, I showed how I applied strategies such as reread and retell, making personal connections, inferring, and formulating a hunch, then testing it. As children wrote about their reading, I was able to help them stretch words prior to writing them.

Both interventions allowed children to successfully interact with print, work at a rate comfortable for them, and deepen their understanding of reading and writing. These small-group interventions occurred during morning message and shared reading and can easily be integrated into the day with the teacher and teaching assistant taking turns scaffolding children's learning.

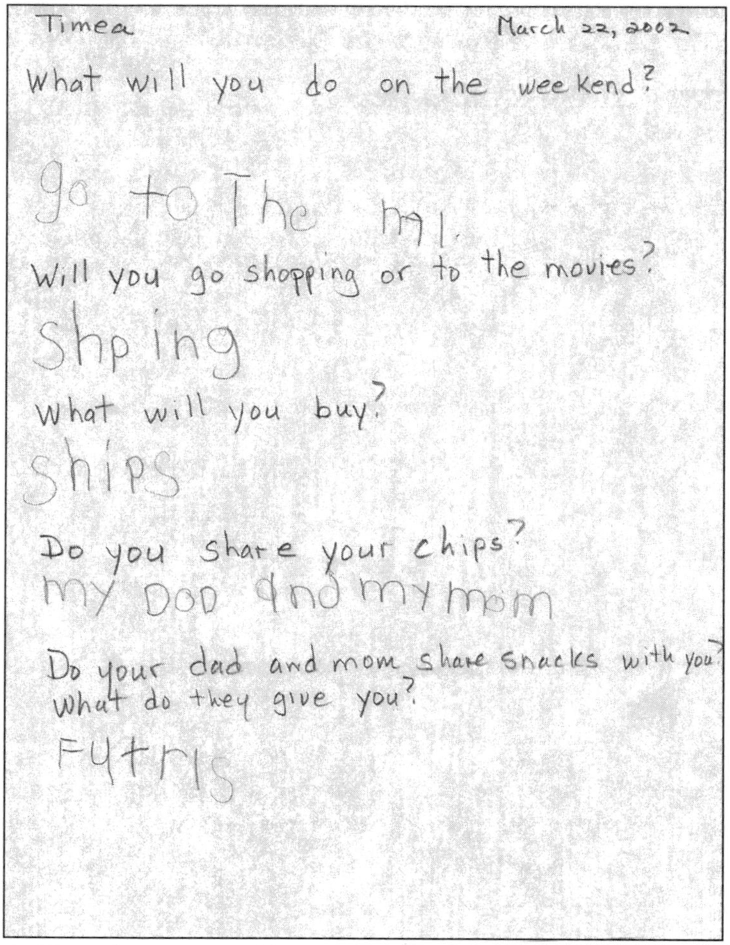

**Figure 4–11.** Timea's progress reflected in a later written conversation
*Translation:* 1. Go to the mall; 2. Shopping; 3. Chips; 4. My dad and my mom; 5. Fruit Roll ups.

## Developing an Intervention Model That Supports Growth

Supportive interventions include a mix of student-centered experiences where children can construct their knowledge of reading and writing and teacher-mediated events that provide scaffolding for the children (Yaden and Tam 2000). The models that follow offer a range of possible interventions teachers can use with children who have limited access to literacy materials as well as children who arrive at school with solid literacy backgrounds. Both groups grow and progress when teachers develop interventions that provide supportive experiences that eventually move these emergent literacy tasks into children's zone of actual development.

## Student-centered Interventions Build Emergent Literacy: Activities That Students Can Do Independently

### A Rich Classroom Library

*Develops book knowledge, concepts of print, the structure of fiction, nonfiction, and poetry. Builds vocabulary and a knowledge of literary syntax and writing.*

❑ Nonfiction, fiction, and poetry
❑ Big books
❑ Charts with poems and songs
❑ Time for independent reading

### Writing Materials

*Develops letter/sound relationships, a knowledge of writing conventions, children's ability to discuss the meaning of pictures, scribble-writing, letters, invented spellings, and reading the written message.*

❑ Paper, markers, crayons, pencils
❑ Journals
❑ Stapled blank books of different sizes
❑ Magnetic or cardboard alphabet letters

### Play Centers

*Offers opportunities for social development, sharing, cooperation, meaningful talk, imaginative and creative thought, and role playing. Equally important, children use reading, writing, and speaking in authentic contexts.*

❑ Home and housekeeping
❑ Grocery store
❑ Post office
❑ Blocks
❑ Drama: puppets, costume box
❑ Restaurant
❑ Science
❑ Mathematics
❑ Listening center

### Painting

*Develops imagination and children's ability to express emotions and ideas in another sign system.*

❑ Finger paints
❑ Easel and paint
❑ Large pieces of paper, crayons, markers, paint

## Teacher-mediated Interventions: Moving Students Forward with Support from the Teacher

### Family Storybook Reading

*Builds a joy in listening to stories; develops book knowledge, concepts of print, as well as how to respond to print and pictures. Also enables children to construct an understanding of how different genres work.*

- ❏ Groups of three to four children
- ❏ Repeated three to five times a day

### Interactive Read-Alouds

*Develops student's book knowledge and an understanding of how readers apply strategies to recall details and construct meanings.*

- ❏ Whole group and small group
- ❏ Big and small books
- ❏ Charts with poems and songs

### Interactive Writing

*Shows children that spoken words can be written, develops concepts of print, writing conventions, letter/sound relationships, and the structures of different genres.*

- ❏ Morning message
- ❏ Written conversations
- ❏ Collaborative writing
- ❏ Letters, messages, notes

### Teacher Modeling

*Makes visible and builds children's mental model of reading and writing by observing how the adult expert applies reading strategies to construct meaning. Models how to creatively use play centers, how to stretch words and match letters to sounds, and ways to plan and develop writing.*

- ❏ Think-alouds
- ❏ Demonstrations
- ❏ Strategy lessons
- ❏ Minilessons

## Closing Reflections

Whether you teach in a preschool, a Head Start program with clearly defined government guidelines for admitting children, kindergarten or first grade, you will find in the following chapters reading, writing, word play, and phonics lessons you can integrate and/or adapt to your children's needs.

One thing is certain: There will be great diversity among the children you teach. This diversity includes the conversations, reading, writing, play experiences, and adult interactions prior to kindergarten. For Literacy Links and all school programs to offer effective instruction that develops emergent literacy, they must build on what children already know and can do. Such programs also consider children's social and cultural lives in their homes and communities (Yaden and Tam 2000). With the assessments in this chapter, you will be able to gather data that provides insights into every child's literacy development. The next step is to interpret these assessments and plan instruction that includes experiences the children can accomplish. In addition, children benefit and grow from independent and interactive free play in centers that permit children to use and apply what they are learning to different situations (Owocki 1999).

# 5

# Constructing a Balanced
# Read-Aloud Program

*Reading aloud to your child opens doors to worlds unknown. You open doors
for your children by teaching them about their world. You can go to places
you could never go in real life through books you read together. You also open
doors for children by sharing values—honesty, loyalty, courage. . . .*

Bernice E. Cullinan, *Read to Me: Raising Kids Who Love to Read*
([1992] 2000, 24)

When my four-year-old daughter, Anina, pleaded "read it again" it felt as if I had read
*Little Red Riding Hood* for the thousandth time. What kept me interested in this
repetitive request, common to all children engaged with storybooks, was observing
my daughter's responses and reactions to the story. Besides talking about the pictures
and simulating the wolf's voice when he answers grandma's observation about big
eyes, teeth, and ears, and besides acting out this story alone and with friends, the
story of Red Riding Hood claimed a deeper place in Anina's mind and imagination.

One day, when Anina's older brother taunted her by singing, "Anina is an
Oscar Mayer Weiner," instead of the usual tears and running to mommy for

assistance and comfort, she quickly retorted, "You act like the big bad wolf." Noticing her brother's shocked reaction, she repeated the phrase again and again, taunting him in a voice that grew shriller and shriller, until he walked away.

That evening, as I reread *Little Red Riding Hood* at bedtime, Anina asked, "Are all wolves bad like this one?" Her question prompted me to visit our local library to find some picture books about wolves. This first foray into nonfiction led to Anina developing an insatiable desire to learn about worms, pandas, tigers, beavers, snakes, trucks, trees, and bugs. Poring over photographs and repeating phrases from nonfiction texts became a daily ritual. However, her attraction to fairy tales and narrative picture books never diminished. I believe that offering Anina nonfiction texts about wolves whetted her curiosity about the world. After reading a narrative, such as Margaret Wise Brown's *Goodnight Moon* (1947) Anina wanted to know more about "the moon and the stars and the sky." Fictional texts opened the door to nonfiction and continual investigations of the natural world, our solar system, and machines.

My experiences with Anina are not unique. They occur everywhere when parents and teachers continually read aloud to children and honor the request of "read it again." In addition to developing emergent literacy, reading aloud sparks the imagination and builds background knowledge about our world. We see this in children's play when they dramatize stories alone, with friends, or transform their dolls and puppets into story characters. We see this when children link the actions and words of characters to situations in their lives, demonstrating a keen awareness and understanding of characters' personality traits and symbols of good and evil. We see this when children's curiosity extends from the narrative to discovering more information about animals, birds, insects, and plants that are part of their beloved stories.

Yes, as an educator, I want children to hear more than a thousand stories before arriving at school so they develop background knowledge of reading and writing. Equally important, however, is what Steven Kellogg notes in this book's preface, for his words mirror the lessons I learned from my daughter and countless other children: "The reading adult's voice unlocks the magic of the story, inviting the child to enter the lives of characters and to explore the landscapes that are delineated in the illustrations." Once connected to the characters and pictures, the child's imagination is free to link these experiences to daily events and to develop personal dreams and values. The elements of a balanced read-aloud program contribute to developing and strengthening children's emergent reading behaviors.

## Family Storybook Reading

Public and school libraries have made books accessible to families of all economic levels. Yet, when I attend programs at my local library, it is the middle and upper-middle class children who crowd the auditorium. In schools where I coach and mentor teachers, I find that few parents living near or in poverty have library cards or regularly bring their children to preschool storybook readings offered on weekends.

Telling parents and caretakers that reading to children is one of the most important things they can do will not create change. Action combined with talk can bring books and families together. Forging this connection is the crucial job of communities, schools, librarians, and educators. Genevieve Patt, a remarkable French librarian whom I met in Williamsburg, Virginia, in September 1990 at an International Board of Books for Young People (IBBY) Conference, told me how she linked books and families. Discouraged by poor attendance at family story hours, Genevieve and her team of associates piled large wicker baskets with inviting picture books and peddled titles door-to-door. Genevieve believed that the first step was to bring the books to parents and reduce the apprehension they might feel about the library, an unfamiliar place. Often, parents living in poverty have had negative experiences while learning in school and avoid institutions, such as the library. Gradually, Genevieve found, after many home visits and conversations with families, groups trickled into the library to check out books and listen to stories with their toddlers.

In 1982 and 1983, Shirley Brice Heath studied adults reading to preschool children which she then grouped in three different communities.

❏ *Children did well in reading throughout school.* Parents in this group read aloud to their children and encouraged their children to interact with the read-alouds by talking about the stories and asking questions. They made sure the children understood the text and provided their youngsters with books.

❏ *Children, in early elementary grades, did well with traditional materials such as workbook pages and drill sheets.* This group, however, fell behind in reading in the intermediate grades. These parents taught their children the names of the alphabet letters, provided them with books, read aloud to them, but not interactively to develop understanding and involvement. During storybook reading, parents read aloud and the children listened silently.

❏ *Children did poorly in reading throughout school.* This group did not offer children books, nor did they read aloud to their preschoolers. Like the other two groups in the study, these parents valued school and viewed education as a way for their children to gain better jobs and a more secure economic position. Yet, they lacked the knowledge of how much reading aloud could prepare their children for reading and writing at school.

It is our responsibility to reach out to all tired, working parents and to parents who have had little or no personal experiences with storybook reading. According to Campbell (2001), Cullinan ([1992] 2000), Neuman, Delano, Greco, and Shue (2001), Taylor and Strickland (1986), and Wells (1986), family storybook reading is the *best* way to develop children's literacy skills, ultimately offering equal opportunities in education for all. Family storybook reading brings adults and children together as families have multiple opportunities to explore everyday and extraordinary happenings. At the same time, family storybook reading develops artistic expression, oral language, and the emergent literacy skills all children need to become successful readers and writers and ultimately productive and contributing members of our society.

## The Case for Recreating Family Storybook Reading at School

At home storybook reading invites parents to cuddle children and snuggle together in an overstuffed chair, sofa, or bed, mixing love and affection with the magic of the story. "The book," as Steven Kellogg writes, becomes "a bridge between two laps, uniting the reader and the audience" (preface). At school, instead of snuggling and cuddling children, I invite readers to have children sit on either side of them so that the children can see the pictures, observe the print, watch the pages being turned from right to left, raise questions, and interact with the reader and the book.

Adams pointed out that children from literate homes enter first grade with more than one thousand hours of storybook reading (1990). In addition, Adams explains that these children spend an equal amount of time writing and playing word games. Those children who arrive in first grade with twenty-five hours or less of storybook reading, according to Adams' research, begin formal schooling at a disadvantage.

Instead of plying this disadvantaged group with worksheets for tracing letters and numbers, instead of having them passively sit at computers and match sounds to letters, instead of copying words and sentences from the chalkboard, I chose a route supported by the research of Adams, Cullinan, Strickland, Taylor, and Wells. I believed that recreating the family storybook reading experiences missed prior to entering kindergarten was the most efficient and authentic way to develop children's book knowledge and concepts about print. By listening to books read aloud in small, safe groups, laughter, questions, and talk about books would develop a genuine interest in books and their structure.

When children arrive in kindergarten hearing no or only a few stories, memorizing the alphabet, copying words, and matching letters to sounds has little meaning for them. My observations in the kindergarten classes of four Virginia schools indicate that children with few literacy experiences become restless during whole class read-alouds. Why? Because story structures are unfamiliar. These children lack the links that connect storybook reading to pleasure, fun, and warm feelings;

## The Importance of Posing Questions and Discussion

The interactive nature of family storybook reading that Heath (1983) and Taylor and Strickland (1986) recommend is crucial to the development of emergent literacy. Encourage the children to ask questions about the story and pictures by modeling the questioning process, then inviting children to ask their own questions. Questions foster discussion, and discussion of texts deepen children's understanding of the story and information as well as the text's structure and how print works (Barrentine 1996, Gambrell 1996, Gillet and Temple 2000, McGee 1998).

they have not developed the listening behaviors read-alouds require, nor do they understand the varied purposes for reading (Heath 1983, Wells 1986). Though literacy-deprived children enter school excited about learning, without positive interventions, their self-esteem and confidence in their ability to learn continually diminishes as they watch classmates quickly answer questions and discuss story events and information (Wigfield 1997).

Research has demonstrated that the best way to develop emergent literacy is not via isolated activities, but through events embedded in authentic contexts such as reading aloud, discussions about books, and play that fosters literacy development (Owocki 1999, Pearson 1996, Sulzby and Teale 1991, Turner 1997). Without prior knowledge about books and print, children have nothing to link skill-and-drill learning to, resulting in time wasted on tasks that don't move children forward but only maintain their read-aloud deprivation levels. In 1998, the International Reading Association (IRA) and the National Association for the Education of Young People (NAEYP) issued a noteworthy joint statement. Both organizations agreed with emergent literacy researchers, stating that the early childhood years are an important time in children's literacy development. Both groups acknowledged that "Failing to give children literacy experiences until they are school-age can severely limit the reading and writing levels they ultimately attain" (197).

### Preparing for Family Storybook Reading at School

My plans to recreate family storybook reading included training teaching assistants to build children's background; integrate read-aloud strategies as they read to small groups, keep records of the books read daily and children's reactions and responses. In fact, I asked schools to always include instructional assistants in study groups and workshop sessions. I believe that the more expertise and knowledge teaching assistants gain, the better equipped they are to assist teachers during reading, writing, play, and word study experiences (Neuman and Delano 2001). However, most of the instructional assistants I worked with did not have formal college training, instead they brought years of valuable experience with young children to our learning sessions and study groups. Several assistants at each school were already involved with helping run a writing workshop, leading the morning message, and reading aloud to the class.

During four training sessions that each lasted one hour, teaching assistants at Quarles Elementary deepened their understanding of how read-alouds build book knowledge, interactive conversations, and concepts about print. We practiced how to think aloud to make visible their responses to pictures and text and the reading strategies they applied. Then I demonstrated the read-aloud process and instructional assistants practiced with one another, trading roles as reader and child. Training for instructional assistants and teachers continued at the schools I supported. At schools far from Winchester, I facilitated monthly meetings in addition to training prior to the opening of school. Study group meetings at schools in Winchester where I lived were bimonthly.

We had years to make up. At Robinson Elementary, in Woodstock, Virginia, children in the Literacy Links kindergartens and the four-year-old Bright Star program listened to books in small groups four times a day. Danielle Waters, who spearheaded the Head Start program at Keister Elementary in Harrisonburg, Virginia, organized small group read-alouds four times a day. At Quarles Elementary, instructional assistants placed beanbags and oversized pillows in the hallways and library. Small groups of children left their classrooms to listen to books three days a week, two to three times a day.

*The Benefits of Acquiring Storybook Reading Hours*   When small groups of four- and five-years-olds experienced daily storybook readings at least four times a day, they listened to twenty books a week. In a 180-day school year, they listened to about seven hundred books—more than 1,400 books read aloud in two years. Add daily read-alouds the teacher presented and children more than logged the one thousand hours Adams (1990) deems necessary to develop emergent literacy.

In Quarles Elementary, when children heard 540 stories by the end of the year, plus the teacher's whole-class read-alouds, they made significant gains. More than 60 percent at Quarles had mastered most letter/sound relationships. Six children had developed some sight words, and all the children could point to the front and back covers, title, and dedication page. They understood that the words told the story and knew that the text is read from left to right. All had developed favorite books and asked for these to be read again and again. Frequently, children begged to be read to instead of working at centers. By the

end of April, teachers observed that all the children had begun to pretend-read during sustained silent reading (SSR).

Children at Robinson Elementary and Quarles absorbed the reading strategy language modeled by the adult reader. Predicting what would happen next, posing questions about new information, a photograph or picture, and making personal connections became part of children's vocabulary as they practiced and applied the reader's strategic language to interactive discussions about texts read aloud.

### Tips for Simulating Family Storybook Read-Alouds at School

Teachers, instructional assistants, and I collaborated to develop and fine-tune our simulations of family storybook reading. We started with picture books that had short texts. As children's desire to listen increased, teachers selected longer texts. Careful records of daily read-alouds were kept on a sheet (see Appendix, page 283). Teachers gathered information on children's favorites and recorded the moment when groups and/or individuals asked for a specific title to be read again. Involvement in a single book meant the children were working hard to understand the story, information, vocabulary, literary language, and structure. Rereading offers children opportunities to absorb themes and get to know characters well enough to transfer story elements to their own play. Like Taylor and Strickland suggest (1986), we found that children raised more questions and conversed more freely about books heard again and again. This was the point that they were ready to absorb and show an interest in learning about print.

For successful family storybook reading at school, adult readers need to reflect on what they have already modeled and the children's responses in order to effectively preplan the day's reading. Here are some suggestions:

- ❑ Read the book before bringing it to the children to make sure the text is appropriate. You need to know the content so that you can decide on your think-alouds and parts you will invite the children to discuss.
- ❑ Discover what children know about the topic.
- ❑ Remain open to questions and comments the children raise. These are crucial to honor and respond to, for a primary goal is for children to interact with the books and feel comfortable asking questions.
- ❑ Be dramatic and imitate the voices of different characters in narrative texts, breathing life and drama into the story.
- ❑ Read fluently and with expression, for you are modeling good reading to the children.

Take time to preplan your read-alouds by reflecting on these suggestions and choosing to include those elements that your children are ready to receive with modeling and support.

*Recordkeeping Supports Preplanning*   The records you keep for the groups you regularly read to will provide you with the information for making planning decisions. Each day, after storybook readings, instructional assistants and/or teachers note the titles of books on log sheets (Figure 5–1). Many times, the adult decides to read a book again. This is an excellent way to model how to move deeper into a story and how with each reading listeners hear more and see more in the pictures. There were times, however, when the children were outspoken and said, "Don't do that one again. Read another." Respect these requests, permitting children to progress in ways that fully allow storybook reading to enter their lives.

By the third week of summer school, Jessica and Dantoe are into Mem Fox. This is a crystal moment in their storybook-listening lives, for it's the first time they have asked to hear stories again. All week, they beg to hear *Night Noises* (1989) and *Koala Lou* (1988) every day. During free play, Jessica croons to a doll, "Koala Lou, I do love you." Jessica tells me she's pretending the doll is Koala Lou. Dantoe's favorite is *Night Noises*. He loves being "scared" and the oversized red print, "Yell, Clatter, Bang, Bang, Bang." He hands me the page and asks, "Can you read it to me?"

When the children start asking for titles to be read again, it's time for teachers to begin to point out print features over several rereadings. The children's responses and growth become guides for teaching decisions, and that's why recordkeeping is important.

Terri Auckland's Class

**LOG OF STORY BOOKS READ EACH WEEK**

Week of  2/26/01

| TITLE & AUTHOR | NUMBER OF TIMES |
|---|---|
| **Monday:** | |
| Farm Morning — McPhail | 2 |
| Happy Birthday, Dear Duck - Bunting | |
| Danny the Dinosaur - Hoff | 2 |
| **Tuesday:** | |
| The Very Hungry Caterpillar - Carle | |
| Koala Lou - Fox | 3 |
| **Wednesday:** | |
| The Doorbell Rang - Hutchins | 2 |
| The Wind Blew - Hutchins | |
| **Thursday:** | |
| Chicka Chicka Boom Boom - Martin & Archambault | |
| The Cat in the Hat - Seuss | 2 |
| Is Your Mama a Llama? | |
| **Friday:** | |
| The Day the Teacher Went Bananas - Howe | 3 |
| Silly Little Goose - Tafuri | 3 |

**Figure 5–1.** Sample log of family storybook reading

In addition to the book log, adult readers should also note children's behaviors during storybook reading. Nancy Reedy, instructional assistant and reading tutor is in charge of Quarles Elementary's summer school. The summer program is for kindergarten children who continue to need extra support to develop emergent literacy. Nancy completes checklists of storybook reading for each of her ten students at the start of summer school and then four weeks later. In June, when she asks Jessica to show her the part of the book that tells the story, Jessica points to the front cover. The June checklist (Figure 5–2) also shows that Jessica is not

---

### CHECKLIST OF BEHAVIORS DURING STORYBOOK READING

Name _Jessica Haynes_      Grade _Literacy Leaks_
                                                          6/2000

**Behaviors**                                              **Date Observed**

✓ **Listens well.**

__ **Asks questions.**

__ **Discusses pictures.**

✓ **Points to items in pictures.**

__ **Asks to hear story again.**

✓ **Knows front and back cover.**

✓ **Knows title.**

✓ **Knows title page.**

✓ **Knows dedication.**

✓ **Makes sensible predictions.**

**Additional Comments:**

Need to find ways to get
her to react to read alouds.
Maybe one-on-one with
Jaime.

**Figure 5–2.** Jessica's checklist shows she needs support in two areas.

asking questions, discussing pictures, or requesting a story be read again. During storybook and interactive reading, Nancy models these behaviors. Because of the small numbers in this class, Nancy and her student assistant can read to pairs of children, working to draw them into the story and pictures.

Once Dantoe and Jessica ask to hear Mem Fox's books again and again, Nancy models the concepts of print listed in Figure 5–2. After Nancy points to a word, she invites the children to point to another word on the page. These interactions continue *only after* the children have read and enjoyed the book two to three times.

Four weeks later, the checklist illustrates Jessica's growth. Now interacting with the text and reader, Jessica asks questions, discusses pictures, and has favorite books she wants to repeatedly hear. Much progress has been made with concepts of print behaviors (Figures 5–3a and 5–3b). Now Jessica has two areas that need extra support: understanding the direction of print and knowing that the print tells the story.

Reflect on and use the planning guidelines that follow to help you provide effective support within children's teaching zone: Vygotsky's zone of proximal development. The questions you raise foster reflecting on children's reactions and help you focus your read-alouds on connecting children to books. Remember that it is pointless to teach concept of word, directionality, upper- and lowercase letters, and so on, when children have not bonded with books or developed concepts about print.

### Posing Questions Supports Preplanning

1. How will I introduce the book and build background knowledge?
2. What pictures will I use for discussion?
3. What personal responses and reactions will I share?
4. How will I encourage the children to respond?
5. How will I wrap up the read-aloud?
6. How will I involve the children in pictures and story?
7. What reading strategies will I model (predicting, personal connections, visualizing, questioning)?
8. Should I read books that have similar topics, such as books about farms or about friends or books about trucks and cars?
9. Should I reread a book the children seemed to enjoy?

Once you've decided what the children are ready to learn, use the following guidelines to construct children's knowledge of book structure and print.

### Guidelines for Building Book and Genre Knowledge

*Introduce one or two elements at a time and repeat them during each read-aloud until children can identify them.*

## CHECKLIST OF BEHAVIORS DURING STORYBOOK READING

Name _Jessica Haynes_____ Grade _Literacy Links_

**Behaviors**                                    Date  Observed
                                                      7-00

_✓_ Listens well.

_✓_ Asks questions.

_✓_ Discusses pictures.

_✓_ Points to items in pictures.

_✓_ Asks to hear story again.

_✓_ Knows front and back cover.

_✓_ Knows title.

_✓_ Knows title page.

_✓_ Knows dedication.

_✓_ Makes sensible predictions.

**Additional Comments:**

*Jaime read to her twice a day — what a difference — Jessica has begun to talk about books!*

**Figure 5–3a.** By the end of the summer program, Jessica has made much progress.

- ❏ Talk about the front/back covers, end papers, and the title.
- ❏ Explain the job of the author and illustrator.
- ❏ Point out the dedication and title pages.
- ❏ Mention and explain the publisher and the copyright date.

CHECKLIST OF BEHAVIOR DURING SHARED AND STORYBOOK
READING

NAME *Jessica Haynes*      GRADE *LiLinks*

**BEHAVIORS**             **DATE OBSERVED**
                                   *7-00*

✓ Points to a word.

✓ Points to spaces between words.

✓ Points to upper case letters.

✓ Points to lower case letters.

✓ Points to a period.

✓ Points to a question mark.

____ Knows print goes from left to right.

____ Knows that the words tell the story.

✓ Pretend reads.

Additional Comments:

*I think it's working alone
with Jaime that has moved
her so far along.*

**Figure 5–3b.** By the end of the summer program, Jessica has made much progress.

❑ Talk about genre features. *For nonfiction:* photographs and captions, sidebars, table of contents, and index. *For fiction:* setting, characters, problem, outcome, beginning, middle, and end. *For poetry:* shape, stanzas, rhyming words, and repeated lines.

### Guidelines for Building Print Concepts

❑ Track the print from left to right by pointing to each word as you read.

❑ Think aloud and explain that you read from top to bottom and that you turn the pages from right to left.

❑ Think aloud and note rhyming words in texts such as *Big Red Barn* by Margaret Wise Brown (1989).

❑ Think aloud and notice one or a few of these print conventions: spaces between words, punctuation, uppercase letters, dialogue and quotation marks, and paragraphs.

## Family Storybook Reading in Action at School

During the first month of storybook reading to small groups I encourage teachers to share their personal feelings to the story and pictures, so the young listeners observe ways to react to stories. Try to select books with topics that are familiar to the children so you don't have to spend large amounts of time building background knowledge. Comments such as: "That makes me sad," or "This part feels scary," or " I cried when I was lost," show children how to interact with pictures and text. Before reading, take picture-walks through half or two-thirds of the book. Encourage the children to discuss the pictures and share what they are learning about the settings, characters, and problems. If the book is nonfiction, invite the children to discuss what they are learning from the photographs or pictures. Model your emotional reactions to pictures and introduce making predictions or wondering what will happen next before turning to another page.

The purposes for storybook reading during the first two to three months are to bring books and children together, to model the pleasure and joy in reading and listening to stories by showing that some books are wonderfully scary while others are delightfully silly and funny, and to forge bonds between child, books, and reader. From the start, I recommend using fiction and nonfiction, although with children who have few read-aloud experiences, you might want to start with narratives and poems, then add nonfiction.

The excerpts of small-group storybook reading come from audiotapes that I made while I lead the read-aloud and detailed notes and audiotapes of my observations. I've included excerpts from a read-aloud during the first month of school and one completed in the spring.

## Snapshot: Family Storybook Reading, the End of September

The reader plays a key role while simulating family storybook reading. Through think-alouds, children can hear and observe how stories affect our feelings, thinking, knowledge, and provide great enjoyment. Once children catch on to strategies that can help them enter into the world of a book, their talk and reactions start to dominate sessions.

**BOOK:** *The Wheels on the Bus* (1987) is an adaptation of a traditional song by Maryann Kovalski (Joy Street/Little Brown)

**PREPLANNING:** Nancy Reedy chose this book because the kindergarten children were familiar with yellow school buses and had been shopping for school clothing and supplies. She liked the idea that the book was a mixture of story and song. Nancy thought she could read it again during the year, inviting the children to chime in and act out the babies crying, the horn tooting, and so on. First Nancy did a think-aloud about the front and back covers, followed by a picture-walk that focused on two pictures, then she read the book. "I wanted to get them into the story as fast as I could," she explained.

*Think-Aloud for the Front and Back Covers*

This book has a lot of energy. Just look at the children and the grandmother. They're very excited. Look at their faces. They're singing and shouting and their arms are waving, almost like they're ready to fly. I see two shopping bags. I wonder what's in them? I wonder what grandmother bought for her grandchildren. And look at the title. Both letter "e's" [points to letters] look like they're moving, just like a bus moves. [Turns to the back cover and uses an excited voice.] Wow! The bus is red and it's a double-decker. It's like a house with two floors.

*Excerpts of the Think-Aloud for Nancy's Picture-Walk*

Here is Nancy's think-aloud for granny and the two girls waiting at the bus stop at the beginning of the story.

One-two-three-four-five other people are waiting at the bus stop. Two are reading newspapers. Granny and the girls don't look as happy and excited as they do on the cover. Hmm. Maybe the bus is late. This must be in a big city. Look at the tall buildings [points to them]. There are those shopping bags. I'm still wondering what's in them. Maybe the story will help. [She runs her finger over the print when she mentions story.]

Here is Nancy's think-aloud for granny and the two girls waiting at the bus stop close to the end of the story.

Look! It's snowing. White flakes are falling everywhere. And it's getting dark. I know that because the lights in the buildings are on. Oh, my! The bus is leaving the bus stop. Granny and the girls look surprised. They're the only ones left. I wonder why they missed the bus. Let's start this story and try to find out!

I applauded Nancy for creating anticipation for getting into the story. The children's first reactions were in response to the two times she wondered. Children made comments such as, "I hope we learn it," and "Did they get home?" which illustrated the children's entrance into the story.

By the spring, think-alouds explicitly connect what the reader is doing to a specific strategy. Whenever possible, build vocabulary and help the children connect the book to their own lives. It's also important to invite children to write about their reading. This can be introduced sooner than the spring. I like to initiate writing about reading when children's responses show me they are making personal connections to and are truly involved in the read-aloud.

## Snapshot: Family Storybook Reading, Early March

The continual modeling that occurred during every family storybook reading session showed the children how to react to and converse about books. Over seven months children learned how to:

❏ Gather information from and discuss the pictures;
❏ Make predictions and check these as the story unfolded;
❏ Pose questions during the reading about why bubbles burst quickly or how Max was brave enough to talk to the wild things;
❏ Make personal connections to characters, problems, and places, bonding them to stories.

The following transcriptions reveal the transformation from children who had nothing to say about a book to rich conversations that reflect their pleasure in listening to stories.

**BOOK:** *A Rainbow All Around Me* (2002) by Sandra L. Pinkney, photographed by Myles C. Pinkney (HarperCollins).

**PREPLANNING:** I chose this nonfiction book to deepen kindergarten children's understanding of the book's end papers and to reinforce that photographs and captions tell part of the story. I planned to also think aloud about the different kinds of print and discuss reasons for changes in print types. In addition, I hoped this book would broaden children's concept of color to include people, the natural world, food, clothing, and symbols of feelings, hopes, and dreams.

**EXCERPTS:** At this point, the children are totally involved in the small-group storybook read-alouds. They ask and answer questions, react to the book, and display how much they have learned. The excerpts that follow reflect the growth in children's book knowledge, their ability to use information to predict what they'll learn, and their curiosity about print.

### Discussion of Endpapers

ROBB: Look at these endpapers. What's different?
CHANNING: They have ribbons. All colors.

ROBB: Why isn't it one color? [Silence.] [I wait for about one minute, then read the title again.]

TIMEA: It says rainbow. That has lots of colors.

ROBB: Good connecting.

CHANNING: It's like Bashi (see Interactive Read-Alouds, pp. 102–114). Those [endpapers] were from Africa.

UVALDO: And Bashi lives there [in Africa].

ROBB: These endpapers start you thinking about what the book will be about. [Lots of nods.] Look at the cover again and the endpapers. What do you think this book will be about?

TIMEA: Different color people.

CHANNING: Painting colors.

UVALDO: Toys and what you wear.

ROBB: You read the photographs so well. Let's read to see what else you learn about colors from this book. [Setting a purpose to motivate good listening.]

*Excerpts from Noticing Print—Done After Reading the Book*

ROBB: Let's look at the two pages for black. What do you notice about the print?

HOLLY: There's a thing after here—and here. [Points to the apostrophe on *Tappin'* and on *Dancin'*.]

ROBB: The author left off the letter "g" and put an apostrophe in its place. What does that do to the word?

CHANNING: It makes it like it moves. Cause he's dancin'.

UVALDO: Read that. [Points to caption next to photo of feet.]

ROBB: "Moving feet/Dancin' to the beat."

UVALDO: Rhymes—it rhymes. Feet and beat.

ROBB: Good noticing. You used the strategy of close reading. By carefully studying pictures and print you were able to understand more about how the print helped give more meaning to the pictures.

*After Reading Discussion*

ROBB: Before I read the book, you looked at the cover and endpapers and predicted the book would be about people, painting different colors, toys, and clothing.

HOLLY: It was about that.

ROBB: Yes, Holly, it was. But did you learn anything else about colors?

CHANNING: Colors has tastes like pink bubble gun.

UVALDO: Oranges.

TIMEA: Red means love.

ROBB: Hmm. So colors can represent feelings and flavors.

CHANNING: And light. The sun is light. It makes you happy.

UVALDO: Go to brown. It's a bear. A friend.

ROBB: So a color can be a stuffed animal you love.

TIMEA: Colors can be new words. Like nu—nutrous.

ROBB: You mean nutritious, good for your health. You remembered a tough word, Timea.

ROBB: Before you read, predicting what the book is about gets you ready to think about the book. When you read, you learn so much more. Today you learned that colors can make you think of feelings and tastes.

Storybook reading has now become the interactive process Heath's research celebrates (1983). It's the rich give-and-take between the reader and the children that holds the potential for enlarging vocabulary, broadening concepts such as what colors symbolize, and helping children recognize the value of reading and discussing books. The checklist (Figure 5–4) can help you monitor children's behaviors during family storybook reading sessions. Complete a checklist for each child once a month. Reviewing them will help you plan what to model during sessions.

Read-alouds are also the ideal way for teachers to show children in kindergarten and first grade how applying strategies deepens their understanding of written texts and pictures.

## Reading Comprehension Instruction: The Strategy Curriculum and Interactive Read-Alouds

Researchers (Beck et al. 1997; Clay [1979] 2000, 1985; Fountas and Pinnell 1997; Pearson et al. 1992) have demonstrated that reading strategies can be taught. Teaching children the benefits of and how to apply a specific strategy such as predicting, questioning, or rereading fosters meaning-making as they read texts. My experiences support the belief that weaving strategy instruction into read-alouds raises children's awareness of specific strategies and how each one can enhance understanding.

Like Smolkein and Donovan (2001) and Wilhelm (2000), I believe that when teachers weave strategy instruction into their read-alouds and discussions of texts, they model how reading strategies can improve the comprehension and enjoyment of fiction, nonfiction, and poetry.

It's important to keep in mind that I'm not advocating that young children learn strategies before they have developed emergent literacy. My goal is for teachers to integrate strategies into read-alouds once children have book knowledge and interact with stories. It's a great way to allow children to enter your thinking process. By observing, children can discover that reading is strategic, active, and interactive.

# Checklist for Family Storybook Reading Behaviors

Name_____

*Check behaviors you have observed during this monitoring period.*

**Response Behaviors**                                    **Date Observed**

**Book Knowledge**

____ Discusses front/back covers.                   __ __ __ __ __
____ Points to front/back covers.                   __ __ __ __ __
____ Discusses endpapers.                            __ __ __ __ __
____ Understands purpose of dedication.             __ __ __ __ __
____ Points to author/illustrator.                  __ __ __ __ __
____ Asks questions about pictures.                 __ __ __ __ __
____ Makes predictions using pictures.              __ __ __ __ __
____ Connects pictures to self.                      __ __ __ __ __
____ Tells story using pictures.                     __ __ __ __ __
____ Knows print tells the story.                    __ __ __ __ __
____ Points to the place where the story begins.    __ __ __ __ __
____ Points to spaces between words.                __ __ __ __ __
____ Recognizes a book by the cover.                __ __ __ __ __

**Listening to the Story**

____ Looks at book while it's read.                  __ __ __ __ __
____ Makes predictions from the story.              __ __ __ __ __
____ Asks questions about characters.               __ __ __ __ __
____ Asks questions about setting.                   __ __ __ __ __
____ Asks questions about problems characters face.  __ __ __ __ __
____ Expresses emotional reactions.                  __ __ __ __ __
____ Discusses story with peers.                     __ __ __ __ __
____ Asks to hear story again.                        __ __ __ __ __
____ Learns new information from the book.           __ __ __ __ __
____ Recognizes some words.                           __ __ __ __ __
____ Retells part of the story.                       __ __ __ __ __
____ Has favorite parts, characters, and events.     __ __ __ __ __

**Listening Behaviors**

____ Focuses on story.                                __ __ __ __ __
____ Listens to peers' comments.                      __ __ __ __ __
____ Accepts different ideas.                          __ __ __ __ __
____ Shows pleasure in hearing stories.              __ __ __ __ __
____ Asks for more read-aloud time.                   __ __ __ __ __

**Additional Comments:**


**Needs for Upcoming Sessions:**

**Figure 5–4.** Checklist for Family Storybook Reading Behaviors
© 2003 by Laura Robb from *Literacy Links*. Portsmouth, NH: Heinemann.

## *Putting Together an Interactive Read-Aloud*

Interactive read-alouds invite you to think aloud in order to show how you apply a strategy to make meaning while reading. Thinking out loud allows children to step inside your head and observe your reading and thinking processes (Wilhelm 2000). According to Cazden (1983) and Wilhelm, each time you make your reading process visible to children, you provide them with a chance to learn more about reading.

I pause to think aloud to show the children how I'm trying to connect words and ideas in this sentence. "Each species (kind) or polyp lives in a separate colony." During a reading of *Life in a Coral Reef* by Melvin Berger (1994, 3) this is my think-aloud:

> I'm confused and need to think about how species, polyp, and colony connect. I better close read, or think about each important word and how I can understand it. Let's see—there are lots of different kinds of coral polyps like there are lots of different birds. Comparing to birds helped me understand species. But each different kind of polyp lives together in one place called a colony. That means different kinds or species of polyps don't live in the same space. I can use the picture to see that they live in clumps or groups that look like weird plants.

One child points out that robins don't all live together. Another wonders why polyps separate themselves because different people live in one apartment house. A third notices that thinking about birds made me understand the word *species*. A group tells the class that looking at pictures helps, too. Just what I hoped for! The children have become excellent noticers and listeners and have observed that readers can compare, look at pictures, raise questions, and zoom in on key words to close read. Curiosity naturally moved the children to question and comment, the second aspect of interactive read-alouds.

After thinking out loud, invite the children to participate by asking a question, making a comment, or trying to apply the strategy as you continue to read. Sharing how you apply strategies works best when modeled with real books (Cazden 1983, Pearson 1996). Discussing a strategy apart from a text is akin to learning to play tennis by memorizing the rules but never playing with a racket, ball, and opponent.

### Suggestions for Read-Alouds

❏ Select a short passage from a book.
❏ Tell why you have paused to think about the selection.
❏ Name the strategy you are using and explain why you think it can help you comprehend. Use the correct name. For example, avoid substituting the word *guess* for *predicting*, causing children to relearn terms in later grades.

❑ Apply the strategy to make meaning.

❑ Invite the children to question or comment.

❑ Focus on one strategy and one short passage so children can absorb information.

❑ Continue modeling the same strategy over several days before introducing a new one.

Once you've absorbed the process, you will begin to pause during a read-aloud and show the children how your mind is trying to link ideas, understand new terms, or wonder what a character will do next.

## Strategies to Model During Interactive Read-Alouds

When introducing, applying, and discussing the strategy, use the strategy's name. This enables children to process and absorb how a specific strategy you've isolated and modeled supports comprehension and recall.

Gradually draw the children into sharing their observations, feelings, and application of a strategy so the read-aloud moves from modeling to interacting. In this section I offer short shapshots that illustrate teacher modeling and student involvement. Later in the chapter, there are transcriptions of interactive read-alouds for you to reflect on and discuss with colleagues.

*Activate prior knowledge and build comprehension before you begin to read*   Ask the group to share what they already know. Take a picture-walk, present series of short read-alouds that introduce the children to a new concept or topic, or have the children browse through books with splendid photographs and pictures.

To prepare children to listen to *Is There Life In Outer Space?* by Franklyn M. Branley ([1984] 1999), I check out a stack of books from the school and public library. The group browses through and discusses pictures to build their knowledge of space, spaceships, astronauts, and the planets.

*Explain text structure*   Help children understand the difference between narrative stories, information books, and poetry.

After reading and discussing *Life in a Coral Reef*, I use the text to introduce the children to captions and sidebars that are frequently part of nonfiction. You can help children understand that narratives have a beginning, middle, and end, and characters with problems to solve.

*Predict and read on to see if the text matches the prediction*   Give support for the prediction. If the text doesn't match, adjust the prediction. Predicting intrigues children and really engages them for they are itchy to know if their ideas match the text.

*Something Special for Me* by Vera Williams (1983) is a great book for predicting. Here's how I introduce the strategy:

> I love to use what I know to predict. Predicting keeps me interested in the book because I'm always wondering what will happen next. Then I can't wait to read on to find out if my ideas match the author's.

The first time Rosa can't decide what to buy for her birthday, and she and mama leave the store empty-handed, I say then ask:

> I'm going to predict what I think Rosa and Mama will do. I think they'll go to another store. What do you think they will do?

The children predict that Mama will take Rosa home or Mama will tell Rosa that they shop on another day. The text surprised the children because they didn't expect Rosa to cry and wonder why she can never decide. After completing the story, we discussed how they felt about making predictions and checking them against the story. "I couldn't wait for you to read more," was the prevalent response.

*Ask questions and read on to see if the text answers them.* As I read *Is There Life in Outer Space?* I stop on page 15 and wonder out loud:

> My mind keeps asking questions. That makes me want to read more because the book might answer them. Right now I'm wondering if there are living things on the Moon? What do you think?

Inviting the children to speculate involves them with my question and the text. After two to three ideas surface, one child insists that I read on to see what the book says.

*Preteach new words by reading the section of the text and showing pictures that relate to the word.* To help children understand that insects have external skeletons, I read two sentences from *Bugs Are Insects* by Ann Rockwell (2001, 8):

> You have a hard skeleton inside, with parts that move. But an insect has a hard skeleton on the outside, with parts that move.

Immediately, the children recount their experiences with crushing bugs and hearing a crunchy sound. They connect this to the concept of external skeleton and tell me it's [the insect's outside] hard like our bones. And some press their fingers to show me how hard bones are. Sometimes, the children jump right in before I think aloud. That's fine, for it shows me that they have enough experiences to participate with confidence.

*Check understanding of a new word or concept by pausing while reading and involving the children in explaining the concept.* After reading page 10 of *Bugs Are Insects,* I pause and think aloud.

> Let me see. I have to check the idea that insects have external skeletons. It says that lobsters and crabs and shrimp have external skeletons. But they live in the ocean and we eat them. We don't eat insects [lots of yucks and gross]. So, just having an external skeleton is not enough to make something an insect.

The children's responses show confusion. Some insist lobsters are seafood that they eat. Others feel that these could be sea insects. "I think we need more information," I say. "I better read on."

*Show the linkage between the meaning in two or three sentences by thinking aloud and modeling how you connect the information.* Showing children how you connect ideas enables them to better understand some information presented in nonfiction. It also illustrates how readers pause to put ideas together.

First, I reread these sentences on page 18 of *What Happens to a Hambuger?* by Paul Showers ([1985] 2001):

> Some kinds of food stay only two hours. Other kinds stay longer. The food stays until all the lumps have been broken up.

Here's my think-aloud:

> Sometimes I have to connect ideas in sentences to really understand what the author is telling me. First, I'll reread the sentences. Now I will try to connect ideas. Hmm. So, food can't leave the stomach until every lump is gone. That means it stays in the stomach until it is like thick soup. Some food gets smooth sooner than others. Now I understand why some food stays longer.

This is a complex process that I model many times before inviting the children to try to link ideas. If they struggle, support them by asking questions and/or offering suggestions.

*Summarize by bringing important ideas together so children can observe relationships and connections.* The ability to do this is one measure of comprehension.

Author Paul Showers introduces many new terms about digestion in *What Happens to a Hamburger?* On page 14, I pause and say:

> There's lots of information here. I better try to bring the ideas together—that's called summarizing. Your food goes down the gullet or esophagus. A door closes your windpipe called the trachea, so food doesn't go in your lungs and make you choke. Hmm. That's a lot to remember. I think I'll read the page again.

After several demonstrations, I invite the children to summarize and pull ideas together in their own words.

*Visualize by sharing the mental picture the text creates in your mind.* What readers can see in their minds, they understand. Encourage children to create and share their mental pictures.

During the first two readings of Steven Kellogg's retelling of *Chicken Little* (1985), I don't show the illustrations. Instead, I pause and tell the children I'm going to visualize Foxy Loxy imagining he's eating the hen's drumsticks. I also tell them that visualizing parts of stories is like making a movie and if I can picture something, then I know I understand it. Next, I ask the children to visualize and describe their mental pictures. If a child is reluctant to share, be patient. Hearing your and peers' descriptions of imagined pictures will provide the model the child needs to construct mental pictures.

*Share your emotional reactions to the read-aloud, inviting children to observe the way stories stir your feelings and cause reactions.* Emotional responses can bond children to books because the story helps them reexperience the emotions they feel daily.

Before reading Jacqueline Woodson's *The Other Side* (2001), I first tell children that when stories arouse my emotions or feelings, I really get into the book. I can see the characters and pretend I feel like them. I pause after reading page 8 of this picture book to think aloud: "I'm sad and angry that a fence separates the black children from the white children. They should all feel free to play together." After finishing the book, I ask, "What emotions did you feel? What made you feel that way?" Here are some of the children's responses:

"Lonely, like Annie when I have no one to play with."
"Happy that Clover was brave and spoke to Annie."
"Scared that Clover did the opposite her mama said. My mama would whup me good."

Not only did the children provide the part of the story that stirred the emotion, but they also made valuable personal connections.

*Retell short sections in your own words.* Reread to model how this fix-up strategy helps you gather additional specific details. Then read a short passage and have the children retell. Reread to illustrate how hearing fact-filled passages more than once helps readers recall many details.

*Connect the read-aloud to other books or to movies, the school and community experiences.* Making connections shows children that books have great relevance to our lives and knowing several books about the same topic can enlarge our knowledge as we gather different perspectives.

Once the children have heard Brian Pinkney's *Cosmos and the Robot* (2000) several times, I say:

> Lots of times after reading a book I think of another book or a movie or experience that's about the same topic. I like doing this because it helps me understand ideas and learn more because I see how different writers use information. I remember all the books we browsed through to learn about space. Can you connect this book to a movie or another book you heard?

The children offer *Is There Life in Outer Space?* and a book by Franklyn M. Branley, *The International Space Station* (2000). Connecting texts often leads to incredible discussions and comparing information. For example, the children delighted in comparing the space suits the astronauts wore in Branley's book to those Pinkney drew.

*Make inferences using pictures and text to explore unstated meanings.* Prompts can encourage inferring, so I often ask the children to study the picture closely and tell me how a character feels and what the character might be thinking. Then I follow up with, "What in the picture made you say that?" Here are some prompts that can support inferring:

- ❏ How does the picture/passage make you feel?
- ❏ What do you learn from these words the character spoke?
- ❏ What do you think the character is thinking now?
- ❏ How are these two characters alike? Different?
- ❏ What were your feelings when I read this part? Can you explain why you felt that way?
- ❏ How do other characters feel about this character?
- ❏ What do decisions the character made show us?

I always introduce making inferences with pictures, for illustrations appeal to children. Helping them understand that inferring means finding unstated meanings works well with pictures because there is no text. The children read into expressions, actions, and setting. Here's what I include in my think-aloud:

> Making inferences means you all have to be top-notch detectives. Clues are in the expressions on characters' faces, in what they are doing, and where they are. Study a character's face and imagine what he or she is thinking and feeling. First, I'll look for clues on the cover of *Night at the Fair* by Donald Crews (1998). The children are smiling and seem happy. They all look at the word *fair* and feel excited to be going.

You will need to model this many times before inviting the children to infer from illustrations.

*Close read by zooming into a sentence or phrase and discussing its meaning or your reactions.*   Focusing on specific words and phrases can help readers understand the meaning of a new word or idea.

The rich vocabulary in Isaac O. Olaleye's retelling of a Nigerian folktale, *In the Rainfield, Who Is the Greatest?* (2000) lends itself to close reading. Here's the part of the text, in this unpaged picture book, that I focus on during my think-aloud:

> The three bickered back and forth, forth and back. And since they could not agree. . . .

Here's what I say:

> I'm not sure what *bickered* means. I'll pause and close read to see if I can find clues. Close reading means I look at all the important words very carefully. When the rain, wind, and fire bicker they do it back and forth. That means they take turns. Now, they can't agree. That means they are arguing and no one agrees. So *bicker* means they argue and can't agree on an answer.

Next I ask the children to comment and tell me what they notice I did as I close read. Model your process many times, then invite the children to think aloud, supporting one another. If you sense that the close reading process will take too long and interrupt the story, return to a specific section and close read it after completing the text.

*Self-monitor by pointing out passages that seem confusing and showing the children how you apply a strategy to make meaning.*   Children are always shocked to learn that I don't understand everything I read. Letting them know that can relieve anxiety, but it's also important to share fix-up strategies that repair confusions. Here's my think-aloud:

> I always think about what I do and don't understand. It's called self-monitoring. If I understand, I read on. If I'm confused I reread or close read to see if I can understand better. I test my understanding by saying what I read in my own words.

As children have countless opportunities to observe you and interact with you and the text, they often adopt what they see and have come to understand. Terri Auckland and Lisa Tusing (Robinson Elementary School) noticed this transfer during independent reading. Sitting in the silent reading area, Angelina and Colton pretend-read *I Know Where My Food Goes* by Jacqui Maynard (1999). The pair takes turns asking each other questions about pictures. When Angelina asks, "What happens in your mouth?" Colton bares his teeth and points to them. "Teeth chew and spit makes it [the food] mushy." "Yuck," says Angelina, with total delight, and turns to the next page.

## When to Initiate Interactive Read-Alouds

For those children who arrive at school with emergent literacy, add interactive read-alouds to your daily menu of reading experiences. For children in need of family storybook reading experiences, focus interactive reading on reacting and responding to the text and pictures, and on predicting and posing questions. Once these children can talk about the text, make predictions, ask questions, and request books be read again and again, add the strategic element to the read-aloud.

## Selecting Books

According to the teachers I've worked with, award-winning books don't always appeal to four- and five-year-olds who lack emergent literacy. Here are some resources that can help you find books that will appeal to the population you teach. You'll find many in your school and public library or in college and university libraries. In the Appendix, you'll find a list of fiction and nonfiction that children have repeatedly asked for.

❑ School librarians have a superb knowledge of new books as well as those tried-and-true favorites. Ask your librarian for help as well as colleagues who can offer suggestions for books that work well in their classrooms.

❑ *A Guide for Super Storytelling Events: Rollicking Read-Alouds and Terrific Tips from Penguin Putnam Books for Young Readers.* 2001. Judy Freeman. Write to Penguin Putnam Books for Young Readers, 345 Hudson Street, New York, NY 10014.

❑ *A to Zoo: Subject Access to Children's Picture Books.* 1998. C. W. Lima and J. A. Lima. New York: R. R. Bowker. Includes the subject matter of 1,400 picture books for young children. Contains author, illustrator, and title as well as 800 subject categories.

❑ The *Horn Book Guide*, published by The Horn Book, Inc., is a biannual publication that organizes books by genre, subject, and age appropriateness. Reviewers rate books from 1 to 6. I urge teachers to order books with ratings of 1, 2, or 3.

❑ *Multicultural Literature for Children and Young Adults: A Selected Listing of Books by and About People of Color.* 1997. 4th ed. G. M. Kruse, K. T. Horning, and M. Schliesman. Madison, WI: Wisconsin Department of Public Education. Annotations of multicultural books the authors recommend for the books' high quality.

❑ "Children's Choices." A list of new books chosen by children appears annually in the October issue of *The Reading Teacher*. This is a joint venture of the International Reading Association and Children's Book Council.

❏ *More Books Kids Will Sit Still For: A Read-Aloud Guide.* 1995. Judy Freeman. An annotated list of top-notch read-alouds listed by grade, subject, and genre. Also includes tips for finding great read-alouds.

❏ "Notable Children's Books in the Language Arts, K–8." This annual list of outstanding trade books appears in the October issue of *Language Arts*, published by the National Council of Teachers of English.

❏ "Teachers Choices." This annual list of books recommended by teachers is published in the November issue of *The Reading Teacher.*

## Interactive Read-Alouds in Action

I have emphasized interactive read-alouds using information books, for like Nell Duke (1999), I am concerned that teachers of young children emphasize fiction. I discovered that with four- and five-year-olds starting with a narrative text and following up with informational texts on the same or a related topic built the background knowledge children needed to step into the nonfiction book. Moreover, when you read aloud from nonfiction, it's okay to read selections to the children, especially if the text is too long to sustain interest or filled with too much information for young children to absorb at one to two sittings (Vardell 1998).

The following modeled strategies invite children's participation in interactive read-alouds. Since it's possible to model many strategies with one book, it's important for you to focus your interactive read-aloud on one or two strategies that you continue to model with different titles. Otherwise, you risk confusing the children with too much process information.

*Strategy Focus: Inferring with Pictures*

**BOOK:** *Bashi, Elephant Baby.* 1997. Theresa Radcliffe. Illus. by John Butler. New York: Puffin.

**PREPLANNING:** I plan to read this story twice. During the first reading, my goals are to show children how to make inferences using pictures in a book and to help the children understand these words: *baobob tree, trotted,* and *slithering.* In addition, I will use the follow-up reading to engage the children in dramatizing trotted and slithering.

ROBB: On the cover, Bashi has its trunk around the mother's trunk. I think Bashi is showing he likes being close to his mom.

HOLLY: I think they love. Like my mom holds my baby brother.

UVALDO: Like my mommy loves me.

TIMEA: And takes care.

ROBB: Yes. And what did you learn from the story?

HOLLY: The mom saved Bashi from the mud.

TIMEA: And the lions eating him.

UVALDO: Others [elephants] watch Bashi. They make him stay close.

ROBB: I like the way you used the story to show me why you think the cover shows love.

*Note how I start the conversation and then let the children talk. The purpose of my questions is to help children bring in story details that support their inferences.*

*Strategy Focus: Reread to Recall Detail*

**BOOK:** *The Elephant.* 1979. Paula Z. Hogan. Illus. by Kinuko Craft. New York: Raintree Children's Books.

**PREPLANNING:** I plan to read this book and pause to recall the details the author includes on a page. To remember information, I will model how rereading helps me keep details in my memory. Then I will pause and invite the children to tell me what they recall and offer them a chance to rehear the page and enrich their recall. This is an opportunity to model text-to-text connections with *Bashi, Baby Elephant.*

*First I model how rereading supports the recall of all the details in a short section. Then I invite the children to try the strategy.*

ROBB: [I read aloud from the book.] "The mother elephant gives milk to her baby. She must watch it carefully. Lions might hunt for small elephants."

CHANNING: I remember lions hunt the babies.

ROBB: Can you tell me other details? [Long pause.]

TIMEA: Read it again. [I reread the passage.]

CHANNING: Babies nurse from mom—like my cousin.

UVALDO: The mom watches the baby.

CHANNING: That's like Bashi.

ROBB: I like the way you connected the details to Bashi's story.

TIMEA: There were lions in Bashi.

CHANNING: They wanted to eat him [Bashi].

ROBB: Wow! You remember the details after the second reading. You also make such terrific connections to the book about Bashi.

*It's important to celebrate the benefits of rereading by honoring what the children recalled so they view this as a beneficial strategy. I also honored the connections they made to* Bashi, Baby Elephant *because we had been working on connections of nonfiction to fiction. The children did this so naturally here.*

*Strategy Focus: Activate Prior Knowledge*

**BOOK:** *Snow Is Falling.* 2000. Franklyn M. Branley. Illus. by Holly Keller. New York: HarperCollins.

**PREPLANNING:** Since the children have seen snow, I will start by collecting what they know about snow and how they feel about it. Then I will use the book's cover to discuss things children can do when it snows. We will also study the endpapers that illustrate snow crystals, showing how each one has six points with a unique pattern. We'll do a picture-walk through half of the book and before reading, I'll pose some questions to discuss: How long can it snow? What does snow feel like? What time of year does it snow?

> ROBB: What do you notice about the endpapers?
> TITUS: It's got designs.
> RACHEL: It's got blue.
> COLTON: It's like the cutouts we made. Snowflakes.
> ROBB: Good remembering. What do you notice about these snowflakes?
> COLTON: They're white.
> TITUS: [Gets up and points.] 1-2-3-4-5-6 points. Every one.
> RACHEL: They're not the same.
> TITUS: Only the points.
> ROBB: You noticed a lot. Each snowflake has a different pattern. But each snowflake has six points.
> RACHEL: How do you know?
> ROBB: [I open to page 9.] You can use a magnifying glass to make the snowflake bigger. We'll do that next time it snows.

*Though there were pauses between each child sharing what he or she noticed, I did not jump in. Thinking takes time, and it's important to offer children time to process and frame their thoughts into words. Note how I summarized or brought together the ideas they shared. I do that so the children observe how I recap and repeat important information that builds prior knowledge.*

*Strategy Focus: Check Understanding of a New Concept*

**BOOK:** *Pop! A Book About Bubbles.* 2001. Kimberly Brubaker Bradley. Illus. by Margaret Miller. New York: HarperCollins.
**PREPLANNING:** The lesson will open with the children carefully observing me blowing a bubble through a wand. I will invite the children to share their observations, then read the book. My goal is to help children understand how bubbles form, why bubbles are always round, and that a bubble consists of a soapy skin that encases air. After reading and watching bubbles, ask the children to explain how bubbles are like people.

> ROBB: [I read the sentence.] "The air inside the bubble pushes out against the soap skin." Hmm, So bubbles have skin?

UVALDO: It's the outside.

CHANNING: It's the soapy stuff.

ROBB: The skin is soapy?

CHANNING: It holds the air. Like our skin holds us.

ROBB: So people and bubbles are alike because both have skin.

TIMEA: Uhuh.

ROBB: [Continues reading.]

*I paused here because I want to follow up the read-aloud with children thinking about how bubbles and people are alike and different. I also want the children to see how science can extend their understanding of the concept of skin so I pose questions to stir thinking.*

*Strategy Focus: Visualizing*

**BOOK:** *This Is the Rain.* 2001. Lola M. Schaefer. Illus. by Jane Wattenberg. New York: Greenwillow.

**PREPLANNING:** While reading, I will pause and share the mental pictures I am making. Then I will have the children share their mental pictures and discuss how visualizing helps you get into and enjoy a book.

ROBB: [I read, but *don't show* the illustration.] "These are the puddles, big and round, that dot the land, muddy wet ground."

ERIC: I see a puddle by my house.

ANGELINA: Me too. A big one. Brown water.

TITUS: I see lots [of puddles.] I jump in.

ANGELINA: [Laughs.] You in trouble. [Everyone laughs.]

ROBB: You all made pictures of puddles you have seen. Let's look at the pictures in the book. What do you notice?

ERIC: There's a frog and turtle.

TITUS: It's raining. [Points to a drop falling.] [Long pause.]

ROBB: What else do you notice?

TITUS: It's like mostly dirt.

ANGELINA: Lots of puddles. Brown, like I saw.

TITUS: Big and small ones.

ROBB: Making pictures in your mind helped you understand that puddles can be big or small. When mud mixes with water the water turns brown, just like Angelina's picture. But puddles can form by your house, in the park, in the street.

*Whenever possible, connect the children's visualizations to the text so they observe how making mental pictures can improve comprehension.*

### Interactive Reading with Big Books

It's April in Danielle Water's Head Start room and Tanisha and Kaywan have spent two years in this program. By December, in addition to simulating family storybook reading several times a day and reading just-for-fun, Danielle has added shared reading of big books to her read-aloud program. This morning, five-year-old Tanisha and Kaywan pretend to read the big book, *Where Does the Brown Bear Go?* by Nicki Weiss (1989). "I'm the teacher," says Kaywan. He opens the book to the endpapers of a sky peppered with stars, a golden crescent moon, and one fir tree. "What do you notice?" he asks, imitating Danielle's favorite question.

Tanisha points to the moon and says, "Moon." She does the same for tree and stars. "It's nighttime. The sky is black." As Kaywan turns each page, Tanisha responds to his repeated query: "What do you notice?"

At first glance, a visitor to Danielle's classroom might think that formal reading instruction has filtered down to the four- and five-year-olds in this Head Start class. Not so. These children have developed emergent literacy behaviors because of the rich read-aloud program they have experienced over the past two years. And shared, interactive reading of big books has been an important part of that program.

## The Shared Book Experience

Shared reading has its roots in New Zealand in the mid 1960s. Teacher and writer, Don Holdaway, developed the idea of using oversized books with kindergarten children (1979). Holdaway wanted large numbers of children in a classroom to experience the visual intimacy of family storybook reading. To bring the children closer to the print and pictures, Holdaway developed the shared reading strategy using oversized books.

Carefully, Don Holdaway watched the children he worked with and observed that (1) Print fascinates young children. They are curious about letters, words, and punctuation; (2) Young children naturally chime in the reading with great enthusiasm—once they are familiar with the text; (3) Children imitate their teacher and point to the words of a familiar story while reading them—educators call this voice-to-print-match; (4) A result of repeated readings of big books is that children memorize many meaning-loaded words. Often the children can recognize these words out of the context of the story.

For children, shared reading is a safe way to learn about books and print. Chiming in on familiar parts involves the group and doesn't single out individuals. Children who are unsure of their responses and reactions can observe and eventually imitate classmates and the adult reader. The oversized format allows a large

**A Must-Have Shared Reading Resource**

*Perspectives on Shared Reading: Planning and Practice.* 2000. Bobbi Fisher and Emily Fisher Medvic. Portsmouth, NH: Heinemann.

In one book, teachers will explore a wide range of suggestions for planning shared reading experiences and strategies for using shared reading in their classrooms.

group to observe print and illustrations, reinforcing what children continue to learn during daily, multiple, family storybook read-alouds. All the strategy modeling you bring to interactive read-alouds works well with big books during shared reading times.

## Materials for Shared Reading

For shared reading to simulate family storybook reading, children should sit close together in a comfortable space.

*A Rug* Most teachers use a soft rug for the gathering place for the shared reading, teacher demonstrations, and the morning message.

*An Easel* You'll need to place the big book on a sturdy easel that is strong and allows the children to turn pages and point to specific parts of the book.

*Pointers* I purchase pointers in our local hardware store and place a Styrofoam ball or a small pompom at one end. As I read, I point to the words. The children also point to words as they reread parts they've memorized or to point to a writing convention or picture.

*Masking Devices* It's easy to make masking devices from file folders. Make several so children can use them during independent reading time. I prefer masking

**Forge Personal Connections**

Before reading fiction or nonfiction, discover what children know about the topic. Ask them: What do you know about this topic? Can you tell us the experiences you've had that connect to the topic; character; setting? Inviting children to share enlarges what everyone knows and links the children to the book. If children have no prior knowledge, then take the time to build their background before reading.

devices that have a slider and are of different widths so the children can spotlight upper- or lowercase letters, punctuation, words, and parts of a sentence (see Appendix for masking models to reproduce).

*Sticky Notes*   Keep these handy so you can cover words and invite the children to predict what's under the sticky note, then quickly check the prediction.

### Introducing a Narrative Big Book: Take a Picture-Walk

When I introduce a narrative big book, the children and I study the front and back covers and think about the title. I read the dedication and invite the children to wonder about it. Then we take a picture-walk through about half of the book. As the children view and discuss the illustrations, I invite them to create a story line, then use everything they've learned to predict what they believe the story will be about. I always record these predictions, and after the first reading, we return to them to make adjustments. I'm always careful to explain that predictions don't have to match the story at this point, but they should grow out of what we have learned from our preview.

As the children take a picture-walk through *You'll Soon Grow into Them, Titch* by Pat Hutchins (1983), hands shoot up. The air crackles with the children's energy and excitement. "I got a prediction," says Morgan. "Me too," echoes through the room. "It's about getting big. See the plants grow," Morgan shows two pictures.

"The pants and sweater are too big," says Latavia.
"The kid will have to grow so they fit," observes Benjamin.
"Yeah. And the mom's growing," says Devin. [Lots of giggles.]
"There's eggs in the nest. And then there's birds," says Jondon.
"Here they go to the store. He's gettin' pants that fit!" says Devin.
Morgan throws her hands up and says, "Everything's growing."

The pictures have created so much interest and anticipation that the children beg to hear the story "right now." And I read it.

Picture-walks not only prepare children for the reading, but they also introduce the characters, settings, part of the plot, and foster wondering about the story. Understanding narrative structures starts during preparation to read and eventually will transfer to the children's narrative pieces.

### Introducing a Nonfiction Big Book

Balance your shared reading program by including as many nonfiction as fictional big books. As Fisher and Medvic point out, informational texts teach children about the world (2000). Nonfiction also enlarges children's background knowledge about science, math, and history and stirs their curiosity about their environment, the natural world, problem solving, and the past.

When I introduce nonfiction, we look at the front and back covers, the dedication, and then we search for these nonfiction features: table of contents, sidebars, photographs and captions, maps, diagrams, an index, a glossary, and pronunciation key.

Our text and picture-walk help the children explore the book's structure and think about and predict what they will learn when I read it. I record these ideas and return to the list to discuss what the book contained, and what the children want to learn more about. Then the children add more information to the list.

When I introduce Allan Flowler's *The Chicken or the Egg?* (1993) to a group of five-year-olds, the children notice that there is no table of contents. But they're quick to point out that there are photographs. At the end, two pages of photographs have captions under each photo, which I explain is a glossary—a place where the author explains words used in the text. Because the children have seen indices several times, they point out what they've learned: "Eggs have seven pages and chickens thirteen—we'll learn a lot about those," and "Some words have only one page—I guess there's not much [information] on those." Here's what the group predicted they'd learn from this book: different kinds of chickens; eggs are different colors; how eggs hatch; how to take care of chickens.

Both girls and boys display great enthusiasm for informational books and early on are learning about the structures of texts they'll continue to meet in and out of school. Moreover, nonfiction texts offer children the models they require for writing their own pieces.

## Questions That Stir Thinking About the Text

After reading and enjoying a big book, focus children's attention on print and/or pictures with three open-ended questions. These questions stimulate discussion among children and can enlarge their mental models of how print works and the meaning contained in pictures.

1. What did you notice about the pictures?
2. What did you notice about the print?
3. Do you have any questions about the print?

These questions actively involve children with exploring and discovering things about print and pictures; researchers agree that active engagement enables children to construct knowledge of how print works (Teale and Sulzby 1989, Routman 1991).

What children notice becomes your signal for what they are ready to learn. When Devin noticed quotation marks and wondered what they meant, Nancy Reedy discussed dialogue and how quotation marks show what characters say. Nancy continued to point out quotation marks and dialogue in all her read-alouds, and eventually invited the children to try using them in writing workshop. Will all children try writing dialogue? No. In fact, you might not have any takers. But they are hearing correct terminology and learning about its use.

By asking children what they notice, teachers can heighten children's awareness of how print works, develop emergent literacy skills, think about meaning with pictures, and prepare them for the important task of reading (Cunningham [1995] 2000, Fisher 1998).

### Masking Ideas Provide Valuable Information

By inviting the children to come to the easel and mask items that answer your requests, you can determine the children's progress with identifying letters, letters and sounds, words, spaces, sight words, directionality, rhyming words, and print conventions (Fisher and Medvic 2000, Holdaway 1979). Here are some masking invitations:

Please come to the easel and mask:

- ❑ A word that starts with the first letter in your name.
- ❑ A letter that's in your name.
- ❑ The letter _____.
- ❑ The first word of a sentence.
- ❑ The first and last word on the page.
- ❑ An uppercase letter.
- ❑ A lowercase letter.
- ❑ The letter that makes the sound _____.
- ❑ The word that rhymes with _____.
- ❑ The title.
- ❑ A word with x number of letters.
- ❑ The space between words.
- ❑ A compound word.
- ❑ A contraction for _____.
- ❑ The name of an animal.
- ❑ The name of a person.
- ❑ A word that ends in _____.
- ❑ A word with the consonant or vowel_____.
- ❑ A word that starts with the blend _____.
- ❑ A word that starts with a vowel.
- ❑ A question mark.
- ❑ A comma.
- ❑ A period.
- ❑ An exclamation point.
- ❑ Quotation marks.
- ❑ The beginning and end of a sentence.

### Planning a Seven-Day Shared Reading Cycle

As you reread a big book or poem on a chart, engage the children in activities like the following—activities that develop emergent literacy (Fisher 1998, Fisher and Medvic 2000, Slaughter 1993). Depending on the length of the oversized text, the interest level of the children, and the depth of study you are striving for, plan shared reading experiences in four- to seven-day cycles.

To develop the children's voice-to-print match, use a pointer while you read, placing the pointer under each word. Point out that you always read from left to right so you develop children's knowledge of directionality.

*Day 1*   Introduce the book. Take a picture-walk by studying the illustrations, then predicting what the book will be about. Record children's predictions on chart paper.

*Day 2*   Read a narrative text and stop two or three times to gather predictions and support from the story and pictures. Start by modeling how to predict and support, then invite the children to predict/support what will happen next. Record these on chart paper.

Tell the children that each time you stop, you'll collect two to three predictions and support. Setting the guidelines helps children accept that everyone won't participate that day.

Show children how you read a nonfiction big book differently from a narrative. Point out the table of contents, index, photographs, captions, sidebars, diagrams, and glossary. Explain the purposes of these nonfiction features and how they help you learn more about a topic. Encourage children to tell you what they think they'll learn from this book. Record their thoughts on chart paper and add to the list after reading the book.

*Day 3*   Reread the book and ask the children to discuss why they enjoyed it, point to favorite illustrations, and retell favorite parts. Next have them adjust their predictions, explaining that predictions usually don't match the story when you only know part of it.

*Days 4 to 7*   Reread all or parts of the book. Discuss the story, information, print conventions, illustrations, or apply strategies during these four days. Focus your planning and work on one or two skills a day, just as Nancy Reedy and I have done (earlier in the Chapter).

You can monitor children's reactions to shared reading with a checklist (Figure 5–5). Complete a checklist for each child every six weeks. Information gathered can help you decide which concepts about print and writing conventions to emphasize.

# Checklist for Shared Reading Experiences

Name_____

**Key:** O = Observed; N = Not Observed

**Behaviors**                                                    **Dates Observed**

____ Enjoys listening.                                          ___ ___ ___

____ Participates in activities.                                ___ ___ ___

____ Answers questions.                                         ___ ___ ___

____ Chimes in on story refrain.                                ___ ___ ___

____ Chimes in on repeated pattern.                             ___ ___ ___

____ Discusses pictures.                                        ___ ___ ___

____ Discusses text.                                            ___ ___ ___

____ Points to spaces between words.                            ___ ___ ___

____ Points to beginning/end of word.                           ___ ___ ___

____ Tracks print.                                              ___ ___ ___

____ Knows print tells the story.                               ___ ___ ___

____ Recognizes some words.                                     ___ ___ ___

____ Uses pictures for meaning.                                 ___ ___ ___

____ Recalls parts during rereadings.                           ___ ___ ___

____ Uses masking device to isolate:                            ___ ___ ___

    ____ upper- and lowercase letters        ___ ___ ___

    ____ punctuation: ___ period, ___ question marks,   ___ ___ ___

    ____ comma, ___ exclamation point, ___ quotation marks   ___ ___ ___

**Figure 5–5.** Checklist for Shared Reading Experiences

## *Just-For-Fun Read-Alouds*

Two to three times a day, reserve time to read a book, poem, or song for pure pleasure and enjoyment. Follow the children's lead and pause to let them discuss a picture or part of the book that reaches their imagination and emotional center. Display, along the edge of the chalkboard or against a wall, books the children truly enjoy. Occasionally, refer to these titles and ask the children if they would like to hear one read again. You can also fill baskets or plastic crates with books you've read aloud; store these in your silent reading area. Encourage the children to browse through the books and pretend-read them during independent reading times.

Three to four times a year, observe children during independent reading. Figure 5–6 will help you monitor what engages children, their behavior, and provides valuable information that can help you plan meaningful interventions.

## Independent Reading: Building Sight Words and Vocabulary

Four- and five-year-olds can choose from many independent reading activities when teachers invite their students to "read." Immersing children (Cambourne 1988, Holdaway 1979) in print enables young learners to connect the fact that spoken language can be written, develops a concept of word and a sight-word vocabulary, and offers words for children to try during writing workshop. However, a room filled with print on the walls, charts hanging on clotheslines strung across the room and from the ceiling, and dozens of books displayed can overwhelm young children. One child in a room cluttered with print told me that she didn't like to look at the walls or ceiling. Strike a balance and aim for immersion that encourages children to visit the charts, browse though displayed books, and use print as a learning resource.

During writing workshop, when children ask Deena Baker how to spell a word, she usually: (1) helps the child stretch the sounds and write what he hears; or (2) helps the child find the word if it is on a word wall or a label of an object or a displayed book.

## *Labeling the Room*

Like Brian Cambourne (1988), I want children to be surrounded by all kinds of print. Along the chalkboard, display books that will be read aloud that day. On bulletin boards, feature children's writing. Hang on a bulletin board the poem and song you are chanting with the children that week. Gradually, using the children's suggestions, label items in the room.

Often, when I walk into kindergarten classes a few days before school opens, I notice the teacher has labeled the room for the children. However, labeling the room

---

## Checklist of Independent Reading Behaviors

Name_____

| Reading Behaviors | Dates Observed |
|---|---|
| ___ Settles down quickly. | ___ ___ ___ |
| ___ Holds book correctly. | ___ ___ ___ |
| ___ Turns pages left to right. | ___ ___ ___ |
| ___ Pretends to read the book, telling the story. | ___ ___ ___ |
| ___ Chooses books independently. | ___ ___ ___ |
| ___ Reads the same book many times. | ___ ___ ___ |
| ___ Focuses on the book. | ___ ___ ___ |
| ___ Pretends to read with a partner. | ___ ___ ___ |
| ___ Returns book to proper place. | ___ ___ ___ |
| ___ Reads labels in the room. | ___ ___ ___ |
| ___ Pretends to read a displayed big book, poem, or song. | ___ ___ ___ |
| ___ Rereads word walls. | ___ ___ ___ |
| ___ Reads classmates' names. | ___ ___ ___ |

---

**Figure 5–6.** Checklist for Independent Reading Behaviors

© 2003 by Laura Robb from *Literacy Links*. Portsmouth, NH: Heinemann.

gains so much more meaning when you involve the children. Two to three days a week, invite the children to tell you a few things they would like to see in print.

- ❏ Write upper- and lowercase letters properly.
- ❏ Print letters neatly.
- ❏ Spell words correctly.
- ❏ Paste the word or phrase on or close to the item.

During the first month in Lisa Tusing's class, children have asked for *table, computer, book case, teacher's desk, door, chalkboard, easel, window,* and *chair.* Several times a week, Lisa and the children read the words together, as Lisa points to each word, sweeping across it from left to right. She offers reading the labels as an activity during independent reading, and permits pairs to use a pointer and say each word. Once children have had enough practice, Lisa creates a matching game that builds the children's sight-word vocabulary. She prints each word in the room on an index card or a paper strip. Then she invites children to locate and match their word with a word in the classroom. "This only takes a few minutes," says Lisa, "so we play the game after the morning message or as a transition from one reading or writing event to another."

### Key Word Rings

Key words, a concept Sylvia Ashton Warner wrote about in *Teacher* ([1963] 1986) while working with Maori children in New Zealand, can enlarge children's sight and writing words and show all learners the connection between speech and written language. Children sit in a circle with their teacher who asks, "What word would you like to see in print?" The teacher records these on cards. Place children's cards on a metal ring and hang the rings on hooks that children can reach. The first word on each key ring is the child's name.

During independent reading, invite your students to "read" their key ring cards to themselves and to a partner. With four-year-olds and five-year-olds who lack emergent literacy, the teacher and/or teaching assistant becomes the child's partner, supporting the reading of requested words until the child can recognize them. Make children's key ring words available during writing workshop by modeling how they are an idea and spelling resource.

Meaningful nouns and verbs such as *fire engine, race, kitten, bus, cry, truck, bicycle,* are what children request. Too many kindergarten and first-grade teachers drill the Dolch list of high-frequency words such as *on, into, what,* and so on. Isolated from words that have meaning, it's difficult for children to memorize these.

Recently, I observed a kindergarten teacher introducing a group to the first word they would learn to read. I felt the children's excitement and energy as the

teacher told them this was a great moment. As I waited for a meaning-loaded noun or verb, the teacher printed *the* on an index card, then showed and read it. Bright smiles faded. Three avoided looking at the word. Two insisted it really wasn't a word. At that moment I felt deeply for the teacher and her children. A great opportunity was lost to the pressure of having children memorize high-frequency words that have no concrete meaning to children who lack a concept of word and voice-to-print match. A compromise for five-year-olds would be to attach a powerful noun to each Dolch word, such as *the whale* or *in the forest,* giving meaning to each high-frequency word on the list so learning them makes sense. In *Phonics They Use,* Cunningham suggests that attaching children's names to high-frequency words helps them associate meaning with the abstract word ([1995] 2000). Here are some examples; note the teacher underlines the high-frequency word.

<u>in</u> the pool <u>with</u> Uvaldo
a candy bar <u>for</u> Tanisha
William is <u>from</u> Edinburgh, Virginia

### Word Walls

Originally called "Words on the Wall" by Cunningham and colleagues (1989), teachers of young children quickly embraced word walls as a way of developing connections between spoken and written language and building young children's sight vocabulary. There is great variation in how teachers use word walls.

Some teachers list alphabet letters on a large bulletin board or high up on a wall, allowing space between each letter for the placement of words. The first words placed on the word wall are the children's names. As the year unfolds, teachers add words related to themed studies as well as high-frequency words or words children repeatedly ask for during writing workshop.

Others place their word walls under the chalkboard or in other low places around the room that the children can reach. Sharon Mooreland, a kindergarten teacher at Keister Elementary School in Harrisonburg, Virginia, has little wall space. She made a tri-part folding screen from cardboard that's the height of most five-year-olds. With six sides available, Sharon created a word wall that her students interact with throughout the day.

I believe that when children cannot reach and interact with word walls, they are more for display and complying with a school district's requirement than meaningful use. For word walls to benefit children, they need to be interactive, permitting the children to take off and place words under the correct alphabet guide letter. With interactive word walls, teachers and children create games such as matching words, finding your partner's name, choosing rhyming words, gathering words related to a topic such as *spiders*, *homes*, or *the ocean*, or selecting words that start or end with a specific sound.

During their first year of teaching the Literacy Links kindergartens at Robinson Elementary School in Woodstock, Virginia, Lisa Tusing and Terri Auckland observed that the alphabet word wall overwhelmed their children and they never used it. I suggested that they create mini-word walls, using $12 \times 18$ inch construction paper, displayed where children could work with the words. We agreed that starting with four to six concrete words that related to books in storybook reading or daily experiences was a good adaptation. Their mini-words walls had headings such as: *What We Saw in the Cafeteria, Library Words, Weather Words, Polite Words, Ocean Words*, and so on. Helping the children learn about the inside and outside school environment was an important part of Lisa's and Terri's curriculum. With limited community experiences, such as visiting the bank, post office, or grocery store, the teachers used the school and its surroundings to enlarge children's experiences and the words they need to think and talk about these.

Often there were two charts. The first came from words the children suggested; the companion chart was the children's list written in A, B, C order. Lisa and Terri observed that as the year progressed and with continual rereadings of mini-word walls during a specific study or experience, some children were memorizing specific words and using them during discussions.

## Closing Reflections

In the essay "Gifts, Not Stars" (1994), George Ella Lyon expressed two ideas that are worthy of our consideration:

> Nurturing gifts requires belief in the goodness of the self unfolding, related to but not competing with others. Thus, where star is about scarcity—only a few places at the top—gift is about abundance. . . . (29)

> If the product is not outstanding—and for schoolwork, that product is the grade, not the learning—then the process is worthless. (31)

The Literacy Links program is about teaching all children, not creating a culture of those who display talents and ability at an early age and leaving those behind who most need support. It's about teaching the process of reading and writing that enables children to create meaningful and splendid products. How does this belief affect the nature of preschool and kindergarten programs? It places the primary responsibility on each school district to find ways to meet the needs of children without a rich background in family storybook reading. A rich and varied read-aloud program is the pathway I recommend to developing and nurturing children's literacy. It's the pathway those children who arrive at school having heard hundreds of stories have taken. It nourishes children's literacy because of the wide-range and abundance of read-alouds. The program includes:

- ❑ **Family Storybook Reading.** Supports delayed learners by enlarging their background information of concepts and topics, constructing their book knowledge, concepts of how print works, and how readers respond to, talk about, and apply strategies to forge powerful connections to books.
- ❑ **Just-for-Fun Read-Alouds.** Uses books, songs, chants, and poetry to bring joy and delight to reading and language. At the same time, introduce children to different genres in the reading and singing process.
- ❑ **Interactive Read-Alouds.** Enlarges vocabulary, teaches new information, and makes visible the strategies readers use to make meaning from fiction and nonfiction.
- ❑ **Independent Reading.** Includes individuals or pairs pretend-reading big and regular sized books, poems, and songs that teachers make available after reading them. Children can also read word walls, their own and classmates' key word rings and writing, and the labeled items in the classroom.

Constructing a *balanced read-aloud program* is the best way to build emergent literacy. Why? Because it benefits children from diverse literacy backgrounds and enriches the literacy of children who arrive at school with abundant storybook reading experiences.

# 6

## Independent and Shared Writing

*Children want to write. They want to write the first day they attend school. This is no accident. Before they went to school they marked up walls, pavements, newspaper with crayons, chalk, pens or pencils . . . anything that makes a mark. The child's marks say, "I am."*

Donald Graves, *Writing: Children and Teachers at Work* (1983, 3)

Two weeks prior to my October visit to Robinson Elementary School in Woodstock, Virginia, I receive an email from Lisa Tusing and Terri Auckland. It's the first year of the Literacy Links kindergarten program, and both teachers want me to look at the children's independent writing.

"They're still scribbling and scrawling with different colors," Terri points out as she shows me some pieces. "They're not connecting what they are learning about reading to their writing."

"I ask them why they keep scribbling," says Lisa, "and the children give me three reasons: '*I see all the colors.*' '*I never had these [colored markers], and I can't [draw].*'"

After brainstorming a list of possibilities that could bring the children to writing with pictures that tell a story or offer information, we decide to try more explicit teacher modeling. Lisa and Terri agree to demonstrate and think aloud, making visible their process of thinking about a story, then drawing pictures. We hope that such support might spawn changes.

It's April. I check my box in Robinson's office and find a message from Lisa and Terri: "Come see our bulletin boards as soon as you can!" Curiosity immediately drives me down the long hall to both rooms. On bulletin boards that line the walls of the hallway are displays of the children's writing. The title shouts in bold, large print: "Our Writing From September to April." I read. Slowly, one tear rolls down my face, then another and another, as I observe the progress the children have made. They are becoming writers, my inner voice whispers. Even in October, when Matthew wrote, he filled the paper with lines; he did not dictate stories about his pictures. By early April, writing includes pictures and words that tell about his picture (Figures 6–1 and 6–2).

The door to Terri's room opens. Angelina pokes her head outside. "Mrs. Robb's here," she announces. Before Terri can say anything, the children crowd around me. Voices blend, like a chorus, as they point out letters, invented spellings that I can read, and ask me if I like their pictures. Terri and I smile at one another. "They're on their way," she says. You bet, I think. Patience, thoughtful teacher demonstrations, emphasizing elements of the writing process such as inviting children to choose their own topics, holding one-on-one conferences, sharing pieces in the author's chair, and writing every day moved these children forward. When Lisa and Terri abandoned the progress-agenda they originally felt compelled to follow, the children grew as writers. Both teachers carefully nurtured each child by celebrating progress during conferences, by inviting school administrators to hear young authors read their pieces, and by displaying children's writing in the classroom and hallway.

## When Children Lack Everyday Experiences

In addition to a lack of literacy experiences, schools also have groups of children who have few everyday experiences that build a knowledge of children's home and community and encourage them to see, connect to, and think about their world. Experiences such as accompanying a parent to make deposits or withdrawals at the bank, checking out and returning library books, going grocery shopping, visiting a travel agent, or watching the parent surf the Internet for information, or getting acquainted with the firehouse are important to young children's developing knowledge of their environment and available community services.

In addition, the conversations surrounding these experiences are equally important, for exchanges between adult and child can clarify questions the child

**Figure 6–1.** Matthew's writing in October

**Figure 6–2.** Matthew's writing in April
*Translation:* I got to hold the kitten.

raises and observations he makes. Rich daily experiences that become part of children's prior knowledge enable them to create mental images that they can translate
into pictures and writing. Children can then use these experiences to write with a
variety of settings, stories, and information.

Those children who lack community experiences require additional support
from teachers. The suggestions that follow can enlarge children's knowledge of
their surroundings. Those who arrive with a wide range of these experiences will
be able to deepen their understandings.

❑   Include, in your weekly or bimonthly newsletters, community places parents
     can take their children.
❑   Plan field trips to the firehouse, a local factory, the post office, and so on.
❑   Use the school and its grounds to learn about the library, cafeteria, and so
     forth.
❑   Share picture books about a veterinarian's office, a visit to the dentist, the
     firehouse, post office, and so on.
❑   Invite community guests into your classroom to discuss their jobs and where
     they work.
❑   Share your experiences with the children.

Continually enlarge and extend children's new and developing knowledge through discussions and by encouraging inquiries. Hearing responses from you and peers will build those everyday experiences the children will eventually bring to their writing.

## Writing Is a Process, Not a Prompt

When I was in elementary school, I equated writing with torture. Teachers assigned topics that I knew nothing about or I found boring. Some wrote the opening sentence on the chalkboard and told us to write. Usually, the class had forty to forty-five minutes to complete a "perfect piece." What did "perfect piece" mean? It meant well-organized, interesting, and free from spelling and mechanical errors.

In the primary grades, I was labeled *intractable* because I refused to write from a prompt or story starter or copy a text from the board. Instead, I wrote what I felt deeply about. The result? Teachers called my parents to school. In third grade, I remember my mom pleading with me to just do what the teacher asked. But the need to express myself ran deeper than complying and doing it the teacher's way.

By sixth grade, on my report card, the teacher printed, in large, uppercase letters, NEEDS IMPROVEMENT IN WRITING. These words stung like the tentacles of a jellyfish and have been etched into my memory. I loved to write, but not from a prompt or an assigned, specific topic such as "My Stamp Collection" (I didn't collect stamps) or "My Summer Vacation."

Teaching and writing have enabled me to strike a balance between free-choice writing and teacher-directed writing. In real life, writers generate their own ideas and are often asked to write about a topic. However, writers always have the choice about accepting an assignment to write about gardens, manatees, or airport security. I want the same choices for children. Therefore, I offer broad topics for directed writing assignments so that students have choices. Winter or summer sports, the Olympics, pond life, the Revolutionary War are examples of topics that allow children choices as they narrow the focus and zoom in on an aspect that fascinates them.

Unfortunately, even today, teachers offer children story starters or lined worksheets with a topic or prompt. Often, teachers claim that they are preparing children to be successful on state mandated tests. However, I believe that when scoring high on writing tests drives writing instruction, the results are formulaic teaching with the singular purpose of passing the state test. Children who practice writing as if it was a series of steps rather than a recursive process that moves back and forth from planning to drafting to revising to planning, and so on struggle to explore their process and unique ideas (Murray 1984). In one school, primary grade children were given this recipe:

- ❏ Make your topic sentence a question.
- ❏ Write three sentences that answer your question.
- ❏ End by writing your question differently.

Children assiduously practiced this formula through collaborative writing in kindergarten and first grade, and then independently in second and third grade. In this school, when teachers announced, "We're going to write," children displayed excitement at the start of the year. Soon, however, when they realized the repetitiveness of writing lessons, excitement shifted to muttering "boring" and "not again." The only hope of developing writers in such an environment is among children who lead schizophrenic lives: They write one way for school and write with joy and passion and meaning at home.

What a contrast to writing workshop where children generate topics, talk about them, draw and write, revise, and learn about genre structures. In writing workshop, children learn to write well because they care deeply about what they write. For them, writing is personal and celebrates themselves, their family, and friends. And when the teacher announces, "Get ready for writing workshop," the children respond just the way Eric and Rachel, both in kindergarten, did when they shouted, "Yea! It's time for writing!" Children who have daily opportunities to write freely start exploring the language they are learning from read-alouds, teacher demonstrations, sharing their stories and the print in their classrooms.

Like Calkins (1994), Chomsky (1971), Dyson (1987), and Graves (1983), I believe that children feel empowered to write long before they read. And, like these researchers, my observations show me how writing every day enables children to gain control of the writing process. At the same time, writing supports the development of phonemic awareness, children's ability to hear the sounds in spoken words. Writing also develops children's knowledge of the alphabet and letter/sound relationships as children write and match letters to the sounds they hear.

## From Speech to Print

From birth, children are programmed, genetically disposed to learning language (Pinker 1994). Russian psychologist, Lev Vygotsky points out that infants' writing consists of gestures in air. Vygotsky explains that written signs can be thought of as gestures that have been fixed (1962). By imitating the adults who continually talk to them and interact with them, four- to six-year-olds can control the phonetic and grammatical systems of their own language. They arrive at school speaking fluently because from birth, adults have conversed with them assuming the children can participate.

I want every teacher to make assumptions about writing that parents instinctively make about learning oral language. Yet, I have visited preschool and kindergarten classes where teachers believe that children are not ready to write until they have learned their alphabet letters and the sounds letters make. They insist that children write by copying words correctly printed on the chalkboard. Most children arrive at school believing they can write (Calkins 1994, Graves 1983). The message these teachers are sending is that writing is hard and laborious; writing has meaning for the teacher, but not for the children. Too soon, children come to believe they cannot write.

When I pass out paper and invite four- and five-year-olds to write, I'm aware that they have to learn a great deal about writing that differs from speaking. Here's what these children do:

- ❏ Choose a topic and create a setting for their writing.
- ❏ Organize the space on their paper.
- ❏ Print scribbles or letters from left to right.
- ❏ Write symbols called letters.
- ❏ Know the sounds that the letters make.
- ❏ Place letters in a logical order.
- ❏ Keep their idea and message in their head.

It's July 11, the last week of summer school that began in mid-June. I'm sitting at a table in Nancy Reedy's writing workshop for kindergarten children who need additional support. I'm side-by-side with Morgan who's telling me about her picture.

"It's about me and my friend. I share a sandwich with her. Here's the bread; here's the pieces of cheese; here's the table; here's me and Latavia."

"I love your picture," I say. "You have so many details that tell this story. What are you going to write?" I ask. There's a long pause. No answer. Morgan chooses a black marker and starts. Here's what she says as she writes (see Figure 6–3):

"I can spell *All* and *by* [she uses her finger to space words]. I can spell *my*." She stretches the sounds in "self" three times, then writes *sef*. Morgan prints *I*, but stops and says "share" again and again and writes *ch* then *a*. Next, Morgan rereads what's she's written. "I need *sandwich* and *friend*." They're on the word wall, and Morgan brings both words back and finishes her sentence. "Do you want to hear me read it?"

"Of course I do!" And Morgan reads her writing.

Morgan shows me that she can spell some words correctly, she can find words on mini-word walls, and she uses spelling inventions to write some words. Her

**Figure 6–3.** Morgan's picture

sentence starts with an uppercase letter and moves from left to right. And, Morgan can read back what she wrote.

When children first start to write, however, their letters can go in all directions. Some start in the middle and end at the top; others, like Tanisha, write their sentence in a list (Figure 6–4). As children continue to observe you talk about print during shared writing and notice how authors organize print during shared reading of oversized texts, they will absorb the concept that print moves from left to right. You can help them apply what they've learned to their own writing during conferences.

For children drawing pictures, scribble writing, printing letters and/or numbers, writing words using spelling inventions and print in their room is hard work because as they draw and write, they must also hold mental images and words in their memory. Recently, I watched Andrew draw a picture of a space ship soaring to other planets. After writing two words, Andrew abandons matching sounds and letters. "My story's too long," he says. So Andrew takes a stack of scratch paper, and while telling the story, he draws rows and rows of squiggly lines, so that his "writing kept up." Andrew finds the ideal solution that avoids the frustration of creating a long story, but not having the muscle or writing fluency development and word knowledge to write it.

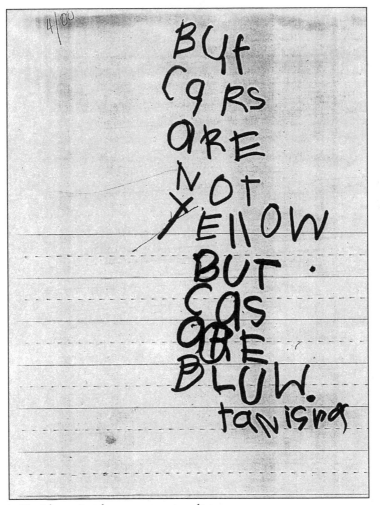

**Figure 6–4.** Tanisha writes her sentence in a list.

## Creating a Writing Workshop for Four- and Five-Year-Olds

Danielle Waters at Keister Elementary and Maryann Sherry at Robinson Elementary have created classroom environments for their preschool children that shout, "You are writers!" Each room has two easels where children take turns painting during writing workshop, free play, and center times. Because they don't have easels and both believe that painting is important for their kindergarten children, Lisa Tusing and Terri Auckland have "painting tables." Stored on a table or a bookshelf are paints and brushes and paper.

A writing center is located on a table or on shelves of a bookcase in each classroom. Stacks of paper, from 24 × 16 inch pieces to 8 × 12 inch pieces, are available for children. In metal buckets or small plastic trays are colored markers, crayons, and pencils. There are staplers to make books, and scissors and tape so the children can cut and paste paper. There are also two stamps and pads to date each piece. Upper- and lowercase letters of the alphabet are on the wall near the writing area, at the children's eye-level as well as above the chalkboard. Taped in the middle of the tables where children work are small strips of alphabet letters.

Some teachers store writing in large folders made from construction paper. Printed on the outside are the children's names. Lisa and Terri devised a different system. They stapled each month's writing into a large booklet. "We found these easier to stack on a shelf and we didn't have to deal with papers falling out," said Lisa. Whichever method you choose, if writing is to inform your instruction and conferences, then pieces need to be dated and kept in the classroom so you can review them, interpret and evaluate them, then create a plan that nudges each child forward (see Chapter 9).

During workshop, at the start of the year, the teacher places a tray of markers, crayons, and pencils on each table. Once children have established jobs and routines, they are in charge of giving out and putting away materials as well as passing out and storing writing folders.

These classrooms are wired for authentic writing experiences. The message teachers transmit daily is that writing is important to communicating and remembering. And writing is an important part of everyday life. Before Lisa Tusing sends a note to the office, she tells the children what and why she writes. "Sometimes," Lisa tells me, "I jot down a note so I remember to give the children the ice cream treat I brought." Lisa always reads her note then passes it around so children can observe how writing can be a memory aid. When the class receives a note from me or the principal, celebrating their writing, teachers read the note and display it where the children can "read" it. All day long, teachers model the ways that writing has become a natural part of daily living. They share and talk about checks for school pictures, thank-you notes, requests from parents, menus from the cafeteria, attendance forms, and shopping lists, memories of field trips to the pumpkin patch and deer farm, continually modeling how writing is part of our lives. Shared and interactive writing show children how the writing process and conventions work. Eventually, many incorporate writing during play, especially when play centers contain materials that encourage children to use writing in real and meaningful situations. Gretchen Owocki (1999) and Nigel Hall (1991) point out that when teachers model how they use materials in centers, the children can develop a mental model and integrate the materials into their play (see Chapter 7).

In the housekeeping center, there's a telephone, a notepad, and pencils so children can take messages. The store center has paper and pencils for shopping lists and receipts. Envelopes and paper for writing letters are part of the post office center. One class had a bank center with checks and deposit and withdrawal slips supplied by a local bank.

## Introducing Writing Workshop

Using Bobbi Fisher's article "Getting Started with Writing" (1991), teachers planned how they would introduce writing workshop on the second or third day of school. Their goal was to establish a routine that children could quickly learn and follow.

*Day 1* Introduce the children to the writing center. Tell them that they will be writing every day. Explain how materials will be selected and passed out.

Discuss materials and how the children can use them. Explain that sometimes they can choose their paper, but there will be times when you will want everyone to write on a particular size. In Terri and Lisa's classes, the children write on 12 × 18 inch pieces of paper most of the time. Both teachers and I agree that large pieces of paper offer children lots of room to draw and write.

Point out that the children can decide whether to write with pencils, markers, or crayons. Explain the purpose of the date stamp and inkpad, scissors, tape, and stapler. I always tell the children that materials need to be neat and returned to the center. We work hard on taking and returning materials the first two to three weeks so that the children maintain an organized writing center.

*Day 2* Explain the four things that Bobbi Fisher recommends the children do with each piece of paper. Using large chart paper, demonstrate how you use the four things when you write. Then invite the children to write. Circulate. Celebrate their pictures, writing, and offer support when children ask for help or say, "I can't write." Engage the child in a conversation of what they did, whom they played with, or how the morning, evening, or weekend went.

When Racheed tells me, "I have nothing to write," I ask him, "Tell what you did last night." After a long pause, Racheed, his voice rising with excitement, explains that he saw a baseball game at the park. "Wow!" I say. "I'd love to know more about it." Before I can complete my sentence, Racheed starts writing.

### Four Things to Do with Your Writing
❑ **Write your name on the paper.**
Even though most young children write with uppercase letters, when you model, show and explain how you start your name with an uppercase letter followed by lowercase letters.

❑ **Stamp the date.**

It's helpful if the teacher does this during the first month, then turns this responsibility over to the children.

❑ **Draw a picture to tell a story or give information on a topic.**

Think out loud, showing how you plan what you will draw.

❑ **Write something.**

Make sure you model that writing can be scribble, random letters, invented spelling, or some words the children know.

I ask teachers to print Fisher's four steps on construction or chart paper and review these until the children have the routine. Nancy Reedy told me that within two weeks of displaying and rereading the chart during independent reading, the children were reading the steps using a pointer. "They imitated me perfectly," said Nancy.

*Day 3*  Review the four steps, model how you write using them, then invite the children to write.

*Day 4*  Discuss how you find topics for writing. I explain that topics are everywhere. I can write about riding my bike, taking a walk and telling what I saw, spilling cereal at breakfast, fighting with my brother, playing ball, riding the school bus, and so on. Then I ask the children to think-pair-share by following these steps.

1.  Think about topics you might write about.
2.  Exchange ideas with your partner.
3.  Share an idea. [The teacher records these on chart paper.]
4.  Read the list of ideas.
5.  Display the chart on a wall or bulletin board.

*Day 5*  Reread the chart of writing ideas. Invite the children to add new ideas. Continue to add ideas, and reread the chart daily at first, then two to three times a week throughout the year. I find that rereading the list often generates related ideas among the children. It also supports children who don't feel confident enough to explore and use their own ideas. When you sense that the list no longer motivates, invite the children to think-pair-share and create new lists.

*Day 6*  Introduce how you use invented spelling. Show the children how you stretch a word and hear the sounds, then write what you hear. When children see you do this during writing workshop and shared writing experiences, they will begin to try to stretch words and hear sounds. Integrate invented spelling into all your writing demonstrations.

*Day 7* Point out some words that are in the classroom and show how you can use these to help you write. Repeat this lesson frequently, especially when there are many labels, two to three mini-word walls, and books on display.

The most effective way to model the writing process is to ask the children to suggest a topic. Interest and investment runs high when the topic comes from the children. I find they attend closely and share the composing process when they can choose the writing idea.

With delayed learners, I use research about spelling development and adjust my demonstrations so they don't overwhelm the children (Bear et al. [1996] 2000, Henderson 1985). First, I model how I hear the beginning sound in a word. Then, I add the final sound I hear. Finally, I'm stretching words and recording the medial sounds I hear.

### Suggested Minilessons for Young Children

All year, it's important to write in front of the children and model your process during writing workshop and when you and the children collaborate to compose. Your observations, conversations, and interactions will inform the minilessons you choose to present to the whole class, to small groups, or to one child. The important thing to remember is to study your students' writing, reflect on their questions, and provide support when they can move forward with your guidance.

At this age, I believe that many of the minilessons I present are like planting seeds in children's minds. I don't expect four-year-olds to try a technique I've modeled. In kindergarten and transition first grades, they might be ready to absorb and apply. However, they have all heard and watched my process many times. When the children are ready to try dialogue or plan a story with a beginning, middle, or end, support them.

Variation in the content of minilessons occurs annually, for each group that steps into your classroom in the fall will differ. Moreover, the growth in children during the year varies greatly. The goal is to respond to the needs your children reveal by offering them support.

If the children reject support, then back off and learn by watching them write, listening to their talk about the writing, and taking notes. Your intentions for writing might not match the children's intentions. Dyson (1990) cautions teachers of young children to create writing environments that accommodate and allow for the variation in writing explorations of this age group. Dyson notes,

> Children's progress, in even our much valued holistic literacy activities is fed by all kinds of intention-guided experiences we may not value. We must consider not just the intentions important to us as teachers, but the intentions important to children and how we might help children build from those intentions. (1990, 211)

Decisions to scaffold, then, should build on what the children are trying to learn and communicate, not what the teachers feel they *should* be writing. After Uvaldo, Timea, Channing, Holly, and Megan have acted out parts of *Bashi, Baby Elephant*, I invite them to write about the story. I notice that all the children but Megan are drawing a part of the story that spoke to them. Megan's picture is about her family (Figure 6–5). She tells me it says: "My mother is going out to dinner. I am going to my daddy's house." After celebrating Megan's detailed drawings and the message her picture communicates, I ask her why she wrote about her family. Her answer is very logical and reveals excellent personal connections, "Bashi has a family like me."

Young children develop as writers, feel empowered to communicate their texts to others, and find joy in writing when they can choose their topics. Recalling my writing history in elementary school, I always extend the invitation this way: "You can write about our trip to the bank or you can choose your own idea." The majority of my invitations encourage children to choose their own topics as they write independently every day.

*Plant Writing Seeds with These Suggested Minilessons*   Keep minilessons short—five to six minutes. Spread them out over several days, for young children cannot listen and sit still for a long time. Repeat minilessons. Children need to hear and observe

**Figure 6–5.** Megan draws her family and connects it to Bashi's family.

these minilessons often to absorb the information. Whenever possible, encourage the children to participate. Reserve time for the children to pose questions about the demonstration and to tell you what they noticed. This enables you to gain insights into what the children have absorbed. Connect your writing demonstrations to shared reading to emphasize that published authors use these writing techniques.

- ❏ *Left-to-right sweep.* As you write in front of the children, think out loud, explaining how you move across the page from left to right. Show them how you return to the left side of the page at the end of a line.
- ❏ *Spaces between words.* Whenever you write, model how you use your index finger to create spaces between words. Use big books to show the spaces between words. Explain how spaces help you read the words with ease because all the letters don't run together.
- ❏ *The room as a word resource.* Whenever I write in front of the children, I consciously model how I use print around the room to figure out how to spell words using book (correct) spelling. I also show the children how a word or list or poem pops a writing idea into my head.
- ❏ *Titles.* Explain how titles help you know what you will read about. Share, again and again, the titles of children's favorite books; discuss these. Help children understand that effective titles are short.
- ❏ *Sentences.* As you model writing, point out how you start your sentence with an uppercase letter and that you end it with punctuation.
- ❏ *Planning.* I discuss how writers plan their pieces, knowing that most four- and five-year-olds are not ready for planning. The two kinds of plans I model are generating a list of ideas, and picture plans. Demonstrations include: drawing pictures of the beginning, middle, and end of a story; drawing a setting, character, the character's problem, and the outcome; drawing a list of instructions such as how to care for a puppy, spring flowers, bugs in my yard, and so on.
- ❏ *Sequencing.* Since following directions is an important part of the children's day at home and at school, I introduce sequencing by starting with the children's lives. Together, we sequence setting the table for dinner, brushing your teeth, making a sandwich, our daily school schedule, preparing for morning and lunch recess, and so on. Once children understand the concept of time-order, we start looking at and discussing sequencing in books I read aloud. We discuss how ordering events improves understanding and our ability to recall and discuss information.
- ❏ *Details.* I want the children to know that good writing has rich details. When I'm modeling, I point out how details come from planning writing. I also tell the children that when I write I pretend I'm a camera taking a

picture describing everything I see with words. Sometimes we practice adding rich details to a dull sentence. Here are the details one group of kindergartners added to "I play."

> I play on the swing. I pump and pump. My feet touch the sky. My head is dizzy. I get scared. I slow down.

Do I expect these youngsters to transfer the interactive demonstration to their own writing? Of course not. I am planting seeds.

❏ *How genres work.* During the year, connect writing to authentic situations and show children how to write invitations, thank-you notes, letters, messages, wish lists, and notes that help you remember. When we read nonfiction, fiction, and poetry in writing workshop I demonstrate how those texts work by writing short pieces, often with the children's help. My goal is to expand children's knowledge of how various genres work. So, if they choose to explore a genre, they have reading and writing experiences to build on.

## Invite Children to Sit in the Author's Chair

Reserving a chair for young authors to sit in while they read their writing builds pride in writing and sharing with an audience (Calkins 1994). During author's chair, children share part of themselves by reading their pieces. Equally important are the many opportunities they have to listen to classmates share pieces and learn from peers. It's an opportunity to practice speaking clearly and slowly as well as holding your paper so everyone can see it. Listeners can gather ideas about writing a piece. Every class has children who are at different levels in their writing development. Observing peers' writing can show a child how to draw a car or how to mark the ends of sentences or how to use the class job chart to see how to spell "Tanisha."

In my writing workshop, I always offer the choice to share or not to share. Children put their pieces on a specific table or bookshelf if they want to share.

Otherwise, writing goes into their folders for me to look at later. I invite the children to share two to three times a week, setting aside about fifteen minutes for this valuable experience. Larger classes share one day's writing over two consecutive days. Children usually want to share immediately, and I find waiting several days removes the excitement and detailed descriptions I want them to communicate to classmates.

Some children are cautious and wait a few weeks before volunteering to share. Others, like Uvaldo, are shy and lack confidence in their work. A few feel their piece is too personal or too sad to share. Whatever the reason, respect the children's decision. As soon as the children observe that it's safe to share in the author's chair, they risk doing it and continue as long as author's chair is safe.

To make the author's chair a safe place, I ask the teacher to be in charge of responding to the children's writing. By observing the teacher, the children learn what is appropriate and supportive. In one class, a child asked the reader why she didn't put a period at the end of the sentence. The reader couldn't respond because she had no idea that she needed a period. Allowing such comments to continue makes workshop a place where children set the expectations for one another and have multiple opportunities to send the message that sharing writing can be embarrassing and humiliating.

Author's chair holds the potential for assisting and facilitating growth as children observe where they can go and identify peers who can support them. At the start of the year, I am the only one who comments on writing. Gradually, as the year unfolds, I turn the commenting and questions over to the children. Here are the kinds of responses I model and then invite the children to imitate.

❏ *Noticing and liking comments.* These call attention to specific details in a drawing and/or in the print. My attention is on the writer, not what others in the class do. The children's noticing and liking experiences raise their awareness of writing possibilities because they observe what classmates are trying and doing.

First, I notice what the children draw and say things like: *I like the way your bike looks so real. I notice that you drew all of your friends who came to your party and then printed their names above each one. I notice that you started your sentence with an uppercase letter. I like the way you have the car pulling the trailer.*

❏ *How did you do that?* This question invites the authors to explain their process or share where their idea came from. I focus on the pictures or the writing and ask questions such as: *How did you make the garden look so real? How did you put curtains on the windows? Where did you get the idea of using quotation marks? A question mark? Indenting to show a paragraph?*

143

❏ *"What happened next" questions.* To encourage the author to think about continuing the story, ask questions such as: *What happened the next day? Will you write more about swimming at the beach? Do you have other stories like this to tell?*

Once you sense the children can take over responding to classmates' writing, negotiate some guidelines with them.

## Tips for Making Students' Responses to Writers Productive

Before allowing students to respond to the child in the author's chair, I negotiate behavior guidelines with the children. Display these near the author's chair. Reread them before each session to refresh the children's memory, reminding them that helpful responses are positive.

❏ Start with "I like . . ." or "I notice. . . ."
❏ Ask questions that encourage the writer to talk about her piece.
❏ Call on different people so everyone has a chance to respond.
❏ Invite the author to reread a part you liked.

The focus during author's chair is to celebrate what each child is doing and to ask for information that explains the child's thinking and writing process. This way, the children can work at their individual writing levels, move forward at a rate that's comfortable for them, learn new possibilities from peers, and build the confidence in their writing ability which is needed in order to risk trying new techniques and strategies.

## Journal Writing

Kindergarten teachers and Melissa Foltz, Robinson Elementary school's transitional first-grade teacher, all incorporated journal writing into their curriculum. The teachers extended invitations for children to write in journals at different times.

❏ Prior to their morning gathering.
❏ After morning recess and snack.
❏ About twenty minutes before dismissal in all-day preschool and kindergarten classes.
❏ At home where children wrote each night in their journals and read entries to their parents. The next day, at school, the children read their journals to their teacher, teaching assistant, or classmates.

In some classes, teachers invite the children to write in notebooks with primary lined paper or in journals the teacher made. During the first month of school, four-year-old Kat knows the story her picture tells, and she dictates it to her teacher (Figure 6–6). Kat's classmate, Danny, draws Power Rangers, his favorite

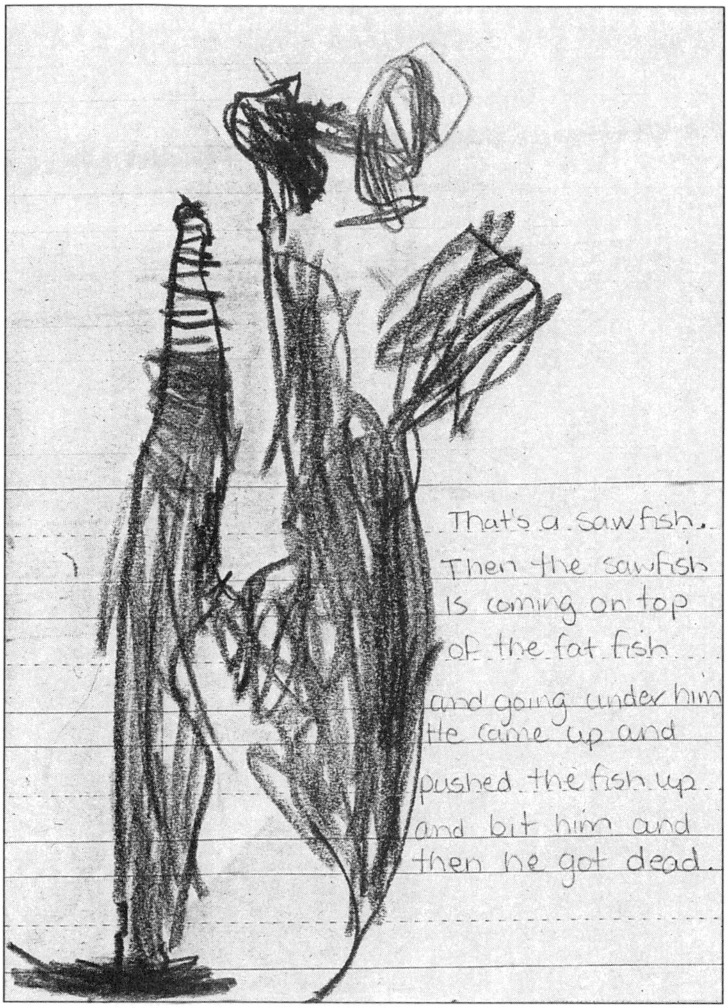
That's a sawfish.
Then the sawfish
is coming on top
of the fat fish
and going under him
He came up and
pushed the fish up
and bit him and
then he got dead.

**Figure 6–6.** Kat's dictated story

toys. Danny understands that authors communicate with print (Figure 6–7). Marks, mingled with letters Danny can write, fill his journal page. When Danny tells his teacher what the story says, like Kat, he observes her write, "The Power Rangers are fighting." Sitting side-by-side the teacher as she writes their dictated texts enables children to repeatedly see that words tell a story and that writing moves across the pages from left to right. In May, Kat's entry with her own writing illustrates how she has taken control of writing the story for her picture (Figure 6–8).

Nancy Reedy and Melissa Foltz mingled free-writing with directed writing, using journals they made for the children. During Literacy Links summer school,

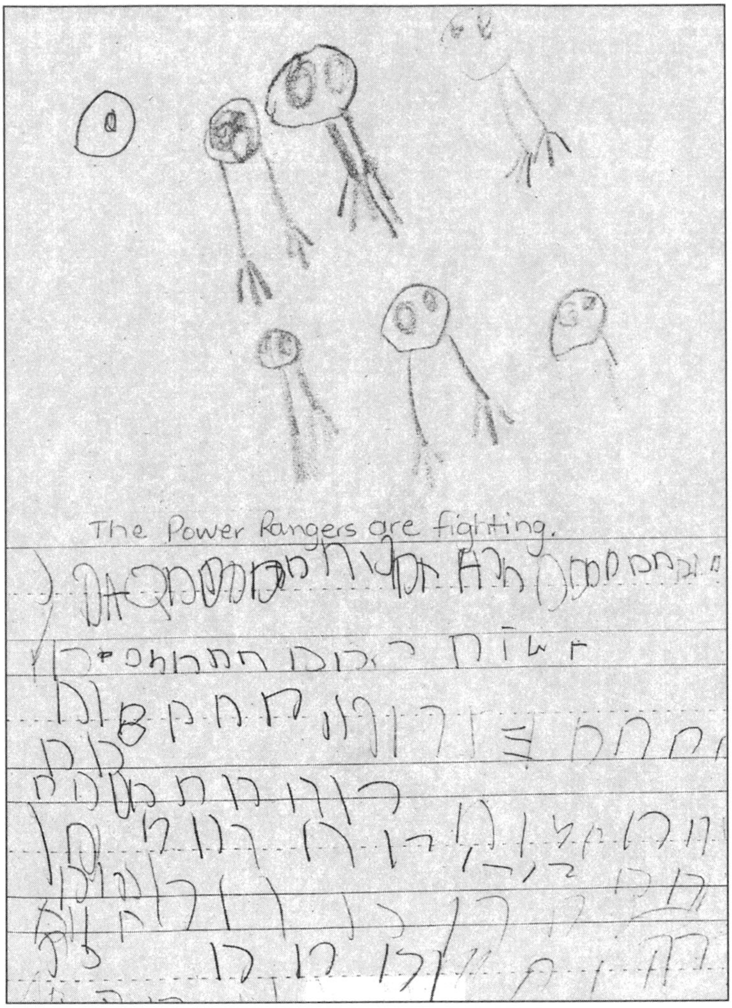

The Power Rangers are fighting.

**Figure 6–7.** Danny shows he knows print contains the message.

Lateivia practices writing the days of the week, information she needs to know before entering first grade (Figure 6–9).

Melissa teaches the transitional first grade at Robinson Elementary in Woodstock, Virginia. In September and October, children write on unlined paper, for Melissa wants to see how they organize and use space. Once children consistently write and draw, Melissa gives them journal pages that have a box for a picture and lines for writing. Keyana's journal entry in September shows a detailed drawing of her cat having babies and a sentence about the cat (Figure 6–10). "I want to help the children elaborate and extend their ideas with details," Melissa says. "So as they read me their journals, I write questions I have and invite them

**Figure 6–8.** Kat can now write a story for her picture.

to answer" (Figure 6–11). Keyana's May journal reflects the progress she's made with writing and drawing, for she now elaborates ideas with teacher questions (Figure 6–12). Progress results from a rich and balanced writing program that includes journal writing, teacher-student collaborations, independent writing, authentic writing in play centers, shared reading of oversized texts, and preplanned minilessons.

**Figure 6–9.** Lateivia practices writing the days of the week.

## Teacher Modeling Dispels Myths and Mysteries

Modeling how you write should continue throughout the year as part of writing workshop and during shared and interactive writing times. When you continually make your thinking and decision process visible, you build children's background knowledge and offer them a model they can apply to their writing when they are ready to adopt it.

In Lisa Tusing's and Terri Auckland's Literacy Links kindergarten classes, the kinds of modeling these teachers offered developed from responding to the children's writing. To move the children from random scribbling, Lisa, Terri, and I

**Name** Keyana _____ Date: 9-26-00

MY CAT GUC
heD BABS

My cat just
had babies

**Figure 6–10.** One of Keyana's September journal entries

demonstrated how we drew a picture of a house, car, doll, book, cat, dog, and person. It took time, practice, and reflective thought to break down how to draw a picture so the children could observe and hear the thinking that went along with the entire process. In one lesson, Lisa demonstrates how she draws a house. Note the connections she makes to what the children know. We felt this was crucial so they could link the model to their knowledge. During writing workshop, Lisa did not require that the children draw a house. Her ideas for modeling and Terri's came from what the children were trying to draw and their discussions. Completed on chart paper, the teachers made these available to the children and periodically returned to each model for review and discussion. Here's what Lisa said:

> My house looks like the side of a box. It has two floors. I need to make it tall enough
> to have two floors. I'll draw that. Now I'll put on a roof. Hmm. The roof looks like a

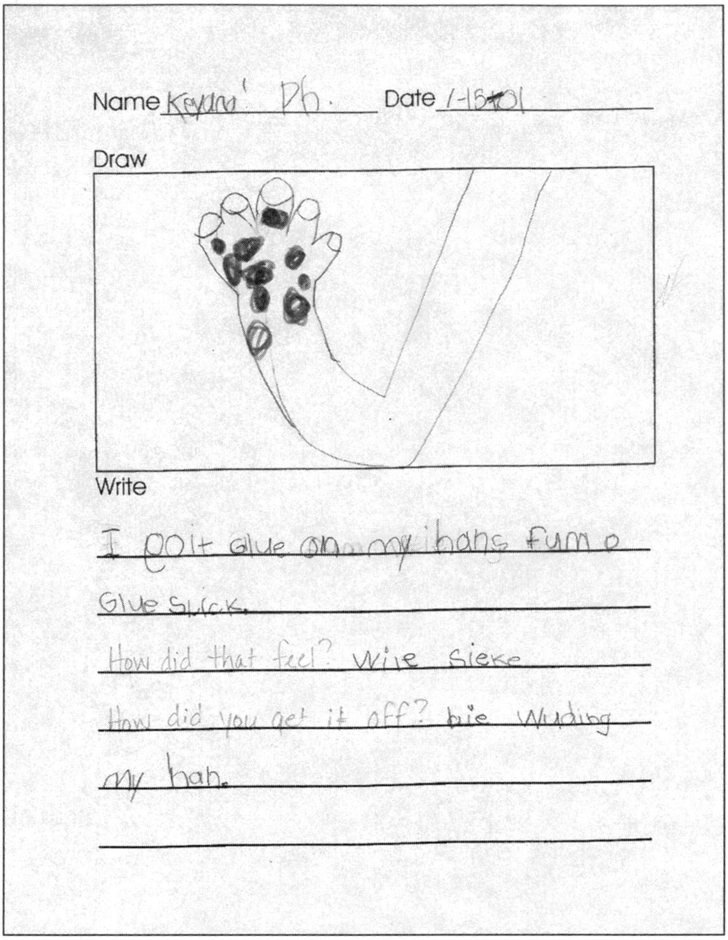

Name Kevin Ph. Date 1-18-01

Draw

Write

I poit glue on my hans fum o
Glue stick.
How did that feel? wire sieke
How did you get it off? bie Wuding
my hah.

**Figure 6–11.** Questions help children elaborate entries.

big triangle. [Lisa shows a plastic triangle.] Now I'll draw it. I have to make it cover the house. [Next, Lisa invites the children to participate.] Show me where I draw the door. Show me a door I can think of as I draw. [Children point to classroom door.] Show me where to put a window on the first floor.

Lisa continues until the house has a door, four windows, and a path. First drawings, Lisa explains, were simple. As the year progressed, Lisa modeled adding details such as a chimney, flowers and trees, a shed, dog, cat, chickens, and so on. Dallas' early pieces of writing, up until the end of November, consisted mostly of scrawls. His later work reflects the benefits of Lisa's demonstrations as well as one-on-one conferences (see Figure 6–13).

We discover that the more we engaged the children in conversations about the weather, school grounds, library, cafeteria, gymnasium, playground, a tree,

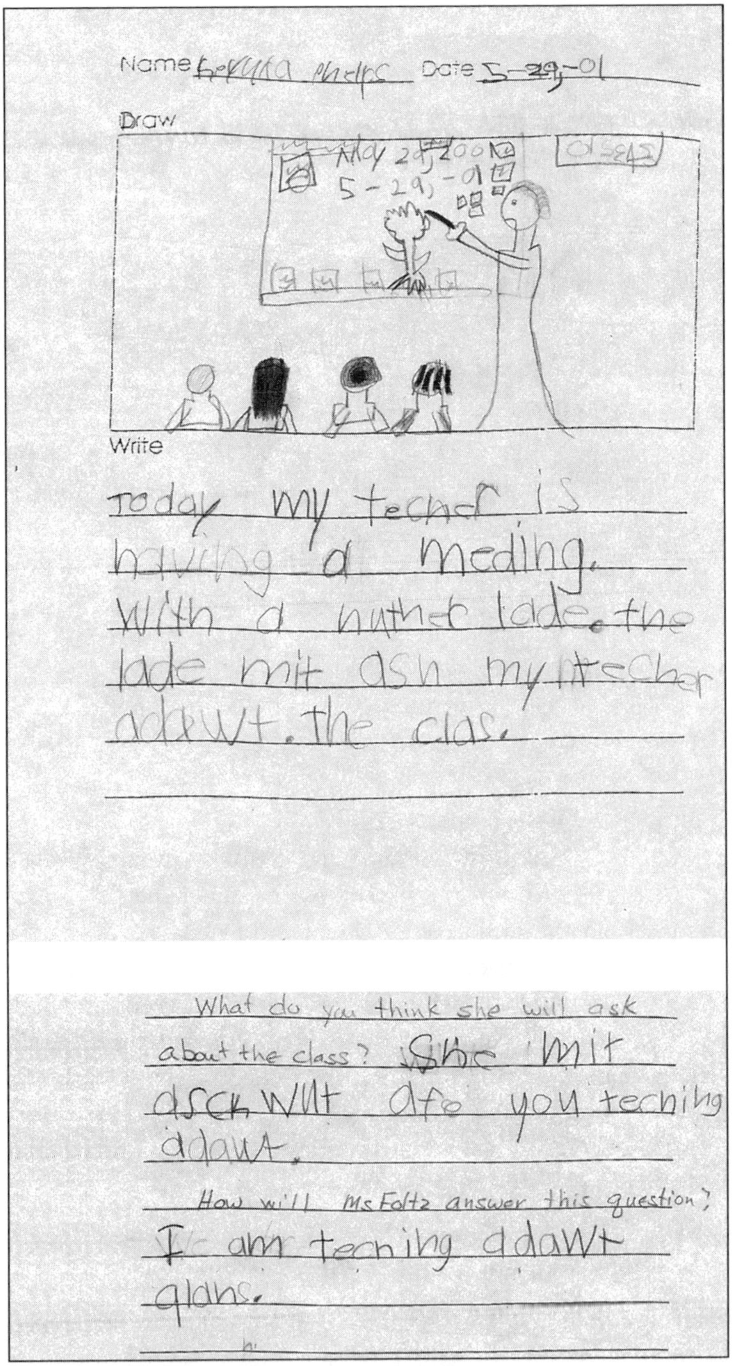

Name Keyana Phelps   Date 5-29-01

Draw

Write

Today my techer is
having a meding.
With a nuther lade. the
lade mit ash my techer
adawt. the clas.

What do you think she will ask
about the class? She mit
asck wut are you teching
adawt.

How will Ms Foltz answer this question?
I am teching adawt
plans.

**Figure 6–12.** A journal entry for May reflects Keyana's progress.

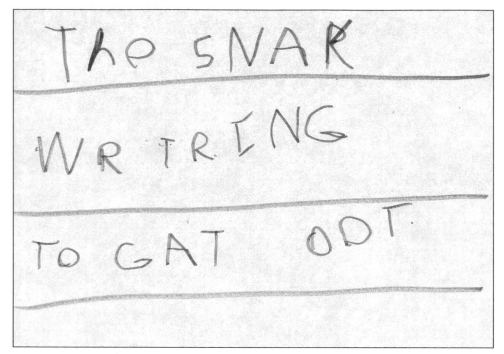

**Figure 6–13.** Teacher modeling supported Dallas's progress in writing
*Translation:* The snakes were trying to get out.

a bird's nest, cars in the parking lot, serving and eating a snack, lunch, cleaning up, field trips, and so on, the more these experiences enter their writing. Moreover, these discussions help the children *see* their world instead of quickly glancing. Most of us take these simple, everyday occurrences for granted. However, many children arrive in preschool and kindergarten with a limited knowledge of their community because they rarely go grocery shopping with a caretaker or visit places like the post office, bank, or garden center. Conferring with children during writing workshop, journal writing times, and while children work at centers enables teachers to help children transform their mental images and thoughts onto paper.

### Conferring with the Children

Whiteboard in hand, Terri sits with Denzel during writing workshop. "What are you going to write about today?" asks Terri.

"My birthday," says Denzel. "That's me, and here's my mommy. She's happy. [Denzel draws a wide smile.] How do I draw the cake?" he asks Terri.

**Figure 6–14.** Denzel's writing early in the year

Using the whiteboard, Terri asks Denzel questions before she draws a birthday cake.

"Writers ask questions to get details and a clear picture of what they want to say. Let me ask you some questions. What was the shape of your cake? How many candles did it have?" Terri takes Denzel's responses and uses them to draw a simple, round cake on the whiteboard. Before she can add candles, Denzel says, "I can do it." And that's exactly what Terri wants to hear.

When Denzel finishes his piece (Figure 6–14), he shares it with Terri, and she's recorded exactly what he says about it: "That's me. That's my mommy. That's my birthday cake. That's another birthday cake. That's flowers. These are words." Terri can meet for four to five minutes with half of her ten children two to three times a week. The whiteboard is always nearby so she can use it to respond to the children's questions and/or her observations.

Conferring with children before writing encourages them to think through an idea from beginning to end and can result in more detailed pictures and text (Dyson 1983, Routman 2000). To hold these prewriting small-group conferences, gather three to four children around you. I prefer sitting on the floor with the

children for it makes these conversations more informal and intimate. And talk flows. I open the gathering with my wonderings: "Hmm, I wonder what I'll write about today." Then I share my idea with the children, asking myself questions that help me add details. Next, I invite them to tell me what they might write about. I use the word *might* because I don't want the children to feel they have to use the idea they spoke about that day. And, several always do choose different topics that pop into their heads as a result of these interactive talks.

The purpose of these interactive group conversations is

- ❏ to develop a habit of thinking about writing before taking pencil to paper;
- ❏ to eventually transform group conversations into internal conversations that occur all the time.

Children's author Johanna Hurwitz told me that she writes a book in her head for almost a year before she actually starts drafting. Her in-the-head writing of the next book occurs while she is working on a novel. Most writers experience conversations with self before and while they are writing. I want to harness children's pleasure and skill in talking by spending short bursts of time focusing these talents on writing ideas and plans. Notice how I pose questions in these two conversations with kindergarten children in November to help the children add details. I always start with the open-ended, "Can you tell me more?" in order to not be directive.

DALLAS: My dad got a new trailer. It's big.

ROBB: Tell me more about the trailer.

DALLAS: It hooks on our car. My dad took me for a ride.

ROBB: Tell me more about the inside.

DALLAS: You can eat and sleep in it. I want to ride in it every day. Dad says we're using it for trips.

ROBB: I can't wait for you to tell me about your first trip, Dallas.

ANGELINA: I have a bike.

ROBB: I have one, too. Tell me more about yours.

ANGELINA: It's blue. Got two wheels.

ROBB: I ride my bike on the weekends. When do you ride yours?

ANGELINA: I do it every day. It's a good bike. It has a basket.

ROBB: Perhaps you'll write about riding your bike one day.

During conferences, prompt children and help them extend and elaborate ideas. Such conversations foster richer discussions among children who arrive at school delayed in their ability to converse with adults and peers. The children will show you through their writing, their questions, and their discussions when they are ready to move deeper into the writing process. If the children don't incorporate in their writing what you've discussed in a conference, that's fine. They will take what they are ready to understand and the time for this differs with each child.

## Other Topics for Conferring with Children

- ❑ Placing spaces between words.
- ❑ Stretching words to listen for and write the sounds heard.
- ❑ Writing from left to write.
- ❑ Using print in the classroom as a resource.
- ❑ Using uppercase letters at the start of sentences. Placing punctuation at the end.
- ❑ Adding a title.
- ❑ Adding more details to pictures and writing.
- ❑ Making a book from paper.
- ❑ Visualizing an idea.

As you circulate during writing workshop, visit with each child for a few minutes. Bend down so you are at eye level. Look for things to praise—use phrases that affirm their emerging and fragile sense of what it means to become a young author.

*Prompts That Celebrate What the Children Do*

These sample prompts recognize and praise children for what's working, and for their attempts to try new writing techniques. Use these as a guide to continually honor children's writing.

- ❑ That picture has so many terrific details. Please tell me about it.
- ❑ Wow! You're writing words. I'd love you to read what you wrote.
- ❑ This piece looks so exciting. I can't wait to hear you read it when you're finished.
- ❑ You're working hard to space those words. I appreciate your efforts. It helps me and your classmates read your piece.
- ❑ What a terrific title! Would you like to share it with the class?
- ❑ The extra details help me imagine exactly what you see.

As children write daily about topics they select, I also want them to write about some of the books you read to them.

## Writing About Reading

Writing about a book that you read and reread to the children is an effective way to gain insights into what they have learned, remembered, and the information, event, or characters that had a huge impact on them.

When I read a book to the children and sense it has affected them deeply or stirred their curiosity, I use that book as a springboard for writing. Responses should follow discussions that open children's minds and hearts to the book's content—discussions where the children link the text to their lives and experiences.

Terri Auckland has just read dozens of books about bears. "The children were sad when the study ended," she said. During free play, groups pretended to be bears in the woods, bears asleep in caves, and bears feasting on fish and berries. "When I told the children they could write about bears," Terri said, "they cheered." First, the children help Terri create a web that contained facts and feelings about bears. Then she asks them to write about bears. Written in May, Denzel's piece (Figure 6–15) illustrates how his writing has developed from only pictures in September to a text with three complete sentences. Writing enables Denzel, who was designated at-risk, to use invented spellings to write and to develop a large sight vocabulary. On a sticky note, Terri notes, "He circled and corrected his work independently."

The group of students I work with at Virginia Avenue/Charlotte DeHart school loved Cynthia Rylant's *Scarecrow* (1998). The invitation to write came from the children. "Can we draw about this one?" Timea asked. Five others echoed, "Please, please." They spent more than forty-five minutes working on their pictures and writing. When Uvaldo shared his piece, there was so much for the group and me to notice (Figure 6–16). In a room with the group he's worked with for three months, Uvaldo's self-esteem and confidence in his ability to write has improved.

**Figure 6–15.** By May, Denzel has made great progress in writing. (He circled and corrected his work independently.)

**Figure 6–16.** Uvaldo writes about *Scarecrow* by Cynthia Rylant.

Slowly and seriously Uvaldo reads: "I like my scarecrow. I like Mrs. Baker [their teacher]." Holly notices the pumpkins. Then Uvaldo points out the green squash. Channing likes the clouds and the straw dripping from the scarecrow's arms and legs. "It looks real," she adds. What I notice is that the children are trying to stretch some words with the assistance of me and Deena Baker. They celebrate one another's progress and all the time the children are teaching each other about responding to books they love. I do not direct the children's responses to literature unless they are writing innovations based on patterned and predictable stories such as Eric Carle's *The Very Hungry Caterpillar* and *The Very Busy Spider*.

## Innovations on Patterned Books

Children learn a great deal about writing, illustrating, and researching material when they collaborate to write an innovation on a text. Innovations or adaptations of books are invitations for the children to write a text using the author's patterned language while changing the topic. During Literacy Links summer school, children's innovations on Eric Carle's *The Very Busy Spider* cover a range of ideas: *The Very Fast Cat, The Very Flying Birds, The Very Angry Lion, The Very Happy Bear*, and *The Very Slow Horse*. Nancy astutely observes, "When the children have a pattern to follow, they learn about the story's construction and gain confidence because they have a guide for writing" (see Figure 6–17).

After a kindergarten class at Powhatan School spent two weeks reading and rereading *The Very Hungry Caterpillar*, I ask the children to brainstorm a list of animals, insects, birds, and so on that they could use to compose their own version of this beloved patterned book. Two days of discussing their list enable the children to choose a topic: *The Very Hungry Parrot*. While planning the pages, they realize that "we got to find out what they [parrots] eat and what colors [feathers] they have."

The children ask the school's librarian for books about parrots. As I read parts of texts, the children tell me when to stop and jot down notes we might use in our

**Figure 6–17.** Books with patterns give students a guide for their own writing.

Dedicated to:
the new Kindergartners

The very Bright
Lightning Bug                by: Donrae

I LiK To   Kash Lightning Bug

Ou nin I was kah
Lightning  Bue Lit icanek
        and      out

One night I was
catching lighting bugs
and a lot came out

**Figure 6–17.** *continued*

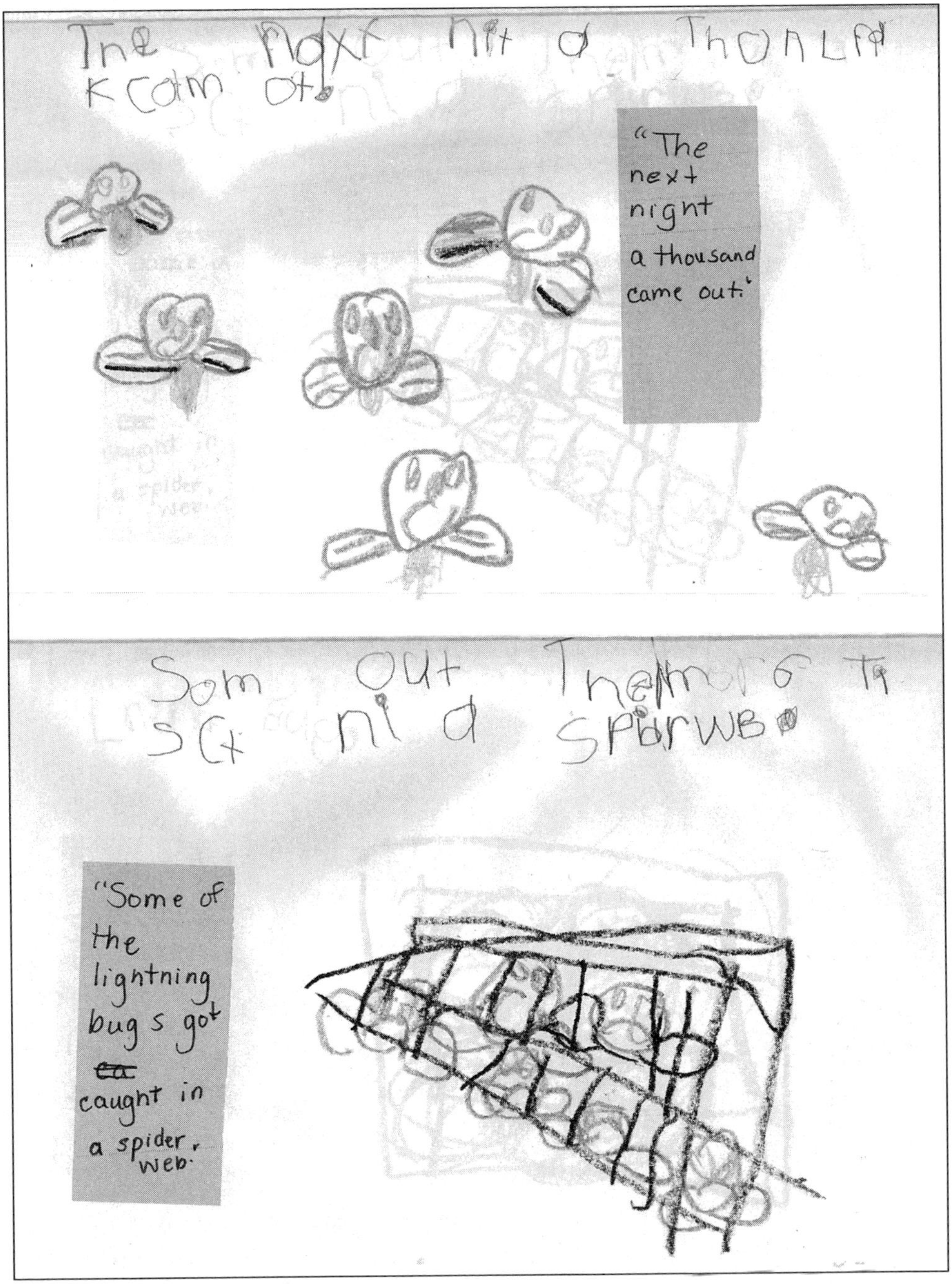

The ndxr nht a ThonLpt K Cam ot.

"The next night a thousand came out."

Som out Themor Tr SCt ni a SpbrwB

"Some of the lightning bugs got ~~Etu~~ caught in a spider web."

**Figure 6–17.** *continued*

**Figure 6–17.** *continued*

class book. Researching teaches me and the children that besides eating fruit and seeds, parrots love to munch on hard-boiled eggs. When the children compose the following sentence, several say, "We got that from research."

On Friday she pecked through 5 hard-boiled eggs, but she was still hungry.

Laminate books so they hold up after countless readings. Books written by the class or individuals are frequently checked out the most. Display the finished book on an easel. During shared reading, read and discuss the story and illustrations. Display individual books at the bottom of the chalkboard by setting them in the chalk tray so children can reach them. Place children's innovations on books in your classroom library so future classes can enjoy them and learn about the process.

## Guidelines for Writing Innovations on Books

Initiate individual or collaborative innovations after the children are thoroughly familiar with the book. In fact, most of the children will have memorized the simple text. Before individuals write their own innovations, confer with each child to help them decide on text changes and select a topic.

Small-group or whole-class collaborations permit young children to observe the writing process from start to finish and to experience researching a topic and selecting details for their book. Even though they are not ready to apply this recursive process to their own writing, they will come to understand the process because of their collaborative experiences.

1. Decide on where in the text you will make changes or innovations. Begin with one or at the most, two changes.
2. Brainstorm ideas to use. Collect the children's suggestions on chart paper. Write each child's name next to his or her contribution.
3. Complete research to make sure you have accurate information.
4. As you write, think aloud and make your process visible. Talk about: How I start and end a sentence; Why I need to begin a new line; How I remember a word's spelling; How I find a strong verb. The goal is to show the children the composing process.
5. Read the piece out loud and listen for places where you might have omitted a word. Model how you use a caret to insert words.
6. Print the revised text on the pages of your class book.
7. Give each child one or two pages to illustrate, depending on the class size.
8. Plan the cover, dedication, and title page. I let chance decide who will draw the cover and title page by drawing two names out of a bag that contains each child's name.

Authors, then, also teach the children about writing, especially when teachers raise children's awareness of words and story structures while reading aloud.

## Authors as Teachers

"I want to write a book," Kristina says. "Can I?" During the first months of their Literacy Links kindergarten classes, the children write on large pieces of paper. The day a child asks to write a book, Lisa Tusing and Terri Auckland inwardly shout "Hurrah!" As soon as one child writes a book, others start writing narrative and nonfiction books. Writing books seems as contagious as chicken pox. Now, the children use staplers and paper to make their books. They read their texts to one another with pride and delight. Before Kristina read *I Love David Next Door*, she announced, "I did everything myself, but not writing the title." During author's chair, when one child notices a dedication page or a table of contents, others start including these features in their books. Observing writing possibilities and connections classmates have made as well as hearing the positive comments of teacher and peers can support children who take the risk of trying something new.

The books also help teachers see what the children have absorbed from the read-aloud program. Teachers look for: front cover with title, author, illustration, back cover, dedication, text and pictures, and features specific to narrative and nonfiction. Brandon's book, *A Storm by the River*, places text on one side and pictures on the other (Figure 6–18). "I wanted room to write lots," he tells me. "And some books are like that. That's how I knew."

A varied and rich read-aloud program offers multiple opportunities to call children's attention to an author's use of words, phrases, and playfulness and creativity with our language. Pause and call children's attention to language you find intriguing and appealing. Place these on mini-word walls and reread them with the children. The word lists that follow are examples of calling children's attention to the delights of language, then immersing them in words and phrases by hanging these charts around the classroom. For some children, these charts become resources for their writing, and they incorporate words and phrases into their pieces.

**Words We Liked**

| | |
|---|---|
| frisking | snoring unawares |
| flapped | peeked |
| splished and splashed | macaroni elbowed in |
| ripply pool | spuds |
| drifted | scowled |

Words and phrases are from *Down by the Cool of the Pool* (Mitton 2001) and *Food Fight!* (Shields 2002).

**New Words We Learned**

| | |
|---|---|
| clamshell jaws | cab |
| cargo | escort cars |
| telescoping forklift truck | sanitation truck |
| destination   monster truck | |

Words and phrases are from *Seymour Simon's Book of Trucks* (Simon 2000).

Children collect ideas about writing from authors. Ideas include topics to write about as well as how to arrange pictures and print on a page. Structural elements discussed during shared reading—beginning, middle, end, character and problem, sidebars, pictures, and captions—frequently find their way into young children's texts. Kristina, author of *I Love David Next Door*, explains that she has writing on

**Figure 6–18.** Brandon writes his first book.

**Figure 6–19.** Kristina's story has a beginning, middle, and end.

one page and pictures on the next and pictures and writing together. "That's how they [authors] do it." Kristina also shows me and Terri Auckland that her story has a beginning, middle, and end (Figure 6–19), a concept Terri has been discussing with the children during shared reading.

Teachers can deepen children's understanding of authors' planning and writing processes by inviting the children to interact and collaborate with their teacher to compose class texts that model all or parts of the writing process.

## Shared and Collaborative Writing

An excited email arrives from Maryann Sherry, inviting me to watch Pam and her facilitate the morning message, sending me to their classroom the moment I arrived at Robinson Elementary. Gathered around Maryann and Pam who both teach three- and four-year-olds in the Bright Star program are ten children, intently watching the chart paper. Today, Pam sits cross-legged on the rug with the children. Maryann slowly says the word *morning*, repeating the /m/ sound. She does the same for *message* and one child says that it's like morning. "That's terrific," says Maryann, "*Morning* and *message* both start with the same letter—m—" and she says the /m/ sound. Next, Maryann asks children to raise their hand if they would like to write a message; she chooses two children. Each child selects a marker pen from a box, writes, then tells Maryann their message (Figure 6–20). On another sheet of paper, Maryann prints what each child said using book spelling, reads it to the group, and asks the children to read it with her as she points to each word.

The children tell me that they can write. Maryann shows me pieces of writing with pictures, scribble marks, and the meaning in book spelling. "I was

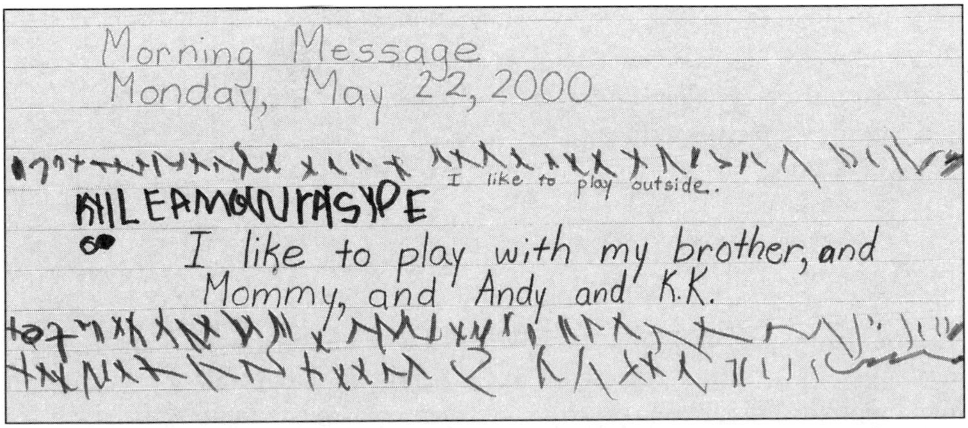

**Figure 6–20.** A morning message by children in the Bright Star program

167

willing to try the morning message when you introduced it during our study group session," Maryann confessed, "But I wasn't sure it would work with my group. I found that my writing and talking about what I am doing fascinates the children. And they are learning that what they say can be written on paper using words."

First Maryann and Pam model and think aloud to demonstrate how the morning message works. "Within two weeks," Pam notes, "'Can I write?' echoes through the room. We have no choice; we must share the writing with the children." Observing shared writing allows children to watch the formation of letters, words, and writing conventions that communicate thoughts to others. Sharing the pen with the children empowers them as writers and communicators.

### A Closer Look at Shared Writing

Simply put, shared writing is writing texts with the children's input as well as inviting them to share the pen with you. There is no one correct way to integrate shared writing into your program. Sometimes you will do all of the writing for the children, especially when the task is complex and beyond them, such as planning and writing a fantasy or realistic narrative. Other times, when generating lists or writing the morning message, the children can successfully share the pen with you. You'll find dozens of ways to integrate shared writing into your day. Here are some suggestions:

- ❏ Retelling a story.
- ❏ Constructing a graph: whether you prefer green or red apples, gloves or mittens, pen or pencils, or surveying the class to discover who walks to school, who rides the bus, or comes in a car.
- ❏ Writing a letter, invitation, or thank-you note.
- ❏ Recounting a field trip.
- ❏ Gathering ideas for, then writing a class newsletter.
- ❏ Noting observations of the weather, a tree, class animal, and so on.
- ❏ Writing up an experiment.
- ❏ Collecting what students know or have learned.
- ❏ Brainstorming ideas.
- ❏ Innovations on texts.
- ❏ Mini-word walls.

Your curriculum and interactions with the children will provide you with many ideas for shared writing. Sometimes you'll spend five minutes on a list or fifteen minutes on the morning message or writing part of a long narrative. Shared writing can be completed at one sitting or continue for short bursts of time over several meetings. It develops children's sense of authorship and pleasure in communicating with others through writing.

To plan a shared writing lesson it's helpful to:

❑ Know the lesson's purpose for writing and communicate this to the children.
❑ Be aware of the writing conventions you plan to emphasize (base these on assessments and what the children are doing in their writing).
❑ Decide whether you will work with the whole class or a group.
❑ Think about whether you will do all of the writing or if students will share the pen with you.

Once the children can stretch words and are writing with invented spelling, I encourage teachers to integrate the children's spelling inventions during shared writing. With one color marker, record the children's spellings; with another color marker, print the book spelling. Doing this honors the children's ability to stretch words and match what they hear to letters. It also makes visible how their words look written in book spelling, something they have been immersed in from shared reading and from the print displayed in the classroom. Kindergarten teacher, Julie Stringer, uses this strategy with the morning message. "I always get real excited about the parts of the word they heard, and point to these. I tell them that's how you learn to spell and that eventually, they'll be able to use book spelling." Using the phrase *book spelling* honors the children's development, eliminates the negative connotations of correct or incorrect, and provides a model for the children to observe and to reflect. For example, in Julie's interactive morning message, the children dictated "The cat ran ovr the mos," and then Julie wrote the book spelling: "The cat ran over the mouse."

## The Morning Message Can Deepen Students' Knowledge of the Composing Process

Invite students to participate in writing the morning message at different levels. Increase student involvement when your observations tell you they are ready to share the pen.

❑ Invite the children to compose the message. Help them form ideas by asking:

Can you tell me something that happened to you this morning? Yesterday? On the way to school? On the weekend?

❑ Repeat each sentence before writing.
❑ Model how you decide where to write the date and start the message.

- ❏ Think aloud and show how you use your fingers to put spaces between words. Explain why and where you start a new line of text.
- ❏ Use students' names in the message.

> Titus said that he built a snowman yesterday.
> Titus: I built a snowman yesterday.

- ❏ Prompt students to hear sounds and help you spell part of or all of a word.
- ❏ Share the pen and invite students to write a word, phrase, or complete sentence. Ask them to say their sentence before writing it. When young children work hard to match letters to sounds, they forget their sentence. Saying it out loud allows you to remember their words for them.
- ❏ Reread as you write and when the message is complete. Use a pointer as you read to foster voice-to-print match.
- ❏ Ask two to three children to use the pointer and reread the morning message or invite the group to choral read with you.

### Interactions with Completed Morning Messages

The children enjoy coming to the chart and using a marker to underline or circle specific items in the morning message. You can also gather extra ideas from the suggestions for masking during shared reading on page 118. Ask the children to point to and circle or underline:

- ❏ Their name.
- ❏ All the letters that are the same as the first letter in their name.
- ❏ A classmate's name.
- ❏ A word with one, two, three, or more letters.
- ❏ A prefix or a suffix.
- ❏ Rhyming words.
- ❏ Words that start or end with the same letter.
- ❏ End of sentence punctuation.
- ❏ High-frequency words such as *in, the, of, by.*

I recommend that teachers use a 24 × 16 inch chart tablet because it easily fits against the wall under the chalkboard. By midyear, four to five tablets are at the children's eye-level. Encourage children to read the morning message tablets and charts that contain the children's dictated innovations on books during choice and independent reading times. The children can quickly find their contribution when you print their name after their sentence. Not only do you honor the young writer, but the child's name becomes a reading-from-memory reminder. The children can spot their name and remember their dictated words. Encourage pairs to reread these stories. By reading together, the children learn to read their classmates' words and have opportunities to enlarge their sight word vocabulary and knowledge of how to construct sentences.

## One-on-One Written Conversations: A Powerful Literacy Tool

Conversations on paper intrigue young children who collectively create a text, then observe the text unfold as the teacher or adult records the children's words (Hall and Robinson 1994, Gallagher and Norton 2000). Interactive written conversations document a thoughtful journey that can build children's confidence as writers and readers. Meaningful interactions, where children observe adults writing, then respond by writing, foster the development of crucial elements.

*Trust*   Working closely with children over a long period of time shows them that writing together is a safe and joyful experience. Therefore, accept what children offer and write what they say without changing their words. Set up behavior guidelines that prevent embarrassment by not insisting that every child in the group must participate. Time and the recognition that you have constructed a writing sanctuary will eventually bring all the children into the process. Try one-on-one conversations with children who don't participate with a group.

*Self-confidence*   When children hear you praise and honor their efforts, self-esteem rises. For children like Holly, Megan, Corey, and David, written conversations develop their ability to stretch words, match letters to sounds, and feel they could "write like them [classmates]." Instead of dreading writing, workshop became an activity the children enjoyed.

*Insight in the Child's Personality*   Writing together enables teachers to get to know each child on a deeper level. We learn about pets, friends, family, favorite foods, games, and children's dreams, concerns, and fears.

*Print and Word Knowledge*   By watching the adult write, children observe that writing and reading move from left to right. They hear think-alouds that make visible when to use upper- and lowercase letters, punctuation, and spacing between words. Because the adult says the words while writing, the child observes how speech transforms into a text.

*Spelling Inventions*   Again and again, demonstrate how you stretch the sounds in the children's words and try to figure out the letters you hear. On February 26, Holly writes strings of letters to convey her message (Figure 6–21). By March 22, written conversations reveal that Holly has begun to match sounds and letters (Figure 6–22). Written conversations and using short bursts of time during the day to help Holly successfully stretch words and hear sounds enabled her to progress.

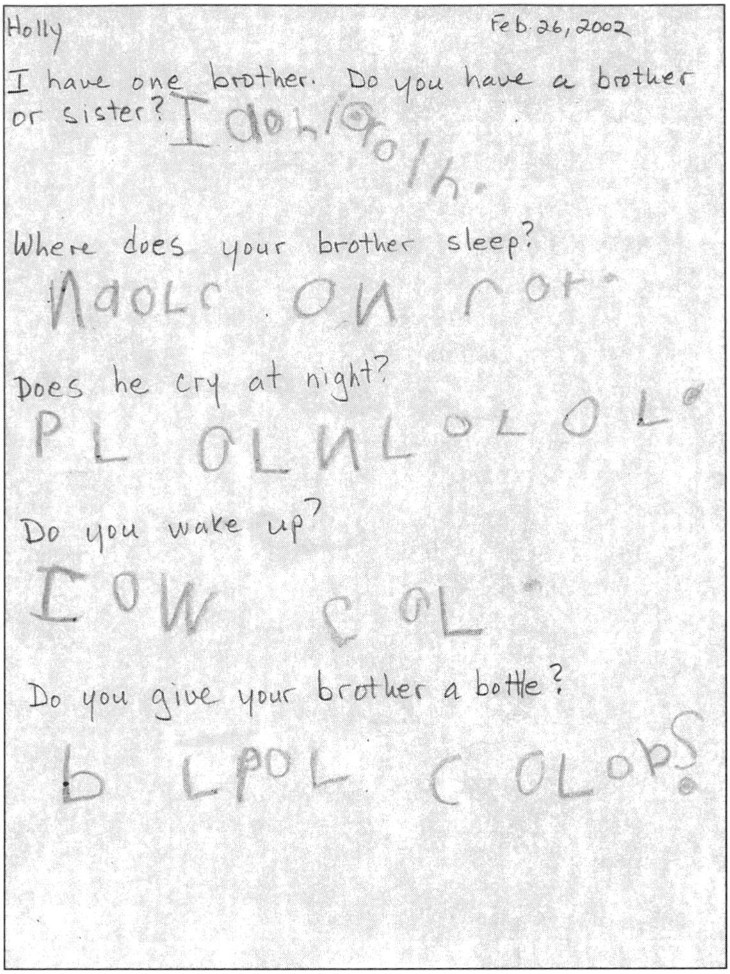

**Figure 6–21.** Holly writes with strings of letters.
*Translation:* 1. I have a baby brother. 2. In his crib. 3. He cries at night. 4. I wake up. 5. I give him a bottle.

Whole-class interactive writing did not facilitate the level of progress that one-on-one work did.

*Reading*    Read and reread the children's text so they come to know the relationship between speaking, writing, and reading. With one-on-one conversations, reread what you have written and invite the child to reread his words. Sometimes, as with Holly and Channing, young children who just begin to write with invented spelling can not reread their work. Repeatedly supporting children by pointing to each word as you reread their words with them can help them encode what they've written.

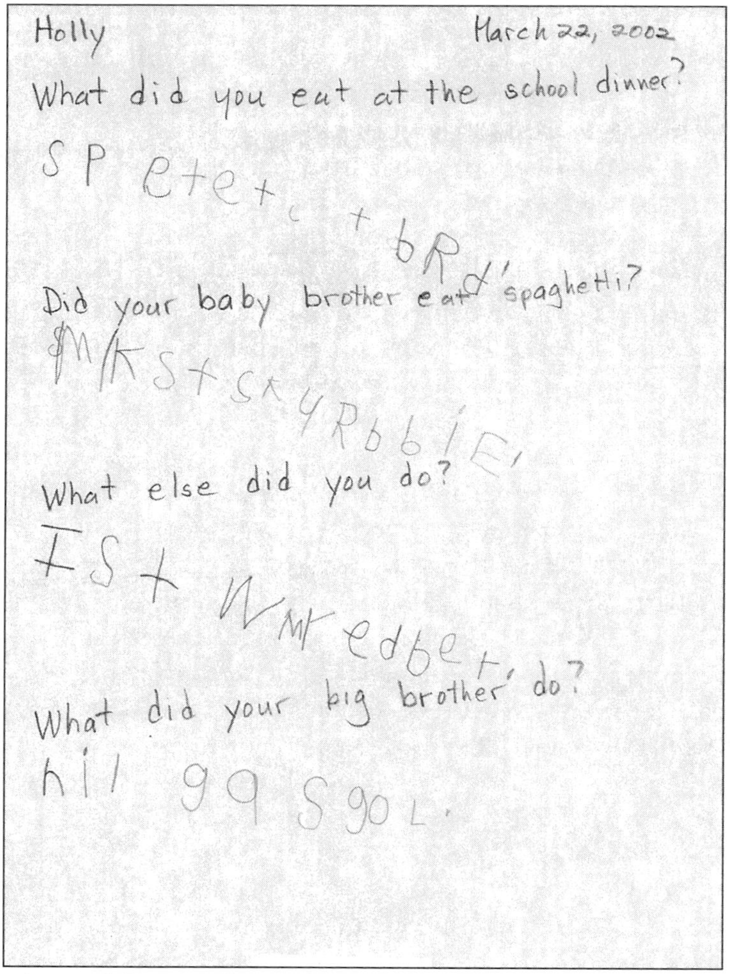

> Holly                    March 22, 2002
> What did you eat at the school dinner?
> S P e t e t c   t b R
> Did your baby brother eat spaghetti?
> M K s t s x y R o b b i E,
> What else did you do?
> I s t   W M e d b e t.?
> What did your big brother do?
> h l l   g g   s g o L.

**Figure 6–22.** A month later, Holly matches some sounds to letters.
*Translation:* 1. Spaghetti bread. 2. Milk. [Writes letters and brother's name, Robbie.] 3. I sat with my mommy and daddy. 4. He sang a song.

## Guidelines for Productively Using Written Conversations

Engaging children in written conversations requires thought and planning by the teacher. Teacher reflection includes knowing the interests and play patterns of three-, four-, or five-year-olds as well as being sensitive to the cultural and socio-economic background of each child.

Beware the pitfall of turning written conversations into recitation games where the teacher asks a yes/no question, such as "Do you have a bike?" (Gallagher and Norton 2000). Instead, ask questions that invite the art of conversation to develop: What do you do after school? Can you tell me about your friend? Dog?

173

Cat? What did you learn when the nurse visited class? Why did you enjoy our trip to the ASPCA? You came back from music humming, can you tell me why? Can you tell me about your favorite game?

The following guidelines are a combination of suggestions for productive written conversations by Gallagher and Norton (2000) as well as ideas developed from my experiences.

❑ Recognize that children's level of writing will range from scribbles to random letters to matching one or more sounds in a word.

❑ Think of the first conversation as a baseline piece that you analyze to see what the child can do and build on these strengths. Compare later written conversations to this first piece to point out progress to the child.

❑ Initiate the process by assuming the child can and will want to write. If you meet resistance, model how pictures, marks, scribbles, and letters are writing. When Timea told me she could draw her family, but couldn't write all the people, I told her that drawing them was a great idea.

❑ Get to know the child if this is your first conversation. Introduce yourself briefly and then ask the child to tell you something about herself. This should take two to three minutes. I usually start by saying, "Hi! I'm Mrs. Robb, and I am a teacher and a mom. Tell me something about you." After the child responds, I say, "Today we are going to talk and write on paper. That's called a written conversation." I always use correct terminology and look for the day the children use it. "Another written conversation?" Uvaldo asks when I appear for our third one.

❑ Place pencils, crayons, and markers on the table and ask the children to choose which one to use for writing that day.

❑ Put the child's name and the date at the top of each paper.

❑ Prepare a second sheet of paper so you can record what the child says before he starts writing.

❑ Say out loud what you are going to write.

❑ Stretch two to three words as you write to model how you try to match letters and sounds. Call children's attention to leaving spaces between words, starting the sentence with an uppercase letter, and placing punctuation at the end.

❑ Ask the child to say her response out loud, just as you did.

❑ Encourage the child to write the sentence. If necessary, remind the child that he can use marks, scribbles, letters, pictures, or numbers.

❑ Write back and forth for a few minutes. The child's body language and waning enthusiasm for responding will help you decide when to stop.

❑ Reread your questions and the child's responses. Take the child's index finger and place it along each word you read.

- ❏ Use the sheet that you've recorded the child's responses on to support reading the child's text.
- ❏ Close by valuing the interactions and set the stage for the next meeting. I say to Timea, "I enjoyed watching you draw your family and write about them. I can't wait to come back next week and have another written conversation with you."

## Snapshots of Written Conversations

It's February when I start working with a group of six children in Deena Baker's kindergarten class. "The children have come a long way from the first day of school," Deena tells me. "I'm concerned that they know their classmates can all use spelling inventions to write, but they're not at that point yet." We plan a program where Deena, the teaching assistant, or I work daily with the children one-on-one or in a small group.

It's obvious to Deena and me that when this group is with the whole class during the morning message, shared writing and reading, and writing workshop, their participation levels are tentative and reluctant. Deena and I agree that this group of six delayed learners don't process as quickly as their peers. Feeling daunted, they become silent during discussions and during author's chair sessions. To change that pattern, I suggest initiating one-on-one written conversations and small-group read-alouds with follow-up discussions, drama, and writing. With written conversations, my goal is to help the children stretch words, match sounds to letters, and build their confidence as writers, listeners, and readers of their words.

The first written conversation takes from twelve to fifteen minutes because of the introductions and short explanations. After that, I find that I can complete a conversation in eight to ten minutes. By the third time, when I walk into the room, the group gathers around me asking, "Can I go first today? Did you remember the paper? Will you read to us after?" Confidence builds quickly, especially when they hear classmates wistfully say, "I wish I could do what Uvaldo is doing."

Written conversations can provide the scaffolding delayed learners need to make progress within their zone of proximal development. All learners can benefit from these one-on-one exchanges. At the start of the year, written conversations teach children about print and writing conventions. Those who arrive in kindergarten able to write with invented spellings can learn about sentence structure, elaborating ideas, and punctuation.

## Literacy Insights Gained from Written Conversations

To demonstrate the learning that takes place through written conversations, consider Channing. Channing is seven years old, more than one year older than her kindergarten peers. This is her first year of formal schooling, and Channing has made much progress with listening to stories and playing with peers. Her first responses consist of random strings of letters for her responses to my queries (Figures 6–23 and 6–24). Channing's last written conversation occurs after she posed for photographs that might appear on this book's cover. Quite dramatically, Channing prepared for the photo shoot by mugging fashion model poses. "I l-o-v-e fashion," she repeated many times. Capitalizing on this interest, I start the conversation by asking, "Why do you like fashion?" What's remarkable about this last conversation is that Channing stretches words independently, she spaces her words without using her finger, and she rereads all of her responses,

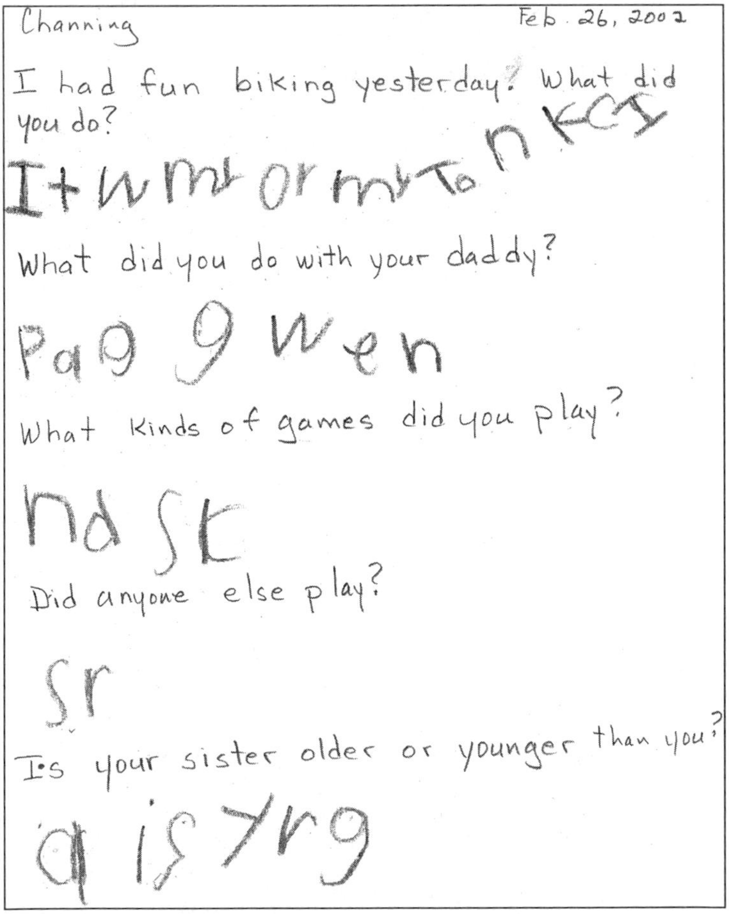
Channing Feb. 26, 2002
I had fun biking yesterday? What did you do?
It Wmr or mrTo n KCI
What did you do with your daddy?
Pa9 9 Wen
What kinds of games did you play?
nd Sk
Did anyone else play?
Sr
Is your sister older or younger than you?
q is Yr9

**Figure 6–23.** Channing writes with random strings of letters.
*Translation:* 1. I spended time with my daddy. 2. We played games. 3. Hide and seek. 4. My sister. 5. She is younger.

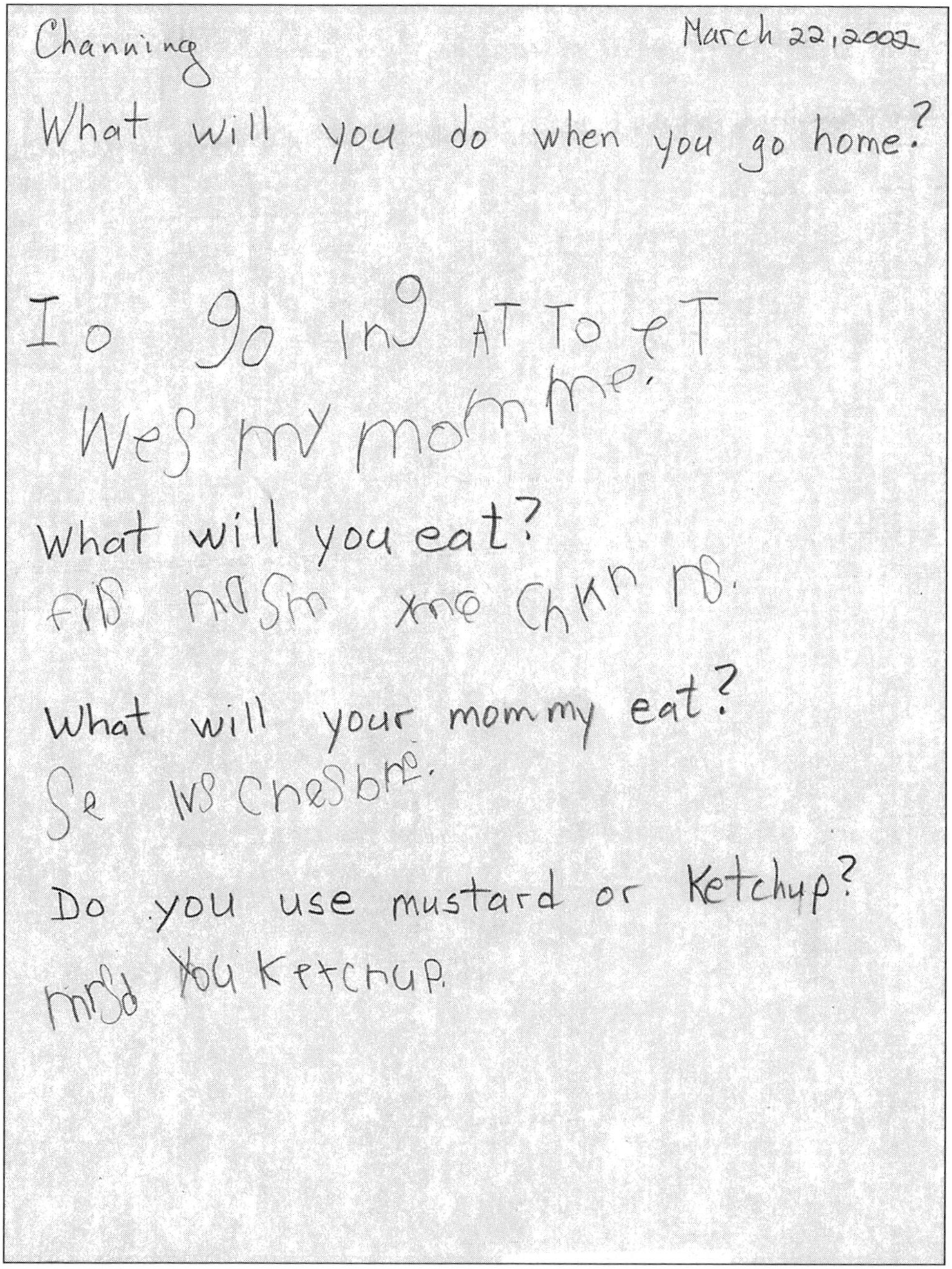

Channing                                    March 22, 2002

What will you do when you go home?

I o go in g AT To eT
Wes mv mom me.

What will you eat?
Fis nasm xno Chkn ns.

What will your mommy eat?
Se ws chesbne.

Do you use mustard or Ketchup?
mrsd You Ketchup.

**Figure 6–24.** Channing writes with random strings of letters.
*Translation:* 1. I'm going out to eat with my mommy. 2. Fries and some yummy chicken nuggets. 3. She loves cheese burgers. 4. My mommy uses mustard and ketchup.

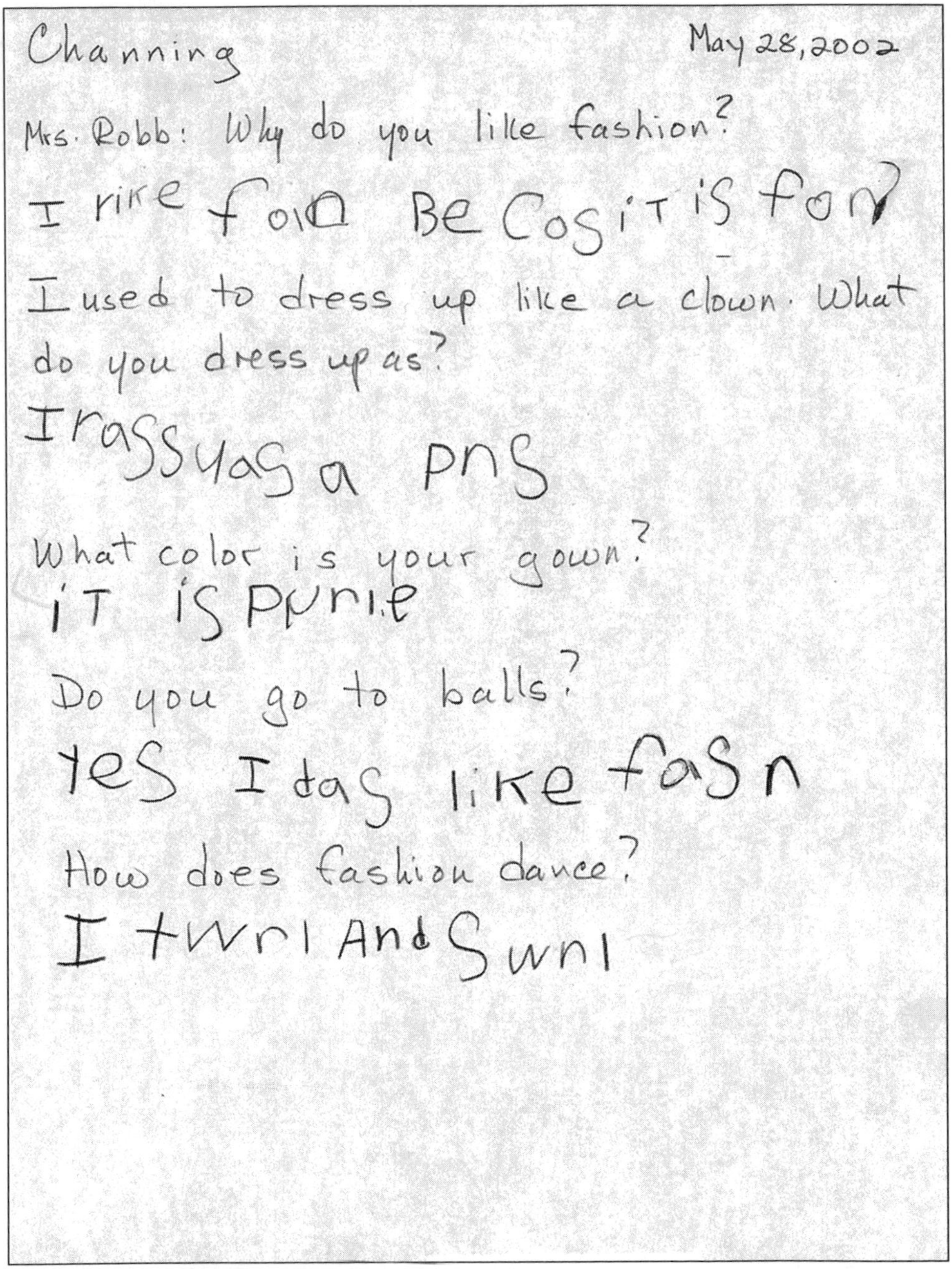

Channing            May 28, 2002

Mrs. Robb: Why do you like fashion?

I rike foα Be Cos iT iS fon

I used to dress up like a clown. What do you dress up as?

I rassyag a PnS

What color is your gown?

iT iS Pυrie

Do you go to balls?

yeS I das like faSn

How does fashion dance?

I twrl And Swnl

**Figure 6–25.** By April, Channing writes with confidence.
*Translation:* 1. I like fashion because it is fun. 2. I dress princess. 3. It is purple. 4. Yes. I dance like fashion. 5. I twirl and swirl.

something she was unable to do until mid-April (Figure 6–25). Moreover, Channing writes with confidence that she can spell the words that communicate her thoughts. At this last meeting, she took my index finger, held it (just as I had done to her), ran my finger under each one of her words, and led the reading! Her grin outdid the Cheshire cat, and her eyes sparkled. "I can write *and* read," she said.

Adapt the guidelines for facilitating written conversations to your students' needs. You can complete two to three a day. Invite your teaching assistant to watch you, to read Gallagher and Norton's book, then to write on paper with children.

## Closing Reflections

Every parent knows that children write long before they read. My neighbor grumbles about drawings on the kitchen and children's bedroom walls. Etched on his bedroom wall is a unicorn my son drew when he was four. These writing actions are common to all children. Parents and teachers can build on these actions by channeling this desire to communicate from walls to paper. When children write, when they observe adults write, and when they interact with adults while writing, they learn, in authentic situations, about letters, the sounds letters make, words, spaces, punctuation, and translating in-the-head thoughts and images into words.

However, not all children arrive at school with a wealth of writing experiences. During the second week of school, while I was observing a child in Lisa Tusing's class write, I noticed she was filling paper after paper with circles and lines, pressing so hard that rips appeared in the middle. When I asked her why she was writing so many pieces, I learned that this youngster never wrote freely on a blank piece of paper at home. "Sometimes I colored in a book," she told me.

For these children—for all children—writing workshop is ideal because every child can start where he is and progress with the support of his teacher. Moreover, teacher demonstrations, children sharing writing, and including writing in play centers reveals writing possibilities to every child. For example, when Dallas notices that a classmate uses exclamation points, he announces, "Next time we write I'm trying those." And Matthew decides that it's time for him to try quotations when he watches his teacher use them during the morning message.

Preschool and kindergarten programs that offer children rich, varied, authentic writing opportunities and free play that incorporates reading and writing, foster the development of emergent literacy behaviors children need for success in school.

# 7

# Word Play, Pretend Play, and Centers

*Making rhymes and playing with words is one of the most reliable indicators that children are getting control of language. They are becoming aware of words and sounds and can manipulate these to express themselves— and impress others!*

Patricia M. Cunningham, *Phonics They Use* ([1995] 2000, 9)

Teachers do make a difference. In fact, research indicates that the expertise and knowledge of the teacher has everything to do with children's progress. Richard Allington, in an article in *Phi Delta Kappan*, notes, "Good teachers, effective teachers, matter more than particular curriculum materials, pedagogical approaches, or proven programs" (2002, 740). Therefore, schools need to invest time and money in ongoing professional study to ensure that teachers keep abreast of research and research-tested strategies so they can meet the diverse needs of the children they teach (Robb 2000b).

To illustrate this point, I invite you to step into two different kindergarten classes. First, observe the interactions between the teacher and children, then reflect on both literacy stories and decide what lessons can be learned from them. I encourage teachers to observe and reflect throughout the day. Information gathered and mulled over can provide the data for continually making instructional decisions that support children's emergent literacy development.

## Two Classroom Snapshots

It's a Monday morning in the first class on our tour. On the chalkboard, the teacher has written the letter of the week, *Dd*. "This week," she announces, "The letter we'll study is [she points to the chalkboard] uppercase *D* and lowercase *d*."

"What about *F*?" a child asks.

"*F* comes after *D*—we'll do that after we study *E*," the teacher replies. And she continues, "Listen to the sound *D* makes, /d/. (A letter between // denotes the sound a letter or cluster of letters makes.) Now everyone help me make the /d/ sound." The children dutifully practice the sound. As I circulate, I hear a boy mutter, "That's how my name starts." But he never shares this with his teacher.

Next, the teacher says, "Raise your hand if you know some words that start with *D*, the letter that makes this sound, /d/." Children offer: *daddy, dog, David,* and *dentist*. One child points out that *daddy* makes the /d/ sound in the middle. The teacher smiles, nods, and says, "We're listening for the beginning sound—the first sound you hear."

On a chart the teacher prints the children's offerings. "This week," she tells her class, "We will listen for words I say and words in books I read that start with the /d/ sound." As the teacher reads aloud, listening for words they can add to the list takes precedence over enjoying and understanding the story. In fact, there is no story discussion. According to the teacher, the purpose of these read-alouds is to identify all the *d* words. "By the end of January," the teacher tells me, "I've covered all the letters and sounds. That's when I let the children write because they have the tools to match letters and sounds."

A forty-five-minute car ride down the Shenandoah Valley to Robinson Elementary School takes me to the second kindergarten on our tour. Lisa Tusing's Literacy Links class has returned from a field trip to a nearby farm. Excited talk about the farm animals the children petted and watched continues as they step off the school bus and walk back to their classroom. Each child carefully carries a small pumpkin, a gift from the farmer. Once pumpkins have been placed in the children's cubbies, Lisa invites the group to write a thank-you note that Lisa will mail to the farmer.

October 17, 200X
Dear Hill High Farm,

> Thank you for letting me have a pumpkin.
> Thank you for letting us play on the farm.
> Thank you for letting us see the animals.

Mrs. Tusing's class

181

First, Lisa compliments the children for remembering to say thank you for all the enjoyable things they did at the farm. "This letter," she tells the children, "will show the owner how much we appreciated our visit, and the gift of the pumpkins. Can you think of other times you might write thank-you notes?" Lisa writes the children's suggestions on a chart: for a birthday present, for a trip, for Christmas presents. "As we think of other ideas this year, I'll add them to the chart," says Lisa.

Next, Lisa invites the children to find a letter in the thank-you note that matches the first letter of their names. Using masking devices, the children spotlight letters and with classmates, say the letter and the sound it makes. Then Nicholas raises his hand furiously. Once he's recognized by Lisa, he charges to the chart and with his finger underlines the -ing in Lisa's name and in *letting*. "They're the same," he says.

"Great noticing," says Lisa. "The letters 'i-n-g' work together and make the /ing/ sound. Does anyone notice other words or word parts that are repeated?" Children come to the chart and with their masking device frame *thank, you, for,* and say these words with Lisa. What's interesting is that at this point in the year, not one child knows every alphabet letter; assessments completed in August revealed that most can recognize half or less or none.


## Interpreting Both Literacy Stories

These stories illustrate teaching styles separated by a wide gulf. In the first classroom, the teacher's instruction emerges from the belief that children must learn one alphabet letter at a time and cannot write until they have received this information. She follows her prepared agenda and is unresponsive to the children's comments if they do not relate to the lesson.

The research of Cunningham ([1995] 2000), Dahl et al. (2001), and Moustafa (1997) challenge this teacher's practices. The teacher is

- ❏ Missing the opportunity to match children's names to words that start with the same letter.
- ❏ Brushing aside the child's query about the letter *F* and refocusing on the letter of the week.
- ❏ Reading stories for the first time for the sole purpose of finding specific beginning consonant sounds.
- ❏ Not responding to the teachable moment when the child observed that *daddy* made a /d/ sound in the middle.
- ❏ Permitting children to write independently only after they learned their alphabet letters and sounds.

In direct contrast, Lisa Tusing uses an authentic writing experience, composing a thank-you note, to illustrate why we write thank-you notes and to discuss additional situations that people thank others in writing. From this writing experience, she invites children to use and build on what they know, their names, to frame letters with a masking device. Lisa is a responsive teacher who follows up what Nicholas notices about -ing to noticing other repeated words. Instead of viewing learning language as moving from the parts to the whole, the belief that drove the first teacher's lesson, Lisa recognizes that children can learn letters and words through shared writing (Dahl et al. 2000, Gallagher and Norton 2000, Hall and Robinson 1994, McCarrier, Pinnell, and Fountas 2000, Payne and Schulman 2000) and through shared reading (Fisher and Medvic 2000, Holdaway 1979). Lisa's teaching decisions grow out of her research-based knowledge and daily teaching events that corroborate what she reads in professional texts.

❏ Children can learn sight words by recognizing the whole word unit, even though they don't know the alphabet (Cunningham [1995] 2000, Moustafa 1997).

❏ Alphabet knowledge develops from the varied reading, writing, letter, and word play experiences teachers offer (Dahl et al. 2002, Moustafa 1997).

❏ As students learn more words, they use patterns and analogy in addition to phonics to decode—like the -ing ending Nicholas observed (Cunningham and Cunningham 2002).

❏ Rich, authentic experiences (the thank-you note) enable students to learn about letters, words, patterns, or written language conventions from the same activity. Reaching a wide-range of children's developmental levels means diminished boredom and frustration. Cunningham, Hall, and Defoe (1998) point out that when teachers provide experiences that have multi-levels of learning, more children progress over time. Those children in Lisa's class who did not detect the -ing pattern observed it and other repeated words because Nicholas was able to share with everyone.

## Suggestions for Helping Children Learn the Alphabet

❏ Read alphabet books often. Encourage children to pretend-read them during sustained silent reading.

❏ Compose class alphabet books that focus on a theme such as the ocean, weather, or food. First, collaborate with the children to write the text. Complete three to four letters a day. The teacher prints the text on large paper, and each child illustrates one to two pages, depending on the number of students. Invite children to reread their class book many times. Place it in your classroom library.

❏ Place alphabet charts in children's journals and writing folders. Encourage them to use these to match letters to sounds as they complete independent and shared writing.

❑ Invite the children to use drama to learn letters by creating letter shapes with their bodies and making the sound of each letter.

❑ Name and make the sounds of letters in words that label parts of your room.

❑ Play the games with children's names that are in this chapter.

❑ Invite the children to make letters from clay, yarn, or pasta. Have them say the letter's name and make its sound.

Like Allington (2002) and Pressley and coauthors (2001), I agree that teachers with a strong knowledge base do make a difference in children's learning. Theoretical knowledge can inform teacher's instruction and decisions about how to respond to the developmental diversity in their classrooms. Having a wealth of information to draw on—information about how children learn—enables teachers to reach all learners.

Therefore, before describing and discussing language play, I believe it's important to explain terms related to playing with language—terms that have been used interchangeably as well as misused and misunderstood. These are *phonological awareness*, *phonemic awareness*, and *phonics*. Understanding the meanings of these terms can not only make you more knowledgeable, but will also enable you to connect to the reasoning behind my recommendations.

## Phonological Awareness: What Is It?

*Phonological awareness* is the umbrella category that describes children's ability to hear and manipulate sounds in words, syllables, and phonemes or units of sound in spoken words represented by individual letters such as *c, b, o, t* (Bear et al. [1996] 2000, Cunningham [1995] 2000). Children's acquisition of phonological awareness is developmental and occurs in stages (Bear et al. [1996] 2000, Opitz 2000). Even some children who enter school with rich literacy backgrounds will not have developed every aspect of phonological awareness. Cunningham describes the stages of phonological awareness this way:

> First, young children become aware of words and understand that words can form sentences. Next children come to know that words are made up of parts called syllables. Finally, children gain what researchers call phonemic awareness, the ability to hear phonemes or individual sounds letter make in syllables and words. ([1995] 2000, 10)

### Phonemic Awareness

Children who develop phonemic awareness understand that words consist of individual sounds made by single or a combination of letters blended together. Phonemic awareness also includes the ability to select rhyming words from a group such as *mat, boy, swing, hat,* and produce a rhyming word for a given word, such as *small* for *tall.* Young children who can hear beginning consonant sounds that are alike—*sip soup silently*—and can think of words that start with the same sound have developed another aspect of phonemic awareness. These children can also hear and separate the sounds in a word such as *dog* by making the sound for each phoneme or letter /d/o/g/. They can also reverse the process and put the whole word together when they hear the single phonemes /s/a/t/ spoken or when they hear the onset (consonants that come before the vowel) and rime (the vowel and other sounds that come after it) spoken, such as /c/-/at/ for *cat* or /spl/-/ash/ for *splash*.

Phonemic awareness has everything to do with hearing spoken sounds. Phonemic awareness does not mean a child can identify all of the alphabet letters or associate a sound with a written letter.

## Phonics

Phonics instruction focuses on decoding words by matching sounds to printed letters. Readers who connect sound and symbol in order to pronounce words in isolation and in continuous text are using their knowledge of phonics—the sounds letters make of words in print.

Theodore Clymer ([1963] 1996) dispelled the myth that systematic phonics instruction creates strong readers when he showed that traditional phonics generalizations are unreliable. Clymer studied forty-five phonics generalizations present in four popular reading programs. He concluded that many generalizations taught have limited value for children learning to read. In contrast to Clymer's study, the National Reading Panel used its scientific research studies to conclude that explicit systematic phonics instruction is superior to hit-or-miss or no phonics instruction. The panel also agreed that they could find no significant differences among the systematic phonics instruction programs available for teachers (2000a, 2000b).

However, the National Reading Panel excluded recent field research that shows that children need more than phonics to decode words. They need a knowledge of word patterns, such as the varied long *a* sounds: *ay, ai, a-consonant-silent e, eigh*. Phonics will not help a child sound out *weight* (Bear et al. [1996] 2000). However, knowing that the *eigh* pattern makes a long *a* sound will support decoding. Familiarity with word families and patterns is also helpful, for readers can then use analogy to decode new words (Cunningham and Cunningham 2002). For example, if a child can read *flight* and *night*, they can use their knowledge of how to pronounce *ight* to say *might*, a new word. Moreover, decoding is not synonymous with comprehension, and as children learn to read, they must also learn to make meaning (Moustafa 1997, Robb 2002).

When preschool children have been exposed to storybook reading, nursery rhymes, songs, poems, and word games and interactive talk with adults, they usually arrive at school with all levels of phonological awareness (Snow, Burns, and Griffin 1998). Moreover, by the end of kindergarten, when children engage in shared, interactive writing experiences, a balanced read-aloud program, and can use invented spelling to write and read back what they have composed, a large number enter first grade able to read or with the developmental skills they need to learn to read (Cunningham and Cunningham 2002, Neuman and Bredekamp 2002, Moustafa 1997). In direct contrast, children who arrive at school with no phonological awareness usually have not been read to and have not played language games with adults nor engaged in meaningful conversations.

## *What Research Has to Say About Phonological Awareness*

Some research points to a high correlation between phonological awareness and learning to read (Lundberg, Frost, and Petersen 1988). In their article, "Supporting Phonemic Awareness Development in the Classroom," Yopp and Yopp (2000) make the case for the importance of phonemic awareness to future reading success. In an alphabetic written system, language users record the smallest units of sound of their spoken language, phonemes, to write words. However, both Yopps agree with Richgels (2001) and the Cunninghams (2002) who believe that phonemic awareness is one of many emergent literacy skills children need in order to experience success when learning to read.

In 1990, when Adams published her comprehensive review of research about beginning reading, she had a huge impact on classroom practices that developed. Adams pointed out that research supported the belief that early word identification depended on phonemic awareness. As a result, numerous books have been written that offer language games that develop phonemic awareness (see Appendix) and phonemic awareness activities have been incorporated into kindergarten and first-grade programs for thirty to forty minutes a day (Cunningham and Cunningham 2002). In "What We Know About How to Teach Phonics," both authors point to the negative impact that devoting so much time to phonemic awareness activities can have on young children: "Such single-level instruction can only bore and even confuse those who already have or would learn phonemic awareness without it" (2002, 93). I would add that when programs recommend large chunks of time be spent on out-of-context phonemic awareness drills, they reduce to less significant other emergent literacy behaviors and take away precious time to develop them.

## Integrate Phonemic Awareness into Daily Literacy Events

Embedding phonemic awareness activities in authentic experiences such as shared reading and writing and writing workshop, immerse young children in activities that develop their knowledge of the sounds of speech from rhyming, to hearing syllables, to understanding onset and rime, and finally hearing letter or phoneme sounds.

Chants make superb transition from one activity to another and you are improving listening skills while have a great time with language. In two to four minutes, you can reinforce what you are teaching with these language games. Here are some chants to incorporate into your day:

> I know words that start with /d/.
>> Dog, dance, dog, dance.
>>> Do you know a word that starts with /d/?

You can play this game with beginning and ending consonant sounds, with consonant blends (sl, br, str) and digraphs (ch, th, sh) and with rhyming words that build children's knowledge of word families (un, at, all, an). Other variations include saying the sample words with onset and rime, and having the children do the same.

> I know a word that starts with /m/.
>> /M/-/om, /m/-/om/.
>>> Can you say a word that starts with /m/?

Each time a child says a word with onset and rime, ask a classmate to blend the parts together and say the whole word.

Create sound play with parts of popular songs that children know. Here's one for the refrain of "I've Been Working on the Railroad."

> Fe-Fi-Fiddly-i-o
>> Fe-Fi-Fiddly-i-o-o-o-o
>>> Fe-Fi-Fiddly-i-o
>>>> Strummin' on the old banjo.
>>>>> Now try it with /z/ or /m/ or /str/.

Turn "The Farmer in the Dell" into a rhyming song and invite the children to create their own innovations. Sing the refrain after each line.

Refrain:
> The farmer in the dell,
>> The farmer in the dell,
>>> Hi, Ho, the derrio,
>>>> The farmer in the dell.
>>>>> The farmer takes a cat,
>>>>>> The cat takes a rat,
>>>>>>> The rat takes a hat,
>>>>>>>> The hat takes a gnat
>>>>>>>>> The gnat takes a bat
>>>>>>>>>> The bat takes a mat
>>>>>>>>>>> The cheese stands alone.

I cannot provide time recommendations for integrating phonemic awareness activities into daily reading and writing experiences. Why? Because the emergent literacy behaviors children bring to school differ widely. The most effective word and language play, however, has several levels of learning and reaches the diverse development in a class of children (Cunningham and Cunningham 2000). My hope is that all instruction responds to the needs of individual children as they grow and change throughout the school year.

Like Snowball and Bolton (1999), I suggest you look at children's writing to determine their level of phonological awareness. When Stephen Burns entered Deena Baker's kindergarten class, he did not write letters or scribbles but dictated the message for his journal pictures (Figures 7–1 and 7–2). By the end of October, Stephen can spell *we* and *to* correctly and hear and write the first and last sounds of words and the short *e* in *went* and the long *a* in *hayride* (Figure 7–3). His March journal entry shows highly developed phonological awareness (Figure 7–4). At this point, phonemic awareness games are pointless for Stephen. However, not all children develop as quickly as Stephen, but once children gain phonemic awareness, their writing reflects their knowledge.

**Figures 7–1 and 7–2.** At the start of the year, Stephen dictates his messages.

**Figure 7–3.** Stephen's progress by the end of October

**Figure 7–4.** Stephen's March journal reveals his developed phonological awareness.

Ashley, in Lisa Tusing's kindergarten class starts the year with random scribbles (Figure 7–5). In October, she adds strings of letters and numbers to her pictures and shares her story with her class: "The bird is trying to get into my house. Then I said what you doing in my house. He was so mad" (Figure 7–6). In May, her writing reveals her growth and ability to match sounds to letters (Figure 7–7). Both Lisa and Deena's kindergartens have balanced read-aloud programs, shared and independent writing, and rich language play that they integrate into authentic learning experiences. These teachers respond to students' needs and work one-on-one during writing workshop to help students

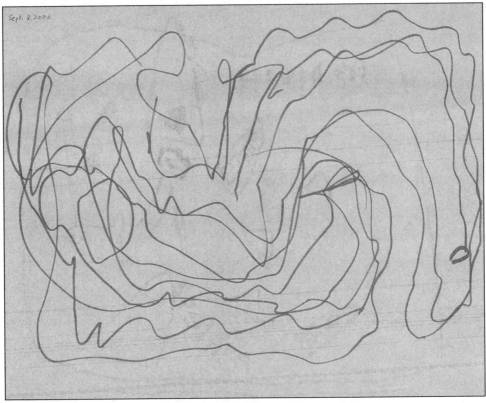

**Figure 7–5.** Ashley writes with random scribbles at the start of the year.

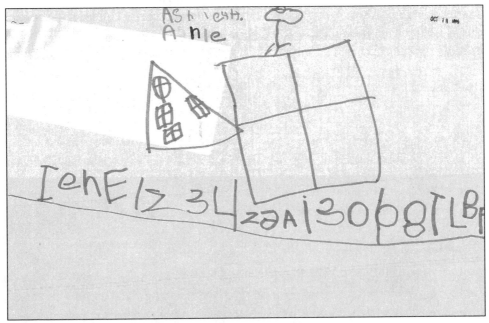

**Figure 7–6.** In October, Ashley writes with strings of letters.

**Figure 7–7.** In May, Ashley can match sounds to letters.

apply their growing knowledge of the sounds heard in spoken language to their independent writing.

Composing and reflecting on the morning message, a collaborative story, a letter, a retelling of a book, or a written conversation can become a multilevel experience that develops children's phonemic awareness and writing conventions. Multilevel learning opportunities encourage all the children to participate and at the same time hold the potential of raising children's awareness of how our language works.

Be selective; don't include all of my suggestions in one lesson. Know your students and choose ideas that respond to their diverse needs. Give all individuals opportunities to successfully participate at some point during the day. Under related items, I've identified the phonemic awareness task it supports. Ask the children to come to the chart, big book, or poem to:

- ❏ Find a word that starts with the same letter as their name.
- ❏ Find a word that ends with the same letter as their name.
- ❏ Circle a word that starts with this sound: /b/. Do this for other sounds.

*Supports:* Matching beginning and ending sounds.

- ❏ Circle a short word that you clap once to say.
- ❏ Circle a long word that you clap two or three times to say.

*Supports:* Knowing words are made up of parts called syllables.

- ❏ Say a word that rhymes with one of the words in the message.

*Supports:* Hearing and creating words that rhyme.

- ❏ Find and point to this word, and the teacher says the onset and rime. (Examples: s-ing, g-et, st-op, pl-ay)

*Supports:* Hearing and blending onset and rime into a whole word.

- ❏ Point to this word, after the teacher says each phoneme. (Examples: /r/u/n/, /f/u/n/, /s/a/t/)

*Supports:* Hearing and blending single phonemes into a whole word.

- ❏ Take a word such as *sat* and ask the children what word you have if you change the /s/ sound to a /b/ sound. Make several substitutions.

*Supports:* Deleting a beginning sound and substituting another sound to form a word from the same family.

- ❏ Find the groups of words that all begin with the same sound.

*Supports:* Identifying a group of words that start with the same sound, called *alliteration.*

In addition to shared writing, you can also develop phonemic awareness by using pages from a big book or a poem on chart paper. Do this *only* after the children have repeatedly heard and enjoyed the text.

### The Relationship Between Reading Aloud and Listening

A mother, anxious about her four-year-old son, asked me for advice. During a recent conference, the child's preschool teacher expressed concern because her son would not sit with the group during read-aloud times. This youngster had dozens of electronic games, and the family had an extensive library of movies on videocassettes. No family-owned books. No family library card. I shared this mother's worries. Beside giving her Bernice Cullinan's book *Read to Me: Raising Kids Who Love to Read* ([1992] 2000), I urged her to obtain a library card, frequent the library, encourage her son to browse through picture books, check them out, and read to him four to five times a day in a warm, cuddly setting. My gut instinct was to also encourage this mom to hide the electronic games and movies. But I resisted, knowing this might frustrate and anger the child who would not be able to understand the rationale behind such an action. Instead, I suggested that the transition to listening and using his imagination to create his own movies would take time, patience, and calm persistence.

So what does this literacy story teach us? The conclusion is simple. If we want young children to love reading and words, to find pleasure in hearing stories, to use their imaginations to explore other places, worlds, and cultures, and to learn about language, then they need access to wonderful books and poems.

## Snapshots of Children Interacting with Poems

Julie Stringer is a young kindergarten teacher at Powhatan School where I teach. Immediately after calendar work and the morning message, Julie starts the children's day with a song or poem that's printed on chart paper. Reread over five to six days, Julie carefully points to each word, encouraging the children to chime in with her. "My favorites," she tells me, "are Mother Goose rhymes. The rhythms and rhymes and topics really capture the kids' imaginations."

"We do tongue twisters like 'Betty Botter' and 'Sea Shells' (see box) so the kids feel down to their toes the repeated first letters. During shared writing time, I have the children make up their own tongue twisters. It's a great way to play with and learn about beginning sounds. I always start with the first letters of their names." Here are two tongue twisters the children composed using their names:

- ❏ Mighty Max made merry mud masks move.
- ❏ Chris crunched creepy creatures and cried.

**Betty Botter**

Betty Botter bought some butter,
But, she said, the butter's bitter.
If I put it in my batter,
It will make my batter bitter.
But a bit of better butter
Will make my batter better.
So she bought a bit of butter
Better than her bitter butter,
And she put it in her batter
And the batter was not bitter.
So 'twas better Betty Botter
Bought a bit of better butter.

**Sea Shells**

She sells seashells on the seashore;
The shells that she sells are seashells I'm sure.
So if she sells seashells on the seashore,
I'm sure that the shells are seashore shells.

Dramatizing poems helps young children deepen their understanding of new words while enjoying poetry. After reading "Jack Be Nimble" several times, the children had memorized the short rhyme and chanted it before I could start reading from the chart.

> Jack, be nimble,
>> Jack, be quick,
>>> Jack jump over the candlestick.

First, I placed a candle in a candlestick in the middle of our shared reading rug. Next, I invited each child to jump over the candlestick without toppling it while the class chanted the poem substituting the child's name. Then the children and I sat in a circle around the candlestick, and I asked them, "What do you think the word *nimble* means?" Here are notes of a discussion I had with children at Quarles Elementary during summer school.

AARON: You got to be a good jumper.

BRYANA: You do it [jump] without kicking the candlestick.

ROBB: Does anyone have other ideas?

SHAI: It means your legs move good.

JOEL: I think do it fast before I go.

ROBB: I like the way you are thinking about what you did to figure out what *nimble* means. All of your ideas are so good. Let me summarize them: *nimble* means you have to have legs that move quickly so you can jump over the candlestick without knocking it down.

Because dozens of nursery rhymes feature wonderful characters, or animals, you can ask the children to choose and pretend to be a character, silently act out the poem, then have the class recite it. Dylan pretends he's "Little Boy Blue," and falls asleep on a beanbag and snores loudly. Jumping rope, Kirsten asks her classmates, "Who am I?" Several respond by reciting, "Jumping Joan." Shai brays like a donkey and holds his hands on his head for pretend donkey ears. After the group recites:

> Donkey, donkey, old and gray,
>> Open your mouth and gently bray;
>>> Lift your ears and blow your horn,
>>>> To wake the world this sleepy morn.

Shai quickly adds, "Morn—that's short for morning."

Beside Mother Goose rhymes, you'll also want to introduce the children to a variety of wonderful poets: Aileen Fisher, William Cole, Charles Ghigna, Nikki Giovanni, Eloise Greenfield, Nikki Grimes, Lee Bennett Hopkins, Shirley Hughes, Bobbi Katz, Karla Kuskin, J. Patrick Lewis, David McCord, Eve Merriam, Alice Schertle, and Joyce Carol Thomas. Here are some other ways to actively involve the children with poetry and enrich their language development.

*Echo Reading*  Recite one or two lines at a time and have the children repeat them as you point to the words printed on chart paper. You'll find that they quickly memorize short texts.

*Choral Reading*  Assign refrains or parts of poems to the class once the children are totally familiar with the rhyme. You might want to tape-record these choral chants and put them in a listening center.

*Predict-a-Rhyme*  Cover rhyming words with index cards or sticky notes, then invite the children to predict and say the rhyming word.

*Humpty-Dumpty Task*  Print each line of a poem on a sentence strip. Mix the strips up and invite pairs to put the poem together. Children can do this once they have memorized a poem and can track the print while reciting the poem.

*Mini-word Walls*  Plan a word wall that grows out of reading Mother Goose rhymes or other poems. Discuss the meaning of each word before adding it to the wall. When appropriate, invite the children to act out the word's meaning. I recommend organizing words from several poems under a category such as: a word wall of unusual foods, words that describe, money words, and so on (Figure 7–8). Set aside a few minutes several times a week to review words and add others. Encourage the children to use the words in their writing.

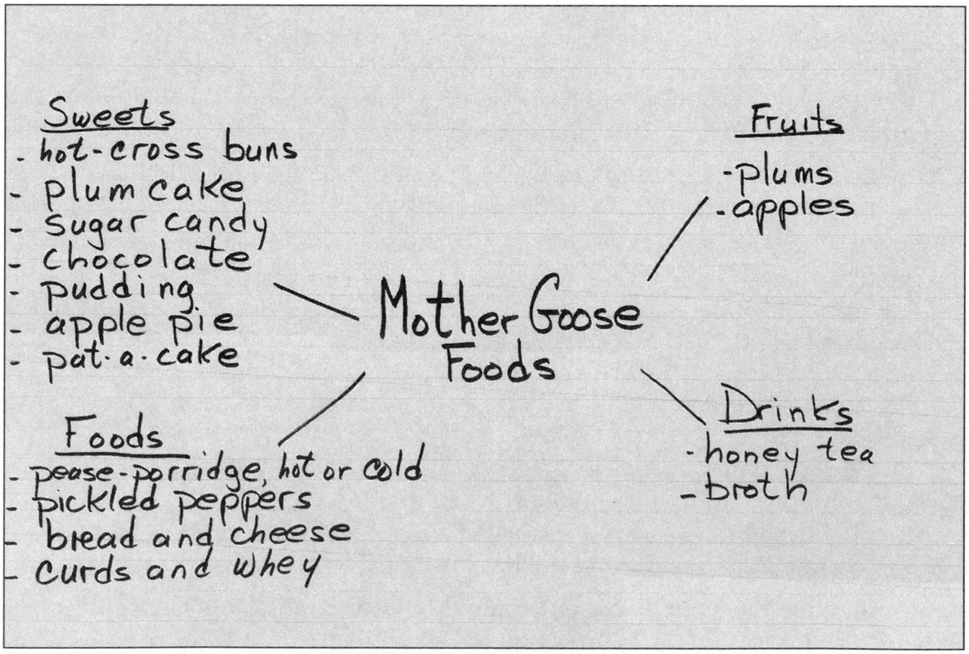

**Figure 7–8.** Children learn about foods from Mother Goose.

*Word or Concept Web*  Brainstorm words that emerge from poems or books that teach concepts such as the seasons, bubbles, colors, specific holidays, weather, space, and so forth. Print children's responses on a word web.

### Snapshots of Children Interacting with Books

Like poems, books read aloud again and again are ideal for building vocabulary, enjoying rhyming words, developing concepts, and learning words that help young readers think about and analyze characters as well as understand other cultures and places. One of my favorite books to foster thinking about character's personalities and giving children the words that describe these feelings and traits is *Noisy Nora* by Rosemary Wells (1973). In a short, rhymed text, Wells paints the character of Nora, Father, Mother, Kate, and Jack, the baby. I make a chart with these emotions and personality traits printed down the left side: *worried, angry, impatient, jealous, sad, mean, spiteful,* and *naughty.* Across the top I print the names of the characters and draw a grid (see Appendix page 285). Then I invite the children to decide who in the story acts or feels worried, angry, and so on. Before I place a check mark on the chart indicating that a character experiences a specific emotion or acts a certain way, the children have to give me reasons from the story. Here are one group's responses for Nora feeling *angry*:

"Jack ate when he was hungry. Nora got no food."
"Dad played with Kate."
"Nora was oldest, so no one played with her."

Use the grid with narratives where characters' thoughts, actions, and decisions show strong emotions and personality traits.

Children can visit the African savanna by reading *Water Hole Waiting* by Jane Kurtz and Christopher Kurtz, pictures by Lee Christiansen (2002). The language sparkles with images and sounds:

Morning slinks onto the savanna
And licks up the night shadows
one by one.

Those opening lines bring children to the illustration of the water hole where animals come to drink. The text is ideal for raising children's awareness of unique rhymes—hippopotami/sky; prance/dance/chance. And the authors provide a magical introduction to *onomatopoeia*—words that conjure sounds in our imagination. A lion walks "slip-slap"; "thrum, thrum," for elephants rumbling along; and "galup, galumpf" describes the giraffe "swaying down the path." Children can feast on strong verbs, sound words, and rhymes during many readings.

After the fifth reading, I invited a group of children to tell me words and phrases they remembered. Several thumbed through the book and found the illustration that helped them recall phrases. Some of their choices that I've included below, reflect how exciting language resonates in children's minds.

"I like the sun doing cartwheels."

"I like the way they say the monkey's thirsty." And I reread, "Monkey's throat is parched and aching."

"I know what it means when giraffe's legs splay. I got it from the picture."

"I noticed that evening can sigh like when I'm tired."

A terrific companion book to *Water Hole Waiting* is *The Water Hole* by Graeme Base (2001). This counting book has lush illustrations and onomatopoeic words.

Bruce Degan fills *Daddy Is a Doodlebug* (2000) with quirky illustrations and fantastic rhymes that invite children to invent other words that rhyme with *doodle*. Playing with language fascinates children, and teachers and I often see their romance with language during center time. In the Appendix, I've listed books that appeal to children and model language play.

## Play Name Games

The majority of kindergarten children can write their first names when they enter school. An ideal way to introduce word play that builds a knowledge of the alphabet, long and short words, and syllables is with children's names. To play these games, print each child's name on an index card or a piece of sentence strip paper. Here are some name-games that children enjoy.

❑ Have each child say his or her name and with the class, clap the beats or syllables. Children place one syllable names in one pile and multiple syllable names in another pile. Later you can sort these into names with two syllables, three syllables, and four or more syllables.

❑ Have children count the number of letters in their names.

### A Must-Have Resource

M. Opitz. 2000. *Rhymes and Reasons: Literature and Language Play for Phonological Awareness*. Portsmouth, NH: Heinemann.

Michael Opitz has compiled a comprehensive list of more than 350 books. The impressive feature is that each piece of high-quality literature listed includes kid-tested, practical suggestions for teachers to integrate into their curriculum.

- ❏ Have the children say and count the number of sounds they hear in their names. Compare the number of sounds heard to the number of letters counted.
- ❏ Invite children to pair-up and learn to read one another's names.
- ❏ Place name strips in a paper bag. Ask children to pull out a name, say it, and give it to its owner.
- ❏ Have the children locate words from shared reading and writing that start with the first letter of their names.
- ❏ Use the alphabet strips on children's tables and near the writing center to have the children line up, holding their printed names, in alphabetical order.
- ❏ Encourage children to learn to read all of their classmates' names. Then, have children take turns giving out writing folders. They can also check attendance by reading the names from the name chart.
- ❏ Help children hear the sound the first letter each classmate's name makes. Once they can do this, help them hear and say the last sound.
- ❏ Point out how children's names are alike and different. For example, Tanisha and Tana start with the letter *T* and make the /t/ sound. They both have the letters *a* and *n* after the *T*. Clap three times when you say *Tanisha;* clap two times when you say *Tana. Tanisha* has three syllables and *Tana* has two syllables.

During the first year of the Literacy Links kindergarten, Terri and Lisa waited until February to introduce picture sorts to develop the children's ability to hear and discriminate between and among beginning consonant sounds. By the end of September of the second year of Literacy Links, their students learned most of the alphabet and more than half were able to hear the sounds at the start and end of their names. That year, Terri, Lisa, and Melissa Foltz, who taught the transition first grade, signed up for a word study class offered by the University of Virginia. All three teachers integrated what they were learning about the emergent stages of spelling into their daily lessons. They explained to me: "We were able to work sooner with those children who were ready to sort pictures by beginning sounds. They developed phonological awareness earlier and scored much higher on the PALS test given in November because we started as soon as children showed us they were ready."

### The Emergent Stages of Spelling

At the start of the year, several children in the Literacy Links kindergartens at Robinson Elementary School were not even at the early emergent stage of spelling development. During this stage, children's writing may consist of scribbles, random strings of letters that have no relationship to the sounds in specific words, numbers, and a mixture of numbers, letters, and scribbles. Their writing lacks directionality and appears anywhere on the page.

The early emergent stage is a period of experimentation when children show us that besides pictures, print contains a message. By February, Holly's picture of a baby elephant and its mother shows their love for one another with hearts. This kindergartner's writing is at the early emergent spelling stage and consists of letters Holly knows (Figure 7–9). Holly's letters do not have a direct correspondence with the words she speaks to tell her story: "Bashi and his mom love."

During the early emergent stage of spelling, children, with the support of teachers, can develop phonemic awareness. Using spelling inventions to write, a few words begin to correspond to the consonant sounds children hear, moving them into the late emergent spelling stage. Five-year-old Uvaldo's writing is a good example of late emergent writing where he hears and prints *pl* for *played* (Figure 7–10).

The checklist that follows, based in part on the research of Bear and colleagues ([1996] 2000), enables you to monitor children's progress as they move from early to middle to late emergent stages (Figure 7–11). Evaluating children's progress supports planning appropriate learning experiences. Your observations and notes on the checklist will also enable you to know when you can introduce a child to picture sorting for initial consonant sounds.

Once children demonstrate through their writing their emerging understanding that there is a correspondence between the letter(s) they write and the word(s) they are trying to represent (*b* for *book*, *l* for *like*, *tr* for *truck*), it's appropriate to use picture sorts to further develop their ability to hear and differentiate between beginning consonant sounds.

### Developing Phonemic Awareness with Picture Sorts

In September, Terri Auckland documented the kinds of word study activities she offered her ten students. In addition to observing changes in the children's writing and their responses to the morning message and other shared writing experiences, Terri administered a spelling inventory recommended by her University of Virginia instructor. The spelling inventory, given after four weeks of school, is characteristic of the Literacy Links population. At this point Tyler struggles to form the letters of his name, and he writes the letter *H* to represent each dictated word (Figure 7–12). By November, Tyler has moved to the late emergent spelling stage because he can hear and match the initial consonant sound in each dictated word (Figure 7–13). He's now ready for picture sorting activities.

The results of the spelling inventory matched Terri's careful observations of the children during writing workshop: four children were at the early emergent level, three at the middle emergent level, and three at the late emergent level.

**Figure 7–9.** An example of early emergent spelling

**Figure 7–10.** An example of late emergent spelling

During Terri's reading/writing workshop block, she supported small groups and worked one-on-one in order to move children beyond early and middle emergent levels and to move those at the late emergent level into the next spelling stage called the *letter name stage*. At this stage, children's writing illustrates that they can match beginning and ending sounds of a word and some medial sounds, enabling others to read the writing and the child to accurately encode a piece.

The activities Terri offered her students grew out of shared and family storybook reading and shared writing.

- ❑ Name games with the children's first name.
- ❑ Songs, nursery rhymes, poems, chants.
- ❑ Syllable clapping.
- ❑ Lettersound matching games.
- ❑ Rhyming games.
- ❑ Choral reading.
- ❑ Echo reading.
- ❑ Tracking and other concepts of word activities.
- ❑ Collaborative writing.

## Checklist of Emergent Spelling and Writing Behaviors

Name⎽⎽⎽⎽⎽⎽⎽⎽⎽⎽⎽⎽⎽⎽⎽⎽⎽⎽⎽⎽⎽⎽⎽⎽⎽⎽⎽⎽⎽⎽⎽⎽⎽⎽

**Behaviors**                                    **Dates Observed**

### Early emergent

❑  Draws and scribbles for writing.            ⎽⎽⎽  ⎽⎽⎽  ⎽⎽⎽  ⎽⎽⎽
❑  Holds a writing implement correctly.        ⎽⎽⎽  ⎽⎽⎽  ⎽⎽⎽  ⎽⎽⎽
❑  Scribbles and random letters have
    a message.                                 ⎽⎽⎽  ⎽⎽⎽  ⎽⎽⎽  ⎽⎽⎽

### Middle emergent

❑  Separates drawing and writing.              ⎽⎽⎽  ⎽⎽⎽  ⎽⎽⎽  ⎽⎽⎽
❑  Uses letter-like forms.                     ⎽⎽⎽  ⎽⎽⎽  ⎽⎽⎽  ⎽⎽⎽
❑  Moves writing across the page
    from left to write.                         ⎽⎽⎽  ⎽⎽⎽  ⎽⎽⎽  ⎽⎽⎽
❑  Writes from right to left when
    ready to start a new line.                  ⎽⎽⎽  ⎽⎽⎽  ⎽⎽⎽  ⎽⎽⎽
❑  Writes in a list.                           ⎽⎽⎽  ⎽⎽⎽  ⎽⎽⎽  ⎽⎽⎽
❑  Writes some letters based on
    sound/symbol correspondence
    to represent some words.                    ⎽⎽⎽  ⎽⎽⎽  ⎽⎽⎽  ⎽⎽⎽
❑  Copies names and letters
    displayed in room.                          ⎽⎽⎽  ⎽⎽⎽  ⎽⎽⎽  ⎽⎽⎽
❑  Uses mainly uppercase letters.              ⎽⎽⎽  ⎽⎽⎽  ⎽⎽⎽  ⎽⎽⎽
❑  Pretend-reads own writing.                  ⎽⎽⎽  ⎽⎽⎽  ⎽⎽⎽  ⎽⎽⎽

### Late emergent

❑  Writes consistently from left to right.     ⎽⎽⎽  ⎽⎽⎽  ⎽⎽⎽  ⎽⎽⎽
❑  Matches some sounds with letters.           ⎽⎽⎽  ⎽⎽⎽  ⎽⎽⎽  ⎽⎽⎽
❑  Substitutes letters that sound alike
    when stretched: $d/b$, $b/p$, $p/h$.       ⎽⎽⎽  ⎽⎽⎽  ⎽⎽⎽  ⎽⎽⎽
❑  Spaces words all the time.                  ⎽⎽⎽  ⎽⎽⎽  ⎽⎽⎽  ⎽⎽⎽
❑  Matches letters to sounds in the
    beginning and the end of words.             ⎽⎽⎽  ⎽⎽⎽  ⎽⎽⎽  ⎽⎽⎽
❑  Reads own writing using letters that
    represent words.                            ⎽⎽⎽  ⎽⎽⎽  ⎽⎽⎽  ⎽⎽⎽

**Figure 7–11.** Checklist of Emergent Spelling and Writing Behaviors

© 2003 by Laura Robb from *Literacy Links*. Portsmouth, NH: Heinemann.

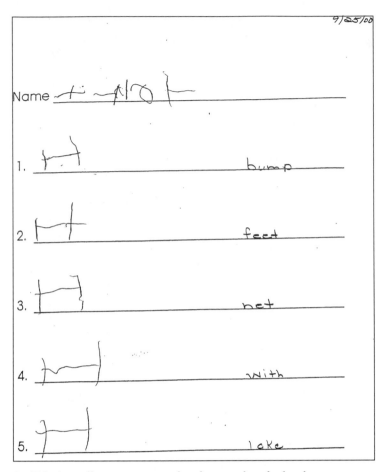

**Figure 7–12.** Tyler's spelling inventory after four weeks of school

- ❏ Morning message and written conversations.
- ❏ Independent writing.
- ❏ Picture sorts for beginning/ending sounds.
- ❏ Stretching words to match letters to all heard sounds.

Here's how Terri and her colleagues conducted picture sorts.

*Use a book, poem, chant, or song as a springboard into picture sorting.* After Terri read *The Giant Jam Sandwich* by John Vernon Lord (1972), the children wrote about sorting *J* and *W* pictures in the book. Next, Terri invited the children to sort objects pulled from a bag that started with /j/ or /w/ sounds. Children placed *J* objects under a picture of a jam jar. They placed *W* objects under their classmate, Wade's name. After completing the sorting of objects, the children tested each item against *jam jar* and *Wade*. For each recommended change, the child

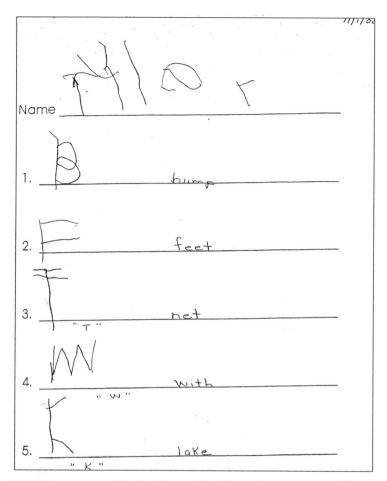

**Figure 7–13.** Tyler can write the first letter of each word.

demonstrated how the sounds did not match by saying the word followed by the key word or picture. Terri took notes after each sorting activity.

- ❑ Tyler had a great deal of difficulty because he tried to sort by color or use instead of sound.
- ❑ Samantha was very quick to notice Tyler's errors and support him. Her tone and words were positive.
- ❑ Wade also sorted incorrectly, guessing more than listening to the beginning consonant sounds.
- ❑ Both Tyler and Wade were able to verbalize the guidelines they had used for sorting. They self-corrected their sorts after I modeled how to listen to the sounds of the key word and the picture.

Once children sorted these consonants quickly and accurately, Terri sent *J* and *W* word sorts home in plastic baggies. Her daily letter asked parents to help their children practice sorting and return the baggie the following day. She continued to invite parents into the sorting process, sending materials home after a child had achieved automaticity in class.

*Respond to what students can do by making sorts easier or harder.*   Start with two single consonant categories, then add a third, and a fourth when you know the children can sort four sounds. Move to consonant blends and clusters once children can hear and sort beginning consonant sounds.

Wade, Tyler, and Samantha can sort pairs of beginning single consonant sounds. Now, Terri invites them to sort pictures that match three sounds. "I add pictures of words that start with *T*, Tyler's name, then I make the task even more challenging by adding pictures that make the *S* sound in Samantha's name." As much as possible, Terri taps into words that start the way her students' names start when making the sorting tasks harder. Terri introduces sorting for three sounds with different consonant combinations.

*Use a key letter and/or picture to head the sorts.*   The key words can be children's names, key pictures from alphabet charts, pictures from books or magazines such as *Scholastic News*, or calendar photographs.

*Direct the sorting activities and think aloud modeling how you do it.*   In kindergarten, Terri and Lisa sit with each child as he or she sorts pictures. Terri models how to name the picture, emphasizing the beginning sound, then says the sound the key letter or word makes. Wade sorts words that start with *b* or *p*. He says, *ball, b-b-ball* and then says *book*, the key picture. Wade repeats *b-b-b-b-ball, b-b-b-book* three times. "I think they're the same," he says and tentatively places the picture of a ball under the key picture, looking at Terri for a sign that he's made the correct choice.

At this point Wade receives lots of positive reinforcement for matching the sounds. "I want to build Wade's confidence," Terri says, "so Wade focuses on hearing the sounds, not worrying about whether he can complete the sort successfully."

*Select pictures that children can easily name and sort.*   Before asking children to sort pictures, make sure they can associate the word with the picture. You'll find excellent pictures for sorting in the appendix of *Words Their Way: Word Study for Phonics, Vocabulary, and Spelling Instruction* by Bear and colleagues ([1996] 2000).

*Say the word for each sorted picture again to make sure it has been placed under the correct key letter or picture.*   In Terri's and Lisa's classes this becomes a habit because children always check their sorts.

Melissa Foltz continues picture sorting with children in her transitional first-grade class. Her students each have word study notebooks. Once Melissa hears each child check a sort, the children paste their sorts into a notebook. Keyana completes picture sorts for beginning single consonants (Figure 7–14), then consonant blends, clusters, and digraphs. Next, she sorts pictures for short and long vowel sounds and pastes correct sorts in her notebook. Melissa has children like Keyana, who are ready to sort words for short and long vowel patterns work with her, then paste correct word lists into their notebooks (Figure 7–15).

In conjunction with developing phonemic awareness, teachers in the Head Start and kindergarten classes that I supported also modeled how to use pretend or imaginative talk and drama to stimulate imaginative play and make it visible to the teacher (Pellegrini and Galda 2000, Wilhelm 2003).

## The Value of Imaginative Talk and Play

The rich, inviting smells of bread baking always transport me back to my Polish grandmother's three-room apartment. Bubbe Annie lived on Wallace Avenue in the Bronx, New York, across the street from my family's apartment house. After school on Friday afternoons, I always stopped at Bubbe Annie's before going home.

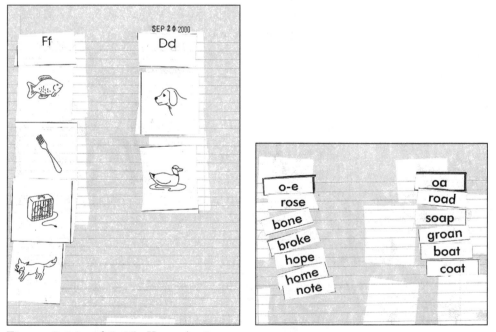

**Figures 7–14 and 7–15.** Keyana's picture sorts

Stacked on the kitchen table were six glistening, braided challahs, special breads that Jewish people eat on the Sabbath. There was one for each of her three daughters, two for her sisters, and one for Bubbe's sabbath dinner.

Bubbe Annie was a collector, and her house was filled with chotchkas or things on living room tables and in an oversized china closet. Every chotchka had a history. The best Fridays, however, were when I returned to Bubbe's apartment to spend the weekend. I never tired of asking, "Tell me the story about this hat, this wine glass, or this statue of a goat."

The stories she told felt mysterious and grand. "The Rabbi's wife sipped tea from this cup. Your Aunt Leah—you're named for her—sewed this locket into the lining of her coat when she came to America. The locket belonged to your great grandmother who wore a wig after her wedding. Religious women cut off their hair before their wedding and wore wigs." Then she'd open the locket and I'd pore over the faded portrait of Aunt Leah and imagine myself wearing a coat with the hidden locket, sitting in the bowels of a steamship bound for Ellis Island.

Bubbe Annie's stories were fodder for my inner, imaginative life. I donned her peach crepe wedding dress, put a white dishtowel on my head for a veil, and became a bride. Or I transported myself to the tiny farm in Poland where Bubbe Annie grew up. Master of the spoken script for these dramatic simulations, I played all the characters and found my props in Bubbe's closets and dresser draws.

One rainy Sunday, when the day lingered and felt endless, I told Bubbe Annie, "I'm bored." I'll never forget her response that I've translated from her Yiddish, "Take you head and knock it against the wall three times." Which I dutifully did.

I recalled that moment many times while playing with friends, raising my own children, and while teaching. Reflecting on Bubbe Annie's words has helped me understand that boredom is extremely beneficial to developing the imagination and pretend life. You see, Bubbe Annie was not about to solve my problem. She was sure that by the third time my head connected with the kitchen wall, I'd think of something to do. In today's world where ready-made visual images from television, electronic games, computers, and videos bombard children's minds, we teachers have to provide opportunities for and model how to engage in pretend play (Pellegrini and Galda 2000, Owocki 1999).

### Pretend Play and Early Literacy

Pretend play is an important part of learning in four- and five-year-old programs. According to Pellegrini and Galda (2000), three-year-olds are able to engage in meaningful pretend play with peers. When pretend play is social, young children learn to use language to negotiate roles and rules, to retell or create original stories, and to include props that enhance and advance their imaginative play.

*Negotiation*    The need to negotiate arises when pairs or small groups of children disagree with roles assigned or classmates' interpretations of a book or event to be dramatized. "That's not the way the story goes," or "I don't think the stepmother talks like that," or "You can be the princess this time if I can be next time," are examples of children initiating negotiations during pretend play. Such interactions help them explore the language of compromise and the words for alternate suggestions. Social play encourages children to clarify what they mean and how they believe characters and people talk and act.

*Narrative Language*    From read-alouds and from observing adults at home, in the community, and at school, children integrate narrative language and story structures into pretend play. Whether they are pretend shopping for groceries or at the doctor's office or dramatizing a fairy tale, play includes becoming different characters, planning the scene with the elements of narrative: setting, problem, outcomes, beginning, middle, and end.

*Props*    Open-ended props such as blocks, cartons, a blanket, and pieces of fabric require that the children devote more time to explaining and negotiating what each prop represents. Explicit props, such as a stethoscope, grocery products, or post office supplies, clearly define the setting, permitting the children to focus on roles, shaping the text and the pretend talk. When a mixture of open-ended and explicit props are in centers, children have opportunities to practice a wide range of pretend play while building important emergent literacy skills.

### Play Centers Can Develop Literacy and the Imagination

Putting books in play centers is an invitation for children to make the story their own through drama. I observe this when Kaywan repeatedly chooses Ezra Jack Keats's *Over in the Meadow* (1971) during SSR. Keats's book is one that Kaywan's teacher, Danielle, has read more then fifteen times. First, Kaywan hugs the book; sometimes he kisses the cover; then he slowly turns the pages, relishing each illustration and retelling the story from memory. Books children come to treasure are ideal to place in literacy play centers.

Pretend play in an airport, grocery, bank center, or doctor's office can foster literacy development and enlarge background knowledge because these centers build on real-life experiences and offer children opportunities to use writing, talking, and reading in authentic ways (Owocki 1999). However, for any center to support children's literacy development, the teacher must first model how to use the center.

*Model How to Use Centers*    Before inviting children to play in centers, consider how children will sign up for centers. In one class, three boys controlled the block center, making it impossible for classmates to play there. I suggest that you alternate free choice with a rotation system. You can use a different color to mark a center. Place each center's color on a corkboard or the chalkboard and students' names beneath the colors. You might have blue for a book center, red for the grocery store, orange for the airport, and so on. In a forty-minute center block, you can have two rotations. If a group is deeply into a drama or simulation, let them remain to complete their play.

Don't put too many centers out at once, for your room will become crowded and cluttered. Moreover, too many choices can confuse young children. Instead, once all children have thoroughly enjoyed some centers, store them and bring in replacements. While you observe or work with an individual, a pair, or small group, children can work productively in centers as long as they understand how to play in them.

Always reserve time to explain and model how to play in centers at the start of the year and each time you introduce a new literacy center.

- ❑ Discuss the materials.
- ❑ Explain the guidelines for retrieving and returning materials.
- ❑ Model, in a think-aloud, how to use the center. Show children how you talk at the grocery store, in the doctor's office, at the bank, and so on. Many have few or no experiences visiting community stores and services. You may have to repeat your demonstrations or even work alongside a group until they can play independently. When I model, I take multiple roles and change my voice. In the veterinary clinic center, I portray the vet, the person with a sick cat, and the cat. At the restaurant, I'm the hostess, the waiter, and the couple ordering and eating dinner. Such scaffolding gives children permission to be dramatic and imaginative while it also builds background knowledge and the specialized vocabulary for pretend play in a wide range of situations.
- ❑ Create behavior guidelines. Discuss sharing materials, listening to one another, negotiating and compromising, taking turns, and noise levels. I encourage teachers to post a list of positive behaviors and reread the items each day to remind children of their responsibilities.

### Play Center Behaviors

- ❑ Speak softly.
- ❑ Listen to friends.
- ❑ Take turns using materials.
- ❑ Take turns playing different roles.
- ❑ Work together to plan.
- ❑ Stay in your play area.

*Suggestions for Creating Centers That Support Literacy*   Literacy rich environments include writing, reading, thinking, planning, and talking. In each play center, include paper, pencils, books, puppets, clothing, magazines, and props that relate to the center's theme.

1.  *Thematic center.*   Stock with props and materials that foster authentic participation. In a bank center, place deposit and withdrawal slips, checks, pens, pencils, a calculator, and play money. For the restaurant, you might have menus, a notepad for orders and pencils, plastic dishes and utensils, a large tray, napkins, aprons, chefs hats, a small chalkboard and chalk for noting daily specials, a calculator, play money, checks, and an outdated credit card.

2.  *Art center.*   Has one or two easels; large, old shirts for artists' smocks; different sizes of blank paper; watercolors; paint brushes; finger paints; crayons; markers; and pencils. You can also include materials to make puppets that children can use for retellings and dramas: socks, colored pieces of felt, glue, and popsicle sticks. Also include projects that relate to what you're currently studying. For example, children can make different kinds of clouds when they study the weather.

3.  *Book center.*   Contains a beloved book and some props that will help children reenact parts of the story. You can also make this a bookstore where you have a display rack with books, paper and pencils for receipts and shopping lists, paper or plastic bags, and cushions and beanbags for reading.

4.  *Writing center.*   Includes different shapes and sizes of blank paper and notepads. Create blank books by stapling paper together. In plastic trays, place marker pens, crayons, and pencils. This center enables children to explore and develop their own writing ideas. Your local printing shop will be happy to supply you with a box of scrap paper of all different sizes.

5.  *Science center.*   Contains a class animal, terrarium, fish tank, rocks, sea shells, and so on, for children to observe, touch when appropriate, and write about. For several weeks, one teacher's science center consisted of a bird feeder outside a window. Include blank paper, crayons, markers, and pencils for recording observations and composing original stories. You can connect this center to your curriculum. In one kindergarten class, the teacher brought in an ant farm so students could observe the ants at work.

6.  *Math center.*   Stock these with calendars, manipulatives for counting, and board games. Store these materials on a shelf and have children take the materials to their table or a space on the floor.

7.  *Solo spaces.*   Sometimes, children don't want to play with a peer in a center. I respect that need by providing quiet places for reading, daydreaming, or playing alone. Have several cushions, beanbags, and a small table or desk

where children can play independently. Discuss this need with the class to build respect for the desire to be alone.

*Start Collecting Those Materials!*   Think about the play centers you want to bring to your students. Plan centers that connect to your curriculum so children can experience the connections between books read aloud, guest speakers, field trips, and play. Here are some tips to get you started.

- ❏ Make a list of your top ten to twelve centers.
- ❏ Brainstorm, for each center, the materials you will need. For example, for a post office collect used stamps, envelopes, boxes, calculator, pencils, pens, date stamper and pad, and a plastic dish to place posted mail. I bring some items from home and visit our local post office and ask for some priority mailing envelopes and boxes. Visit the bank to gather literacy materials. Send a letter home and ask parents to save empty food boxes and cans with smooth-edged tops for your grocery store center.
- ❏ Keep a list of the items you've placed in each center in a notebook. Two to three times a week, check the centers to see if you need to replenish supplies. Note where you obtained materials. Clear records make setting up centers and keeping track of materials easier. Children playing in a center often suggest other materials; jot these in your notebook.

*Finding Room for Centers*   At a faculty meeting, Julie Stringer, one of Powhatan's kindergarten teachers thought out loud, "My room is too small to have lots of centers set up. What can I do?" Many teachers face Julie's problem—a solvable problem once you determine where to store centers.

- ❏ Assess your room and decide where to place centers, making sure there's enough space between each so the children don't disturb one another.
- ❏ Decide which centers can be stored on shelves or in plastic crates, allowing children to take materials to their table or a designated space.
- ❏ Place the contents of centers, such as props for pretending to be a firefighter, nurse, policeman, for dramatizing a fairy tale, a doctor's kit, or grocery supplies, in labeled boxes or plastic crates that can be stacked. During center time, set up those boxes you wish to offer the children. When pretend playtime ends, children can carefully return materials to the correct box or crate and help stack them.

*Suggestions for Pretend Play Literacy Centers*   Once you start thinking about center possibilities, ideas flow. Your curriculum and your student population will help you develop literacy centers. Lisa Tusing and Terri Auckland wanted centers that could enlarge their students daily, community experiences because most had not spent time at the post office or a bank, at the firehouse or a farm.

When planning centers, consider what experiences your students bring with them as well as the themes you have planned. Adapt the list that follows to your student population. Reflecting on it will spark additional ideas.

- ❏ Airport
- ❏ Bakery
- ❏ Bank
- ❏ Book store
- ❏ Dentist's office
- ❏ Department store—clothing
- ❏ Doctor's office
- ❏ Garden shop
- ❏ Gas station
- ❏ Greeting card shop
- ❏ Grocery store
- ❏ Hospital
- ❏ Laundromat
- ❏ Library
- ❏ Movie theatre
- ❏ Museum
- ❏ Nursing home
- ❏ Pet shop
- ❏ Post office
- ❏ Restaurant
- ❏ Shoe store
- ❏ Veterinarian
- ❏ Zoo

Placing a beloved book and some simple props into a literacy center is easy. It's an ideal way to develop children's imaginations and build on their growing enjoyment of listening to stories read aloud.

*Dramatizing Books in Literacy Centers*    Charlotte Huck wrote words that resound with truth: "Never underestimate the power of a real story to take a child into the literacy world" (1992, 522). Reading books again and again foster this literacy development and deep entrance into story.

When I read *Bashi, Baby Elephant* by T. Radcliffe, I listen carefully to the children's talk and actions. Uvaldo and Channing refer to Bashi as if he is real, and he crops up in their conversations during writing workshop. "Bashi was scared in the mud. Bashi thought the lions would eat him up. I can trot like Bashi." The story has captured the children's imagination and they enter the character's life, feeling and talking, and thinking like that character (Coles 1989). These are the kinds of books that I place in centers, so children can dramatize parts that spoke to them. Here's one enactment based on *Bashi, Baby Elephant.*

**CENTER PROPS:** The book: T. Radcliffe. *Bashi, Baby Elephant.* 1997. Illus. J. Butler. New York: Puffin.

**PRE-DRAMA NEGOTIATIONS:** The children discuss which events they will dramatize. The first is when Bashi sinks into muddy water. They agree where the water will be and who will play the lion, Bashi, and mother.

UVALDO:  Help! Help! I'm stuck.

HOLLY:  I'm a lion. I'm hungry.

CHANNING: I'm coming. I'll get you out.
UVALDO: I'm scared. The lions will get me.
TIMEA: All of us will help.
UVALDO: I'm free.
CHANNING: Stay close to me.

**CENTER PROPS:** The book and a list of rhyming words the children created. Beatrice Schenk De Regneirs. *Was It A Good Trade?* [1984] 2002. Illus. Irene Haas. New York: HarperCollins.

**NEGOTIATIONS:** The pair decides that they will make trades that rhyme. "They can't be silly words," says Kirsten, "They have to be real things." Laurie nods in agreement.

KIRSTEN: You have to rhyme the things.
LAURIE: I traded a cook for a book.
KIRSTEN: I traded a bat for a hat.
LAURIE: I traded a cow for a sow. [Giggles.]
KIRSTEN: I traded the sun for a bun.

Books in centers, along with invitations to act out parts or to imitate specific language play, naturally encourage children to integrate literate language into their play.

*Integrated Learning Centers*   Connecting centers to a theme or topic such as the ocean, weather, pets, or gardens raise children's awareness of the links between spoken and written language in several areas of the curriculum. I recommend authentic activities that encourage hands-on learning. Avoid standard worksheets that invite children to color, follow the dots, match pictures and words, and so on. The emergent literacy unit for a study called "Under the Sea" is an example of integration that asks children to continually construct meaning by doing.

### Emergent Literacy Unit: *Under the Sea*

*Art center*   Stock this center with photographs of fish and sea creatures that will help the children make stick puppets or fish masks from paper plates to use in creating pretend play dramas.

*Science center*   Place a fish tank in the center and teach the children the names of the fish and plants. Demonstrate how to observe the fish. In the center, place a chart with a drawing of each kind of fish in the tank and the fish's name. Include blank paper, crayons, pencils, and markers so the children can draw and write about their observations.

*Math center*   Place, in a basket, counting books about the ocean, fish, and unusual sea creatures. Include blank books, pencils, crayons, and markers for students to write original counting books.

*Social Studies center*   Display a map of the world on a bulletin board or a wall. As you study fish and other underwater dwellers, help children tape their first names on the ocean or sea closest to where they live.

*Dramatic play*   Have children pretend they are different fish using sock puppets or masks. Decorate the center with children's drawings of fish. You can also build a fishing supply store and stock it with fish nets, small fishing poles, cash register or calculator, receipt pad, pencils, and a shoe box of pictures of fish children can "catch."

*Blocks*   Help the children imagine that this center has become an underwater sea world. Include flippers, snorkels, and labels for their holding tanks such as, *Dolphins*, *Whale Tank*, and *Please Don't Feed the Fish*.

*Housekeeping*   Discuss foods made from fish, mammals, and crustaceans that live in the sea. In this center, post famous dishes and the country that's known for each one (e.g., herring in Norway, fish and chips in England, smoked salmon in Scotland, whale blubber in Alaska, caviar in Russia, oysters and crabs in Maryland). (You can locate these places on the word map in the social studies center.) Include metal pots, plastic bowls, and spoons so children can pretend cook fish dishes.

Children playing at centers provides you with time to scaffold play as well as carefully observe what the children say and do.

## Observing Children During Center Time

Yetta Goodman coined the phrase *kidwatching* (1978); she encouraged teachers to pose questions about students' literacy learning, observe them at work, and take notes. When you systematically observe children during pretend center play, you add an important aspect to your growing knowledge of their literacy development that their writing and talking also provide. What you observe and note during play can inform your instructional decisions for each child.

### Guidelines for Observing Children

These suggestions enable you to think about and develop a helpful kidwatching process.

- ❑   Observe one to two children during center time. Start with one child if the process is new. Remember, you will most likely divide your time between observing and supporting individuals and groups.
- ❑   Continue these observations for two to three days. Always explain to the children what you are doing and how it helps you and them, avoiding them imagining that you are recording behaviors that aren't productive.

- ❑ Record your observations on sticky notes. I like to prepare a set of sticky notes, then place these on a clipboard. On each note I print the child's name, date, and the center's name.
- ❑ Store notes in a literacy file folder or in a loose-leaf notebook with dividers for each child. Keep observational checklists and samples of students' journal and independent writing in these folders.
- ❑ Reread and reflect on your notes, checklists, and students' written work to interpret these assessments and plan instruction (see Chapter 9).
- ❑ Consider the following questions as you observe; they can support your gathering of important information and help keep your notes objective.

    What knowledge of narrative story structure does play reveal?
    What do I learn about children's ability to share? To negotiate? To compromise?
    Do the children use words appropriate for the center play?
    What do I learn about how children use writing?
    What aren't children doing that it's important to note?
    What have I learned that can help me plan instruction?

Figures 7–16 and 7–17 are observational notes for Uvaldo and Timea taken while writing about Cynthia Rylant's *Scarecrow* (1998). Note how I describe the behaviors and quote words, but avoid editorializing. Objective notes equip me to interpret a range of information during a reflective period, instead of making judgment calls while I'm watching and noting.

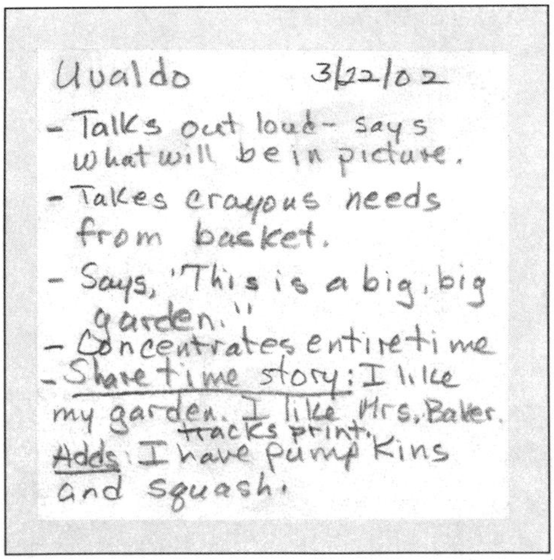
Uvaldo 3/22/02
- Talks out loud- says what will be in picture.
- Takes crayons needs from basket.
- Says, "This is a big, big garden."
- Concentrates entire time
- Share time story: I like my garden. I like Mrs. Baker.
Adds: I have pumpkins and squash.
tracks print.

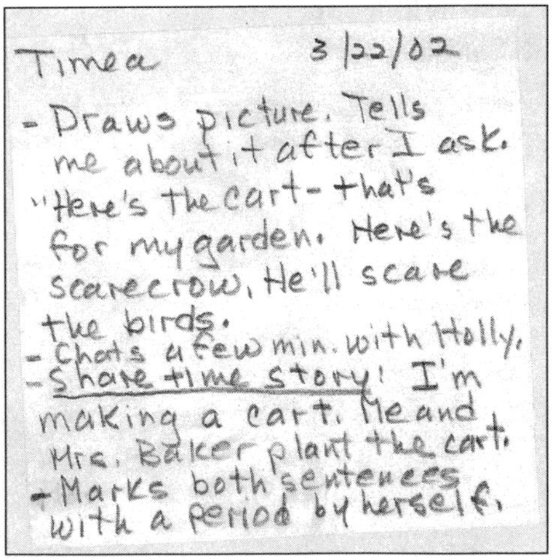
Timea 3/22/02
- Draws picture. Tells me about it after I ask. "Here's the cart- that's for my garden. Here's the scarecrow. He'll scare the birds.
- Chats a few min. with Holly.
- Share time story: I'm making a cart. Me and Mrs. Baker plant the cart.
- Marks both sentences with a period by herself.

**Figures 7–16 and 7–17.** Observational notes for Uvaldo and Timea

# Checklist for Pretend Play in Book and Drama Centers

Name _____          Date observed _____

### Social Interactions                                    ### Additional Comments

_____ Shares materials.

_____ Listens to peers.

_____ Negotiates adjustments.

_____ Has positive outlook.

_____ Uses quiet voice.

_____ Accepts friend's ideas.

_____ Problem solves (roles, script).

_____ Changes roles willingly.

### Narrative and Story Language

_____ Creates stories with beginning/middle/end.

_____ Uses words appropriate for center.

_____ Integrates props into story line.

_____ Retells including story language.

_____ Uses puppets and masks to dramatize and retell.

_____ Includes characters and a problem.

_____ Connects to self during dramas and retellings.

### Book Knowledge

_____ Holds book correctly.

_____ Turns pages right to left.

_____ Tracks print with finger.

_____ Retells using pictures.

_____ Predicts before turning some pages.

_____ Asks questions about pictures/text.

_____ Drama includes characters, settings, problems, events, outcomes.

_____ Points to some print when telling the story.

_____ Reads some print in patterned/predictable texts.

**Figure 7–18.** Checklist for Pretend Play in Book and Drama Centers

© 2003 by Laura Robb from *Literacy Links*. Portsmouth, NH: Heinemann.

## Checklist for Writing Behaviors in Play Centers

Name _____          Date observed _____

**Written language**                    **Additional Comments**

_____ Uses scribbles.

_____ Uses random letters.

_____ Mixes letters and numbers.

_____ Copies words from charts.

_____ Mixes directionality when writing.

_____ Writes from left to right.

_____ Spaces groups of letters/scribbles.

_____ Uses initial consonants.

_____ Uses initial and final consonants.

_____ Uses initial, final, and medial consonants.

_____ Includes vowels in words.

_____ Has some correct spellings.

_____ Spaces all words.

_____ Uses punctuation. (Note which kind.)

_____ Uses paper and notepads appropriately.

_____ Knows writing communicates ideas.

*Additional Comments:*

**Figure 7–19.** Checklist for Writing Behaviors in Play Centers

### *Checklist of Children's Book and Drama Behaviors in Play Centers*

Observing children's book and drama behaviors during center play can provide insights into their developing book and story structure knowledge. Use this list to guide your observations or to replace taking your own anecdotal notes (Figure 7–18) on page 217.

### *Checklist of Children's Writing Behaviors in Play Centers*

In literacy centers, writing is less open-ended because children use writing in the context of the center's theme. Use this list to guide your observations or to replace taking your own anecdotal notes (Figure 7–19).

## Closing Reflections

Because play reveals children's social interactions, their knowledge of narrative, and the language they use in specific places and situations, it is an important part of emergent literacy development.

As I visit kindergartens around the country and talk to teachers, I have discovered that time for play continually diminishes. The pressure from high-stakes testing has caused school districts to introduce reading instruction and bring back skill-and-drill worksheets, diminishing time spent on learning from play, a balanced read-aloud program, and writing workshop. These changes are insidious, slowly creeping into the curriculum and replacing how Gordon Wells described learning.

> We are the meaning makers—every one of us: children, parents, and teachers. To try to make sense, to construct stories, and to share them with others in speech and writing is an essential part of being human. (1986, 222)

Instead of bombarding children with stacks of worksheets or drilling phonics rules before they have book knowledge and concepts about print, create a curriculum that includes pretend and language play. That way you foster meaning making by enabling children to learn about written and spoken language by using it.

# 8

# School, Home, and Community Connections

*What the child is able to do today in conversation with a supportive adult, he or she will tomorrow be able to manage alone in that interior dialogue that he [Vygotsky] called inner speech.*

Gordon Wells, *The Meaning Makers: Children Learning Language and Using Language to Learn* (1986, 111–112)

When Yemi's brother Kokou wanders off while the pair are in the village market, Yemi begins a frantic search to find her younger brother. Reunited, the pair return home, and Yemi thinks out loud, telling Kokou that Mama must be worried. Mama's reply is worth reflecting on:

> "As my mama told me, and her mama told her, I will tell you. You weren't alone today, Yemi. We don't raise our children by ourselves. 'It takes a village to raise a child'" (Jane Cowen-Fletcher 1994).

In this story, the villagers who keep Kokou safe from any impending dangers symbolize the interconnectedness and interdependence of all community members.

Those interconnections place the responsibility for raising and supporting children on parents, schools, and others living in the surrounding community. This doesn't mean that parents abrogate their duties; it means that in addition to parents and caretakers, community members ought to play a role in supporting the young. Support, here, does not mean raising or teaching the children; it does mean that parents, caretakers, and the community work alongside schools to strengthen family and school literacy by forming learning partnerships. What happens, then, is that schools reach out to continually educate parents about literacy, and communities develop projects that support literacy development among parents, children, and schools.

Throughout this book, I have suggested ways to reach out to parents who I believe, want their children to be happy and successful at school. Now, I am also advocating community involvement in children's education. Linking home, school, and community poses challenges to all parties. Some level of literacy learning for each child began in a home that was part of a community long before the child entered school. The challenge is to find reasonable ways to involve parents, community members, and businesses in the literacy development of children.

## Schools Connecting to Homes

In the 1960s, most families of the children I taught had stay-at-home moms. These women signed up to participate in class projects, chaperone field trips, and teach individuals or small groups. Sometimes they took my morning and lunch recess duties, freeing me to scaffold the learning of several children. Each year, I could always count on mustering a core of parents who worked with me daily.

However, families have changed. Today, with working single parents and two parent homes where each has one or more jobs, parents can no longer volunteer to help teachers at school. Moaning about "those good old days" won't reverse these changes. Instead, one mission of schools and teachers is to share information with families by continually communicating with them and by creating one to two programs that tired parents will attend in the evening. Not every parent will be responsive and read letters or practice a skill with their child, but many will.

What follows are some ways you can forge solid home/school connections that educate parents and keep them informed of their children's progress.

### Before School Starts

I still have and treasure the note card my first grade teacher, Mrs. Lombardi, mailed to me before school opened. On the front is a picture of elves dancing in a flower-filled meadow. Inside, she wrote:

Dear Laura,

I can't wait for school to start. Then I will meet you and learn all about you. We'll have a great time reading and writing together.

Love,

Mrs. Lombardi

For years, I reread this note until the edges curled and yellowed from constant opening and closing. Oh! And I can still recapture how grand and important I felt the day my mom handed me the letter. I could read my name and see that my new teacher had written to me!

That's why I recommend sending a note card to each child in your class. Let them know that you can't wait to meet them, hear about their summer, and work with them. You can also invite them to bring a favorite toy or book on the first day. By the end of the first week, every child can talk about what they've brought. Those children who have no books at home and little book experience can observe their peers' enthusiastic talk about cherished books.

Instead of the note card, you might prefer writing a brief letter to the child that includes a copy of a short song, poem, or nursery rhyme displayed in your classroom (Fisher 1998). Invite parents to read and reread the poem to their child. On the first day, when you read the same rhyme to the class, children will relate to it and chime in on rhyming words and repeated phrases.

## Journal Writing

Most teachers use a composition notebook with primary lines. The first time you send the journals home, include a short note that explains what you want the child and parent to do (Figure 8–1).

---

Dear Parents,

Please set aside time in the evening for Justin to write in his journal. Justin can use pencils and/or crayons. Encourage him to draw a picture and then tell you about it. You can also ask Justin to write something about the picture. Please help Justin put the journal in his book bag, so he can show and talk about his writing to his friends at school.

Thank you for helping Justin grow as a writer.

Sincerely,

---

**Figure 8–1.** Letter to parents about journal writing

## Book Bags

Each Friday, send a book home with a record sheet that explains what you would like the parent or caretaker to do (see Appendix for record sheet). I like to start parents reading to children on the weekend when they have time to interact without feeling pressured.

Know your families and be sensitive to those adults who can't read. Consult the principal and last year's teacher if possible to discover parents who struggle with literacy. For this group, don't include the record form. Instead, telephone home and leave a message that explains you would like the adult to hear the child retell the story many times using the pictures in the book.

## Letters and Newsletters

Some teachers send home a weekly or bimonthly newsletter that chronicles the week's highlights, educates the parents about an aspect of literacy development, and can also ask parents to practice a skill the children are learning. During the six weeks of summer school, teaching assistants sent home a newsletter every Friday. Sharon Garber not only informs parents and asks them to help their child retell a story, she peppers the letter with praise for the children (Figure 8–2).

During summer school, Nancy Reedy writes a note home and asks parents to help their child learn a sentence he or she composed. Nancy includes sentences written by other children (Figure 8–3). She hopes the children will want to memorize their classmate's sentences, too. And three days later, all of them can read at least three of the sentences. Nancy's purpose for making this request is to help the children track print. On a large piece of chart paper, Nancy has written each sentence. During morning gathering, she invites children to come to the chart and use a pointer to read a sentence and track print by matching spoken words to the text.

## Scheduled Parent-Teacher Conferences

Most schools have two scheduled conferences a year: one in the fall and one in the spring. This is the ideal time to review children's work, celebrate progress, and show parents ways they can provide support at home. I suggest that teachers prepare for conferences by listing points to cover with parents and selecting pieces of writing to share. On the form there is room to note issues parents raised and teacher recommendations (Figure 8–4) on page 227.

I encourage teachers to divide points to discuss with parents into academic and social issues and work habits. Always start with positive statements so parents feel the child they love is improving. One of the most distressing telephone calls I fielded was from an extremely upset parent who attended a conference where the teacher

Dear Parents and Caretakers,

This was another fast and fun-filled week. We did so much, and there were days when we were unable to complete everything I had planned. What a wonderful group of children I have the privilege of teaching. They are all so interested, attentive, and enthusiastic about reading and writing.

This week we have been reading *Tommy at the Grocery Store* by Bill Grossman. It's about Tommy, the pig, who is left behind at the grocery store by his mother. He is mistaken for a salami, meat, a potato, soda bottle, banana, even a chair until Tommy's mother finds him. We retold the story many times and also looked for rhyming words. Please ask your child if he or she can retell the story to you and recall some rhyming words.

This week we have also been studying word families. We learned the following word families: *an* and *at*. Please help your child form words using these word families.

During writing workshop, the children continue to retell *The Three Bears*, including the beginning, middle, and end of the story. They also are writing their own stories about bears and sharing these with the class.

All of your children have written in their journals at home and brought journals back to school the next day. This shows me and the children how much you value their work. Children who write in their journals every evening for a week receive a special treat or privilege.

Ask your child to show you the word ring that's in a large, brown envelope. These are words your child wanted to learn to read. Practice reading them together, then return them on Monday.

Thanks for allowing me to share this time with your child.

Sincerely,

**Figure 8–2.** Classroom Newsletter

"never pointed out one good thing about my child." Making the list beforehand ensures that you will start with praise. Set priorities when discussing needs. I suggest you raise one or two needs. It's impossible and terribly frustrating, anyway, for parents to attend to myriad behaviors. The lists that follow are a starting point—they contain suggestions you can use that can also trigger other points you wish to raise.

### Academic Progress
❑ Knows upper- and lowercase letters.
❑ Matches sounds to letters.

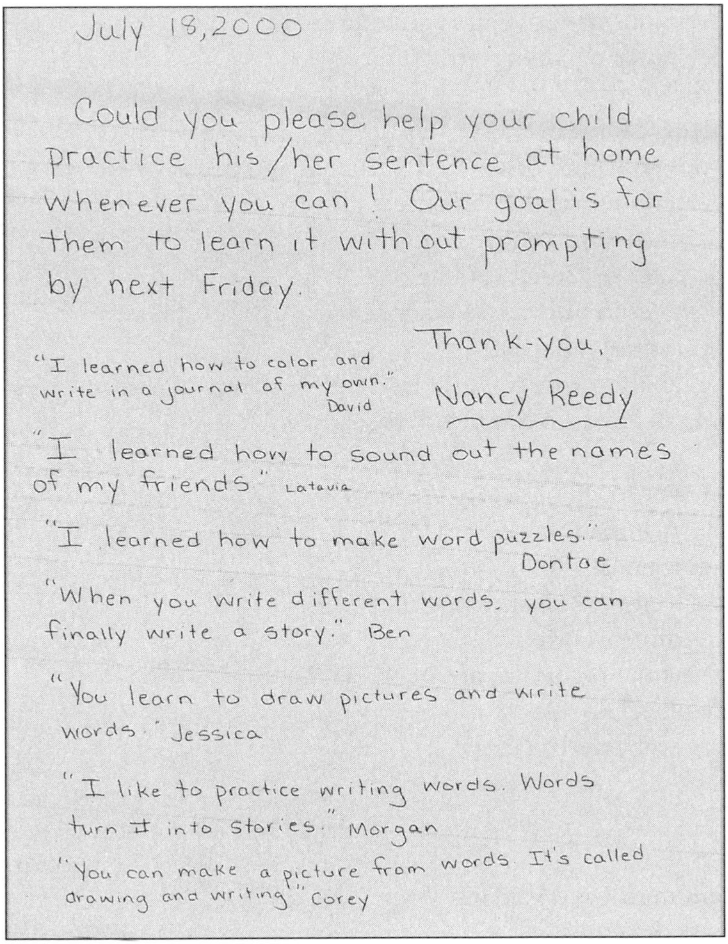

July 18, 2000

Could you please help your child practice his/her sentence at home whenever you can! Our goal is for them to learn it without prompting by next Friday.

Thank-you,

Nancy Reedy

"I learned how to color and write in a journal of my own."
David

"I learned how to sound out the names of my friends." Latavia

"I learned how to make word puzzles."
Dontae

"When you write different words, you can finally write a story." Ben

"You learn to draw pictures and write words." Jessica

"I like to practice writing words. Words turn ⫪ into stories." Morgan

"You can make a picture from words. It's called drawing and writing." Corey

**Figure 8–3.** Nancy's note home to parents

❏ Is developing these aspects of book knowledge: holds book correctly; turns pages from right to left; points to front and back covers, title page, dedication; knows print tells the story.

❏ Is developing these concepts about print: points to first and last word on a page; points to first and last letter of a word; points to spaces between words; points to upper- and lowercase letters; points out punctuation and knows its use; points to beginning and end of a sentence.

❏ Enjoys reading the room.

❏ Is developing these aspects of phonemic awareness: rhymes words, segments individual sounds and onset and rime, puts words together by listening to individual sounds and onset and rime.

- ❑ Understands narrative story structure.
- ❑ Understands nonfiction structure.
- ❑ Pretend-reads.
- ❑ Chooses reading during center time.
- ❑ Extends conversations with the teacher and peers.
- ❑ Discusses books and experiences.
- ❑ Participates in shared writing.
- ❑ Participates in shared reading.
- ❑ Participates in interactive read-alouds.
- ❑ Enjoys writing workshop.
- ❑ Writes about the story: scribbles, random strings of letters, letters and numbers, matches sounds and letters.

## Social Progress

- ❑ Shares materials.
- ❑ Makes friends.
- ❑ Works well with all classmates.
- ❑ Uses manners correctly.
- ❑ Respects the physical space of others.
- ❑ Abides by class rules.
- ❑ Solves problems by talking.
- ❑ Accepts teacher and peer support.

## Work Habits

- ❑ Listens during read-alouds.
- ❑ Follows directions.
- ❑ Completes work.
- ❑ Puts work in appropriate places.
- ❑ Helps with daily clean up.
- ❑ Enjoys nonacademic subjects.

These lists can help you set priorities about issues to discuss whether you are talking to a parent at school or on the telephone.

### Telephone Conferences

In addition to alerting parents to behavior or attendance issues, telephone them to celebrate progress. Terri and Lisa call parents in December to let them know the progress they see. Shana's mom hears that in September, her daughter recognized one uppercase and no lowercase letters. Now, Shana recognizes twelve uppercase and fifteen lowercase letters. And she can say the sound each makes! Terri and

# Parent-Teacher Conference

Name _____          Date _____

**Adults Attending Conference** _____

**Points to Cover During Conference**

**Issues Parents, Caretakers Raised**

**Teacher's Recommendations**

**Additional Comments**

**Figure 8–4.** Parent-Teacher Conference Form

## Mrs. Auckland's Kindergarten

| Alphabet Name | capital | lower | capital | lower | | | | | | | | | | | |
|---|---|---|---|---|---|---|---|---|---|---|---|---|---|---|---|
| Wade Barb | 19 | 13 | 35 | 22 | | | | | | | | | | | |
| Kelsey Barbero | 11 | 10 | 25 | 23 | | | | | | | | | | | |
| Samantha Clark | 22 | 14 | 26 | 23 | | | | | | | | | | | |
| Darrian Dysart | 3 | 3 | 20 | 24 | | | | | | | | | | | |
| Tyler Polk | 3 | 2 | 25 | 23 | | | | | | | | | | | |
| Hayden Ramage | 3 | 3 | 26 | 24 | | | | | | | | | | | |
| Shana Rauch | 1 | 0 | 12 | 15 | | | | | | | | | | | |
| Kali Tamkin | 22 | 21 | 26 | 25 | | | | | | | | | | | |
| Denzel Warr | 9 | 3 | 26 | 24 | | | | | | | | | | | |
| William Waybright | 0 | 0 | 1 | 1 | | | | | | | | | | | |

**Figure 8–5.** Terri's record sheet of children's alphabet language

Lisa use their assessment records to make these telephone calls and enlist parents' support to continue to move a child forward (Figure 8–5).

### Breakfast with the Teacher

I used to have "lunch with the teacher," but with working parents, I have changed these informal encounters to early morning. A pot of coffee and juice is enough. Let parents know what you will be serving so they and the children will eat breakfast at home. Some teachers do this once a semester, others two to three times a year. Schedule these from 7:30 A.M. to 8:00 A.M., which means parents depart before school buses arrive.

Parents will come with their children because they go from school directly to work. Your teaching assistant can read and play with the children. If you don't have someone to play with the children, invite a small group instead of all parents. Set up a play table with books, paper, crayons, and toys to keep the children occupied.

At these informal meetings, I encourage parents to ask questions about the program, not their child. It's also a great opportunity for me to explain what we are presently doing and suggest ways the parents can help children at home. Educating parents about the importance of reading to children and encouraging conversations about books is a challenge that can be met by instituting family reading nights at school.

### Family Reading Night

"I loved being able to read to my children without the telephone or doorbell ringing. No interruptions. Just the three of us and a book." Similar comments were made by several parents when I invited the group to reflect on their first family reading night experience at Cooley Elementary School in Clarke County, Virginia.

Family reading nights bring teachers, school administrators, moms, dads, children, babies, grandparents, aunts, and uncles together for an evening of reading aloud. You can schedule these every month or once a semester. The abundance of books to choose from and the relaxed environment combine to create a pleasurable evening for tired, working families who come to the school to read to their children. Administrators and teachers should attend and read with families for this sends the message that reading aloud is a top priority among educators. Use the following guidelines to help you, along with a team of teachers and administrators, plan and implement successful family reading nights.

- ❏ Meet with the PTO and invite them to support the program by providing refreshments for the first event.
- ❏ Coordinate calendar dates with the PTO and school administrators to prevent conflicts.
- ❏ Work with the school librarian to collect fiction and nonfiction picture books. Teachers can donate, for the evening, some books from their classroom libraries. Make sure the teacher's name is in each book so they can easily be reclaimed at the end of the evening.
- ❏ Two weeks before the first family reading night, write a collaborative letter with your students and send it home. Explain the purpose of the evening and what will happen. Decide on a time frame. I suggest starting at 6:30 P. M. and ending at 7:30 P. M. when the evening is for kindergarten and first-grade children.
- ❏ Ask parents to respond and return the letter. Display these in the classroom.

❏  Have the principal, during morning announcements, talk enthusiastically about the upcoming event and encourage the children to talk about it at home.

❏  Open the event in the school's gymnasium or multipurpose room.

❏  Model how to read aloud using a child who volunteers.

❏  Display picture books attractively so families can choose one or two books to read aloud.

❏  Explain where families can read to their children. You can use areas of the multipurpose room, hallways, and some classrooms. Make reading spaces comfortable and inviting with oversized pillows and beanbags.

❏  Let parents know that they can exchange books and continue reading until about fifteen to twenty minutes before the program is over.

❏  Meet in the library for punch and cookies, reflecting on the evening, and checking out library books.

As a result of attending family reading nights, many families joined a public library and began to read with children at home. Over the years, teachers and I have developed variations on the theme of family reading night in order to maintain interest and a high level of participation. Reading aloud, however, should always be the focus. You might want to try some of these different suggestions.

❏  *Indoor picnics.*  Invite families to arrive earlier, set down blankets in the multipurpose room, have a picnic-style dinner, and chat before reading stories aloud. This evening is quite popular, especially during cold, winter months.

❏  *Reading and desserts.*  Set up a potluck dessert party where families bring their best dessert. Close the evening by sampling goodies.

❏  *Local storytellers.*  Invite a teacher, parent, or community member who loves to tell stories to open and close the evening.

❏  *Feature children.*  Have children recite nursery rhymes, poems, or sing songs before the evening officially starts. An opportunity to watch their children will bring out many parents.

*Tips for Parents on Reading Aloud*   On your first family reading night or on your fall parent's night give a written copy of these tips (see Figure 8–6) to parents, caretakers, and relatives. Use them to model, with a child, the how-to's of reading aloud.

## Parent Centers

Several public school systems in Virginia and all over the country have opened parent centers. Schools usually locate these centers in a room in their central office building or in one of their schools. Stocked with professional books and materials that can educate parents about reading, writing, and ways to assist their

1. Find a comfortable place where you and your child can sit together. Let the book become a bridge between both laps.

2. Talk about front and back cover illustrations and the title. Predict what you think the story might be about or ask a question and think aloud saying, "I wonder if the story will answer my question."

3. Take a few minutes and encourage your child to talk about some of the pictures in the book. Your child might simply point to what he or she sees or make a connection to something similar that happened.

4. Encourage your child to predict what will happen next by stopping occasionally and saying, "What do you think will happen?" Allow lots of time for an answer. If none comes, then you can offer a prediction. Repeating this process will help your child know what to do.

5. Make understanding the story your focus. Every few pages, stop and retell what happened. Talk about the characters and what they do. Then, invite your child to help you retell small sections. Your child will let you know when he or she is ready to retell an entire section.

6. Connect a character or an event from the story to your child's life or your life. Clearly explain the connection and ask your child if he or she wants to add anything.

7. Point to the words as you read. This helps your child understand that print contains the story, and that we read from left to right.

8. Ask questions and give your child thinking time to figure out an answer. If your child doesn't answer after a minute or so, say, "Here's what I was thinking. . . ."

9. Choose books with your child at the school and public library.

10. Read aloud at bedtime and if possible, during the day.

11. Have a great time together and send the message that reading is fun!

**Figure 8–6.** Tips for Reading Aloud to Your Child

children with homework and studying, these centers also contain a television, a VCR, and professional and school-made videos for parents to watch. A checklist explains how parents can check out books as well as when to return them. School librarians, a team of teachers, and administrators organize and order materials for the center.

Open during the day, parent centers also have evening hours two to three days a week, making materials and the space available to working moms, dads, and caretakers. Parent study and support groups can meet there. Some teachers view a video with one or a small group of parents and use this common experience as a springboard for discussing how to read aloud, how to help a child with homework, or understanding and supporting different learning styles.

Funding can come from school budgets, a percentage of dollars raised by the PTO, and contributions by area businesses and corporations. Parent centers can raise adults' awareness of how important their role is in developing emergent literacy.

## Linking Homes to Schools

Like Peter Hannon, I believe that schools should bring children's home literacy experiences to school (1998). Hannon urges teachers to celebrate what parents and children do together at school. You can encourage this by sending a letter home that invites parents to send to school children's writing, drawing, family photographs, favorite books and magazines, collections of sea shells, rocks, toy cars, and projects children and parents complete together such as making a rag doll, a model airplane, or a book.

At school, you can honor and celebrate home literacy by reserving a bulletin board for displaying writing and drawing. Children can also bring projects, books, and so on to class and talk about them during show-and-tell. By linking literacy development in the home to school, you send children the message that reading, writing, and talking about projects adults and children complete together is very important work. Moreover, in the children's minds, you forge solid links between how and what they learn at home and at school. When you extend these links to include community members, you provide children with the kind of foundation that can strengthen emergent literacy and cultivate a lifelong commitment to learning and helping future generations.

## Communities Supporting Literacy

The ancient Chinese philosopher, Confucius, believed that if one person acted responsibly, then that person would influence another, and both in turn would influence two more people, until finally, an entire community changed. The example of one person could influence and transform the actions of a nation. Though some might consider this point of view naive politically, I believe that it has merit regarding community participation in education. Moreover, with tight state and federal budgets, school districts will need ongoing support from the private sector to maintain quality, public school education. Donations can be dollars for funding projects and/or community members working with children.

When one community business or group of citizens supports the education of children, advertise and celebrate their contributions in the local newspaper, by speaking to groups such as the Rotary and Lions Clubs, or by appearing on local television to talk about specific programs. Invite others to provide support and suggest ways that they can make meaningful contributions to children's education.

### Holiday and Summer Packets

At Robinson Elementary, Terri Auckland, Lisa Tusing, and I worried about children backtracking over long winter, spring, and summer vacations. We brought our concerns to the principal, Jane Rea Gaidos, who asked us to first compile a list of what we wanted in different packets. Then Jane said that she would telephone area businesses and large corporations to see if they would provide financial support. We needed for each packet:

- ❑ A box of crayons.
- ❑ A coloring book.
- ❑ Two pencils.
- ❑ A blank notebook.
- ❑ An alphabet card with key pictures to help students pronounce each letter.
- ❑ A double pocket folder.

Children would return their packets after winter and spring breaks, but keep them after summer. In addition to the supplies, Lisa and Terri included a selection of items appropriate to each child's development and progress.

- ❑ Number and alphabet follow-the-dot pictures.
- ❑ Picture sorts to review.
- ❑ Photocopied minibooks to color and pretend-read.
- ❑ Blank books.
- ❑ Copies of *Scholastic News* for kindergarten.
- ❑ Copies of poems and nursery rhymes the children had memorized from repeated readings.

Jane was able to interest several local businesses in supporting this take-home program, enabling Lisa and Terri to purchase supplies and make the packets. Stapled to the outside of each packet was a letter to parents, explaining the contents, explaining how to encourage and help their child, and also suggesting visits to the library to check out books.

School administrators and teachers wrote thank-you notes to the contributing companies and teachers mailed collaborative thank-you letters from the children. I also recommend that samples of the children's work accompany collaborative letters, so business leaders can see the benefits of their contributions. Showing appreciation and how dollars translate into improved learning are steps that can ensure ongoing support.

## Visiting Readers

When my nephew, Douglas, called from Indiana to invite me and his uncle to read to his class, I immediately wished that Winchester, Virginia, was not so far away from Lafayette, Indiana. Sending an audiocassette of us reading aloud was the best my husband and I could do. School read-aloud programs that invite adults to read aloud to children enable children to see that literacy is more than something for school. It sends the message that reading is what people from all walks of life do.

Guest readers can be school staff members, cafeteria workers, the custodial staff, school bus drivers, PTO officials, and administrators. Or schools can invite policemen, doctors, nurses, shopkeepers, waiters and waitresses, and so on to read aloud to a class once or several times.

You can ask guest readers to bring a book they loved to hear or one of their own children's favorites. I suggest keeping a large crate of top-notch picture books for reading aloud in the library, just in case the visiting reader needs some ideas. Let those who accept the invitation know that they can select a book at school a few days before their formal visit. Most readers like to have time to go over a text. Encourage visitors to explain how reading is important to their lives, helping children understand that reading well is for daily life, for professional life, and for the personal pleasure books bring.

## Book Buddies

One morning, I walked into my classroom at Johnson Williams Middle School balancing two cartons of picture books. A kindergarten class at Berryville Primary School had delivered a collaborative letter inviting each of my sixteen seventh- and eight-grade at-risk learners to become a young child's reading buddy. My class eagerly accepted. My students drew names of kindergartners that I had placed in a paper bag, then wrote a letter, introducing themselves to their young buddies.

That morning my students eagerly unpacked boxes of picture books and pairs browsed through them. One student walked up to me, holding an open book in the palms of both hands and said, "So this is a picture book." Never read to at home, this student's main school memory was completing worksheets. I'm sure many of his primary teachers read aloud. The experience, however, was not imprinted in his memory.

For three weeks, older students plunged into the world of picture books. The need to select titles to read to their younger buddies liberated initial feelings of reading "baby books" and freed them to discover authors and stories they had never read. Once they read and enjoyed three to four books, students practiced reading aloud with each other. Training them to read aloud to younger children increased their confidence, but also showed them how to be active and responsive readers, making the book even more enjoyable. My students learned about the parts of a book, making predictions, allowing time for the children to enjoy the pictures and ask questions and make connections. Pairs placed the book on both laps creating a bridge to connect reader and listener. Students practiced alternating roles of reader and young buddy, and during a class period read several books.

On the first meeting between middle school and kindergarten students, sixteen young children, wearing name tags, tentatively marched into their school's multi-purpose room. Older students gently grasped their buddy's hand and led them to chairs, benches, or pillows for thirty minutes of reading aloud. Over several weeks, friendships developed from sharing stories. Comments such as, "My buddy saw me in the grocery store and ran over to hug me," and "My buddy called me as I walked by the front porch of his house. He waved a book he was reading and showed it to me," caused older students to recognize that by reading aloud, they were making a deep impression on the younger children. As a result of the buddy program, several older students' negative attitudes toward reading diminished.

A poll, taken by the American Library Association and Gallup in 1989 surveyed high school seniors across the country. The purpose of the survey was to discover if high school seniors intended to continue to read after graduation. The results were disheartening: 80 percent of those questioned said they would not voluntarily choose to read again. Now, when these students marry and have children, I doubt that most will work diligently to create a literate home environment, for they have not forged connections to books and reading. A book buddy program that requires every student, before high school graduation, to learn the importance of reading aloud, how to read aloud effectively, and how to use these skills with young children, can transform negative feelings toward reading. In addition, young adults can relearn much about the reading process they might have missed. By reading aloud to young children, older students directly experience how to read books as well as the treasures books contain: great stories that reflect our lives and the lives of other cultures, new information, and accounts of the past and future. Hopefully, helping their buddies will also help older students become lifelong readers.

*Guidelines for Creating a Book Buddy Program*

The suggestions that follow can help you plan and implement a book buddy program.

### Setting Up the Program
❏ Contact a primary school teacher near your school. Explain the project and invite the teacher to participate by having her students collaborate to write a letter of invitation to your students.

❑ Work out meeting times with the primary teacher. Scheduling five to seven meetings is a good start. Ask an administrator to arrange transportation for your students. Some schools are close enough for students to walk.

❑ Have the primary teacher give you a list of the names of students.

❑ Read the letter from younger students to your class and post it on a bulletin board or wall.

❑ Help older students choose a buddy. Place each primary child's name on a piece of paper and fold it. Put the names in a bag or small box and have your students choose one. If the ratio of primary to older students is not equal, have some older students work with two book buddies or two older students work with one child.

❑ Reserve time for your students to write a letter to their book buddies. In the letter students can introduce themselves, discuss their hobbies, favorite sports, and talk about what will happen when they meet.

## Training Older Students to Read Aloud

❑ Gather picture books from the primary school's library and/or your public library.

❑ Model, for your students, how to effectively read aloud. In addition to using expression, making dramatic pauses, and recreating characters' voices, have students think aloud and discuss the title, author, illustrator, and front and back cover illustrations. Next focus on the endpapers, title page, dedication, and holding a book so both readers can see it.

❑ Invite students to ask questions about your demonstration. Repeat the modeling until you sense that students understand the process.

❑ Form reading partners.

❑ Invite partners to take turns being older and younger student and read aloud the book each selected.

❑ Circulate around the room and offer support, encouragement, and praise as pairs practice.

## First Meeting

❑ Allow twenty to twenty-five minutes for each book buddy session. (This does not include travel time.)

❑ Encourage older students to talk to their buddies before plunging into reading aloud. Getting to know one another is an important part of this relationship.

❑ Have older students write an enthusiastic letter to their buddies, celebrating this first experience.

❑ Encourage the primary teacher to collect children's reactions, record these on chart paper, and send them to your students.

❑ Continue writing back and forth.

❑ Extend the program beyond seven meetings if both groups can find the time and the school can continue to arrange transportation.

## Pediatricians and Obstetricians

Ask pediatricians and obstetricians for permission to include, in their waiting rooms, school-designed lists on how to read aloud and ways parents can build a strong home literacy environment. Explain to these professionals that the materials they feature can influence parents' attitudes toward literacy.

Suggest that these doctors consider ordering from the International Reading Association, brochures to keep in their office for parents to read. Brochures come in Spanish and English and multiple copies are inexpensive. Write to the International Reading Association, 800 Barksdale Road, PO Box 8139, Newark, DE 19714-8139. Here are some titles that can educate parents:

❑ *Beginning Literacy and Your Child: A Guide to Helping Your Baby or Preschooler Become a Reader*, No. 1028-840.
❑ *I Can Read and Write! How to Encourage Your School-Age Child's Literacy Development*, No. 1029-841.
❑ *Get Ready to Read! Tips for Parents of Young Children*, No. 1017-841.
❑ *Make the Most of Television: Tips for Parents of Young Viewers*, No. 1024-841.
❑ *What Is Family Literacy? Getting Involved in Your Child's Literacy Learning*, No. 1044-841.

You can also share these brochures with parents on registration day, at parents or family reading nights and place them in parent centers. Beside reading materials, community programs that offer parents hands-on experiences with books and using public libraries, can transform adults' attitudes toward literacy.

## An Innovative Librarian's Project: BOOKSMART

I met Noreen Bernstein in Winchester, Virginia; she was the children's librarian at our local public library. Her programming for children always focused on bringing families into the library. Under Noreen's direction, the number of families with young children who used the library and attended programs more than doubled in one year.

Noreen brought her high energy, expertise, innovative programming, and never-waning enthusiasm to Williamsburg and James City County, when she accepted the position of Head of Youth Services for both libraries.

After Noreen read about the Literacy Links program in *Redefining Staff Development: A Collaborative Model for Teachers and Administrators* (Robb 2000b), she telephoned me to discuss an idea the book provoked. Several telephone calls later, Noreen had formulated the BOOKSMART project that would bring library staff, books, parents, and preschool children together for two hours on Monday through Thursday. The next step was to find a grant in order to fund the five-week project. On an Internet listserv, Noreen had read about Square One that offered grants for reading readiness initiatives. With the assistance of a staff member, Noreen completed the grant form and submitted it.

BOOKSMART, a pilot family literacy program created by Noreen Bernstein and the Youth Services staff of the Williamsburg Regional Library in Virginia, served forty prekindergarten children. Now funded by Square One of the Hampton Roads Partnership, the program became a collaborative effort among James City County, Head Start, the Williamsburg-James City County School System, and the library.

The goals of the program were to increase emergent literacy in preschool children and educate their parents about reading aloud and services they could tap into at the library.

*Training Day for the BOOKSMART Staff*   The sixty staff members for the program included the Youth Services library staff, as well as staff from Head Start and Bright Beginnings, from the Child Development Resources Center, and from the primary grades of area public schools. Training day was at one of the two sites where prekindergarten children attended their daily programs. BOOKSMART was held at both these sites so that the library did not have to provide additional bus services. Moreover, everyone felt that it was important for young children to remain in their own school environment.

After the first meeting, Noreen telephoned me and said, "This was the first time these people had been together and it was awesome to feel the energy and enthusiasm for constructing a program we all passionately believed would help children." Each group had areas of expertise and suggested different ways to develop emergent literacy. What Noreen learned from these planning meetings was, "That one of the best roles the library could play in this process was serving as a catalyst to bring these community groups together."

During the training day, adults experienced the program just the way the children would. Noreen believed that these simulations would deepen the staff's understanding of each learning station and better equip them for supporting the children. Noreen and her staff selected the five weekly themes, the weekly giveaway books, and the graduation-from-the-program book. Part of training day was reading the books and discussing the themes.

- ❑ **Weekly themes:**   Colors, Counting, Rhymes, Food, and Animals
- ❑ **Weekly giveaway books:**   Purchased with program funds, these matched weekly themes. Everyone agreed that it was important to get books into the children's homes to be reread and treasured.

1. *The Little Mouse, The Red Ripe Strawberry and the Hungry Bear* by Don Wood.
2. *White Rabbit's Color Book* by Alan Baker.
3. *Feast for 10* by Cathryn Falwell.
4. *Silly Sally* by Audrey Wood.
5. *The Cow that Went Oink* by Bernie Most.

❑ **Graduation book:**   Every child received an autographed copy of *Matthew A.B.C.* by Peter Catalonotto. Graduation concluded with a tea for the staff, children, and the kindergarten teachers they would have in the fall.

*Experiences That Reached the Children*   For each weekly theme, the staff created learning stations that groups of children rotated through at the two sites that housed the program. Noreen divided the twenty children at each site into five groups of four. Each small group spent twenty minutes in a station working on the following.

❑ Book walking to teach concepts about print and build background knowledge by studying illustrations.
❑ Rhyming games with nursery rhymes.
❑ Drawing and telling the picture's story.
❑ Storytelling to develop listening.
❑ Book buddy reading where one adult read to two children.

   Each child received a journal for drawing pictures and recording their stories and responses to what they were learning.

*Educating the Parents*   Every Friday evening, parents met in the library. BOOK-SMART funds provided dinner for parents, children in the program, and siblings. Halfway through the program, parents brought favorite ethnic dishes to supplement the library dinners. If requested, James City County provided transportation to and from the library. After dinner, children attended a forty-five to fifty minute program that BOOKSMART staff chaperoned. While a puppet show, juggler, musicians, or storytellers entertained the children, their parents worked with the library staff on:

❑ Getting acquainted with the library through a walking tour or a treasure hunt that focuses on books for preschoolers and parent resources.
❑ Receiving a library card and checking out books for themselves and their children.
❑ Learning to interactively read aloud to their children.
❑ Experiencing the value of a picture walk through a book.
❑ Telling stories with wordless picture books.
❑ Making stick puppets for retelling stories.

The library gave each parent a tote bag with crayons, scissors, glue sticks, old magazines to cut up, and blank books. Each bag also contained a book for parents about reading aloud and literacy development: *Book Steps* by Alix K. Miller (2000). Twenty-two out of thirty-nine families attended Friday evening programs every week. Several teachers and their spouses also came; some stayed with the children, others worked with the parents.

By the third week, most parents were volunteering to lead picture walks and read-alouds and share personal stories. Noreen emphasized to the parents that literacy experiences don't always require books. "Sharing family stories and cultural histories are also a part of the process." Older siblings often chose to attend the parent sessions instead of the entertainment, learning how to read aloud and tell stories.

*What Noreen and Her Staff Learned* "Space for this type of project is crucial," Noreen pointed out. A small space means reducing the number of children so they can move through the learning stations without interfering with one another. She also recommends avoiding distractions such as a piano or toys, for these can divert children's attention while they are working in small groups as they move to different stations.

Everyone felt that the program should run an entire school year, perhaps once or twice a week. Lengthening the program would offer the children more time to absorb and practice emergent literacy skills and extra time for the teachers to observe students. In addition, they felt that the staff needed more time to exchange stories about the children.

The library's Youth Services staff observed the need to work with and support parents and preschool educators—a need which they hope to fulfill with BOOKSMART and programs like *Feed Me a Story*.

## Feed Me a Story *Project*

Noreen Bernstein developed the idea for this unique partnership with a local supermarket by reviewing data on attendance at library preschool story hours. Data over the last ten years showed a marked drop in attendance. According to Noreen, "Lifestyles have changed. There are so many working moms and single parent families, all with children in child care. And the traditional story times just don't work for them. I believed that what we needed was a storytime that fit into the one-stop shopping mode."

First, Noreen called the manager of Ukrops Super Market, a family-owned chain with headquarters in the Richmond, Virginia, area—a chain known for its commitment to and participation in community projects. The manager loved the name of the project, *Feed Me a Story*, and gave the library's Youth Services a grant toward purchasing books to give away to participants.

Next, Noreen applied for and received funding from the Loleta Fyan Grant from the American Library Association. After the first year, funding for the one-hour program came from the library's budget and donations from Ukrops and other community organizations. Local newspaper articles that celebrated the Saturday storytime program heightened community interest and ultimately involvement.

*Materials for the Program*    Here's how you can organize your own *Feed Me a Story* program. You'll need:

- ❏ Two quilts or blankets to place on the tile floor for children and parents to sit on while listening to stories.
- ❏ Several costumes of children's favorite literary characters that a staff member wears, such as Clifford, Max and Ruby, Arthur, Amelia Bedelia, and so on. This is a big hit among the children.
- ❏ A library book-drop in the store for families to return books checked out of the library. This makes returning books convenient.
- ❏ A healthy snack that Ukrops or the sponsoring supermarket provides each Saturday morning.
- ❏ Books for each child attending the program. The first year, Noreen used most of the grant money to give away books every week. Now, she and her staff select, at random, one Saturday a month to give each child attending *Feed Me a Story* a book.
- ❏ You'll need one hour—about thirty-five minutes for reading aloud, and the rest of the time for questions and a snack. In Williamsburg, the program starts at 10:00 A.M. on Saturday mornings.

*Some Concerns and Adaptations*    Each week there were variations in attendance. On a Saturday morning, twenty-five to as many as ninety children and parents attend story time. Preparing for the larger number is wise as leftover books and packaged snacks can be saved for the following Saturday.

In addition to parents, older siblings started attending the program. Some played games, such as chess, which the library staff brought along. However, most preferred listening to the stories, which is what Noreen hoped would occur. Noreen pointed out, "By listening and observing, they are learning how to share books at home with siblings and eventually their own children."

A major concern of the Youth Services staff was that parents would drop young children off and shop for groceries, defeating an important goal of *Feed Me a Story*—modeling how to read aloud and enjoy books. "Our staff encourages parents to stay, and they do," Noreen explained. "An adult will stay and shop after the program. Two adults often split up; one stays for story time, the other shops. We see more fathers at this program than at any others the library sponsors." Each year, other libraries ask for information about the program. Noreen's favorite was a library in Oregon that was creating *Feed Me a Story* in multiple languages to serve their population. A year's worth of *Feed Me a Story* programs can be found on the Williamsburg Regional Library's website at www.wrl.org.

## Operation READ: *Bringing Books to Families*

Before Jim Kivligham retired as principal of Bessie Weller Elementary School in Staunton, Virginia, several teachers wanted to help Jim make one of his dreams a reality: getting books into the homes of young children. The mission statement of the program named *Operation READ* reflected Jim's fervent belief that children who are read to in their early years have a better chance for success in school and are more likely to become productive, adult citizens. Rather than bring children to school or the local public library, teachers agreed that the best way to support some families was through home visits. Modeling how to read aloud, teachers felt, would be more successful if they worked with one family at a time.

Teachers applied for a grant from Valley Alliance, a civic group in Staunton, because one of its goals was to support literacy projects. In addition to the $1,500 awarded to Bessie Weller by Valley Alliance, other civic groups, organizations, and businesses contributed more than $3,600. Two parent and single parent families with low incomes were invited to participate in a program whose purpose is to help families experience the joys of storybook reading. The program started with twenty-five area families who had children in Head Start, preschool, and kindergarten.

*Gathering Materials and Extending Invitations*   Volunteers and teachers prepared materials. Their goal was to conserve dollars so that more books could be purchased. Groups made book bags, and teachers purchased outstanding picture books, enough to give each child in a family three to four books.

Two adults selected books appropriate for the age of each child in a family. A telephone call arranged a time that worked for the family. During the visit, volunteers show the books, encourage the families to browse through them, then read aloud to the children. The books remain in the home, and the volunteers encourage the parents to read them to their children. Before leaving, parents receive a telephone number that they can call to invite the adult readers back.

The main goal of the first visit is to build trust between the family and volunteers which is why the same volunteers continue to work with a family. *Operation READ*'s goal is for volunteers to visit a family at least four times a year, encourage family storybook reading, and leave new books for the children each time.

## Closing Reflections

The strength of many, families and community members, is far more powerful than that of one person, the teacher, when it comes to supporting children's literacy development and attitudes toward reading.

Many years ago, anthropologist Margaret Mead spoke at Handley High School in Winchester. Wearing an overflowing, dark blue dress and carrying a shepherd's staff that reached at least two feet beyond her head, Mead's speech still rings true today. She explained that the break-up of the nuclear family, where many relatives lived in the same house or on the same street, was a fact that Americans had to accept. Then she suggested that communities think out of the box and recreate the supportive network that nuclear families had provided children, parents, and the elderly: Mixed age groups in suburban and small town neighborhoods. Separating the younger from older people deprived both groups of the assistance and comfort they could offer one another and the expertise each could share. The elderly became the much needed surrogate parents and grandparents; the young, surrogate children and grandchildren.

The African philosophical belief of "It takes a village . . ." illustrates Mead's suggestions. Men, women, businesses, social and religious institutions in small towns and large cities must share the responsibilities of caring for one another and developing literacy among the very young and middle and high school students. Then, perhaps, we can create a literate, educated population where all citizens effectively participate in the democratic process, obtain jobs with benefits, and eradicate poverty.

# 9

# Evaluation and Beyond

*In many ways evaluating is just like reading and writing:*
*it involves noticing details and noticing themes and patterns.*

Peter H. Johnston, *Constructing Evaluation of Literate Activity* (1992, 8)

It's May. Terri Auckland and I are circulating among students during writing workshop. I'm impatient for the day to end. So is Terri. Jane Rea Gaidos has asked Terri, Lisa, and me to stop by her office after the children have been dismissed. We all know that the PALS screening reports have probably arrived. Did the test show the progress we see? I wondered. Will they let the program continue if the results don't mirror the assessments and observational notes the teachers have gathered? These questions that I've struggled to subdue all year creep into my mind. Doubts cling to my inner thoughts and I can't shake them off.

Finally, the three of us are sitting in Jane's office. Slowly, Jane hands each of us a copy of the PALS screening tests for Terri's and Lisa's classes (Figures 9–1 and 9–2). Jane's voice choked as she said, "I knew the testing would coincide with your performance assessments." Silent nods were all we could manage. For several minutes, the four of us reread the results again and again, tears staining our cheeks. Scores were way beyond what we hoped they'd be, but totally aligned with the

| | | Sum Score | Rhyme | Beg Sound | ABC Lower | Letter Sound | Spelling |
|---|---|---|---|---|---|---|---|
| **Benchmark Range** | **Spring** | **74** | **9-10** | **9-10** | **24-26** | **20-23** | **12-17** |
| | **Fall** | **28** | **5-8** | **5-8** | **12-20** | **4-11** | **2-7** |
| Dallas Bly | Spring | 92 | 10 | 10 | 26 | 26 | 20 |
| | Fall | 35 | 7 | *4** | 15 | 7 | 2 |
| Brandon Carter | Spring | 88 | 10 | 10 | 26 | 26 | 16 |
| | Fall | 49 | 10 | 6 | 23 | 6 | 4 |
| Walter "Shaun" Cram | Spring | 89 | 10 | 10 | 26 | 26 | 17 |
| | Fall | 43 | 10 | 7 | 19 | 4 | 3 |
| Ashley Hodges | Spring | 90 | 10 | 10 | 26 | 26 | 18 |
| | Fall | 38 | 7 | *3** | 15 | 10 | 3 |
| Rodger "Chip" Miller | Spring | 92 | 10 | 10 | 26 | 26 | 20 |
| | Fall | 45 | 9 | 9 | 16 | 10 | *1** |
| Ashley Rogers | Spring | 90 | 10 | 10 | 26 | 25 | 19 |
| | Fall | 33 | 6 | 5 | *10** | 9 | 3 |
| Kristina Schultz | Spring | 91 | 10 | 10 | 26 | 26 | 19 |
| | Fall | 31 | 10 | 8 | *10** | *2** | *1** |
| Wallace "Arnold" Shipp | Spring | 92 | 10 | 10 | 26 | 26 | 20 |
| | Fall | 52 | 9 | 8 | 23 | 11 | *1** |

**Students who were below criteria in Fall and above criteria in Spring: 2 (18%)**

| | | Sum Score | Rhyme | Beg Sound | ABC Lower | Letter Sound | Spelling |
|---|---|---|---|---|---|---|---|
| **Benchmark Range** | **Spring** | **74** | **9-10** | **9-10** | **24-26** | **20-23** | **12-17** |
| | **Fall** | **28** | **5-8** | **5-8** | **12-20** | **4-11** | **2-7** |
| Matthew Kingree | Spring | 81 | 10 | 10 | 25 | 26 | *10** |
| | Fall | *27** | 10 | *1** | 12 | *2** | 2 |
| Kayla Smoot | Spring | 82 | 10 | 10 | 26 | 26 | *10** |
| | Fall | *19** | 6 | 5 | *6** | *2** | *0** |

**Students who were below criteria in Fall and Spring: 1 (9%)**

**Figure 9–1.** PALS scores for Lisa Tusing's class

| | | Sum Score | Rhyme | Beg Sound | ABC Lower | Letter Sound | Spelling |
|---|---|---|---|---|---|---|---|
| **Benchmark Range** | **Spring** | 74 | 9-10 | 9-10 | 24-26 | 20-23 | 12-17 |
| | **Fall** | 28 | 5-8 | 5-8 | 12-20 | 4-11 | 2-7 |
| Jeffery Mitchell | Spring | *71** | 10 | 9 | 24 | *19** | *9** |
| | Fall | *19** | 6 | 7 | *3** | *2** | *1** |

**Students who were above criteria in Fall and below criteria in Spring: 0**

(none)

**Students for whom Fall and/or Spring scores were not available: 2**

| | | Sum Score | Rhyme | Beg Sound | ABC Lower | Letter Sound | Spelling |
|---|---|---|---|---|---|---|---|
| **Benchmark Range** | **Spring** | 74 | 9-10 | 9-10 | 24-26 | 20-23 | 12-17 |
| | **Fall** | 28 | 5-8 | 5-8 | 12-20 | 4-11 | 2-7 |
| Donnai Diamond | Spring | (scores not available) | | | | | |
| | Fall | *27** | 7 | *1** | *10** | 7 | 2 |
| William Parkinson | Spring | 86 | 10 | 10 | 26 | 24 | 16 |
| | Fall | (scores not available) | | | | | |

Scores used to create summed scores: Rhyme, Beg Sound, ABC Lower, Letter Sound, Spelling

| Key: | At or above benchmark | *Below *** ***benchmark*** |
|---|---|---|

**Figure 9–1.** *continued*

progress we had observed. A score of 72 is passing; a score of 92 indicates a perfect score in each area screened.

Terri and Lisa felt that some children who met the benchmark still needed continued support before entering first grade. They struggled with listening, tracking print, writing about their pictures, and extending conversation with adults and peers. Because Jane Rea Gaidos agreed that one test a child takes should not be the sole consideration for predicting success in first grade, she relied on her teachers'

| | | Sum Score | Rhyme | Beg Sound | ABC Lower | Letter Sound | Spelling |
|---|---|---|---|---|---|---|---|
| **Benchmark Range** | Spring | 74 | 9-10 | 9-10 | 24-26 | 20-23 | 12-17 |
| | Fall | 28 | 5-8 | 5-8 | 12-20 | 4-11 | 2-7 |
| Colton Bulatko | Spring | 83 | 6* | 10 | 26 | 26 | 15 |
| | Fall | 11* | 3* | 4* | 2* | 0* | 2 |
| Titus Embrey | Spring | 91 | 10 | 10 | 26 | 26 | 19 |
| | Fall | 18* | 10 | 1* | 6* | 1* | 0* |
| Angelina Funkhouser | Spring | 91 | 10 | 10 | 26 | 25 | 20 |
| | Fall | 25* | 7 | 4* | 14 | 0* | 0* |
| Travis High | Spring | 88 | 10 | 10 | 26 | 25 | 17 |
| | Fall | 18* | 4* | 3* | 9* | 2* | 0* |
| Ashley Miller | Spring | 87 | 10 | 10 | 26 | 26 | 15 |
| | Fall | 24* | 4* | 4* | 12 | 1* | 3 |
| Ray Orebaugh | Spring | 88 | 9 | 10 | 25 | 26 | 18 |
| | Fall | 17* | 5 | 3* | 8* | 0* | 1* |
| Molly Tisinger | Spring | 84 | 10 | 10 | 26 | 24 | 14 |
| | Fall | 13* | 3* | 2* | 5* | 0* | 3 |

**Students who were below criteria in Fall and Spring:  2  (18%)**

| | | Sum Score | Rhyme | Beg Sound | ABC Lower | Letter Sound | Spelling |
|---|---|---|---|---|---|---|---|
| **Benchmark Range** | Spring | 74 | 9-10 | 9-10 | 24-26 | 20-23 | 12-17 |
| | Fall | 28 | 5-8 | 5-8 | 12-20 | 4-11 | 2-7 |
| Kristina Shifflett | Spring | 63* | 4* | 10 | 22* | 23 | 4* |
| | Fall | 6* | 3* | 1* | 2* | 0* | 0* |
| Benjamin Stephens | Spring | 30* | 5* | 9 | 9* | 6* | 1* |
| | Fall | 7* | 3* | 2* | 2* | 0* | 0* |

**Students who were above criteria in Fall and below criteria in Spring:  0**

| (none) |
|---|

**Students for whom Fall and/or Spring scores were not available:  2**

**Figure 9–2.** PALS scores for Terri Auckland's class

| | | Sum Score | Rhyme | Beg Sound | ABC Lower | Letter Sound | Spelling |
|---|---|---|---|---|---|---|---|
| **Benchmark Range** | **Spring** | 74 | **9-10** | **9-10** | **24-26** | **20-23** | **12-17** |
| | **Fall** | 28 | **5-8** | **5-8** | **12-20** | **4-11** | **2-7** |
| Jeremy Dommel | Spring | 74 | 10 | 9 | 26 | 20 | *9** |
| | Fall | (scores not available) | | | | | |
| William Parkinson | Spring | (scores not available) | | | | | |
| | Fall | *23** | 10 | *1** | *10** | *2** | *0** |

Scores used to create summed scores: Rhyme, Beg Sound, ABC Lower, Letter Sound, Spelling

| Key: | At or above benchmark | *Below* **benchmark** |
|---|---|---|

**Figure 9–2.** *continued*

recommendations. Before discussing teachers' evaluation process, it's important to understand these terms: *assessment, interpretation, evaluation,* and *interventions.*

## Defining Terms

*Assessments* are the data you have collected about a child. Included are standardized tests, writing samples, concepts about print and book knowledge screenings, spelling inventories, observational notes, and checklists. When reviewing assessments, look at samples from different points during a grading period. As the school year unfolds, save representative assessments in student folders from the beginning, middle, and end of the year. A range of assessments provides you with a picture of each child in many situations on different days. Using a range of materials enables you to form an image that is closer to reality than relying on one teacher observation, one screening, or one standardized state test.

Assessments are valuable for they guide your thinking about a child and help you comprehend the learning process and style of each individual. *Interpretation* occurs when you review and reflect on a range of assessments, taken over time. To interpret assessments, to explore and discover what the collected data tells you about a child's learning, you will combine your expert knowledge of early literacy development with the information you've reviewed to draw conclusions about a child and respond by developing a plan that can support each child's emotional and academic progress (Robb 2000c, 2001).

*Evaluation,* for me, means the process of transforming the interpretations of assessment data into possible *interventions,* which are teaching and scaffolding plans that can improve learning. The reason I use the word "possible" is because our first interpretations might not benefit a child. When this occurs, it's time to reread assessments and search for other ways to support a child.

For example, Terri Auckland was trying to help one of her students segment the sounds in one-syllable three-letter words. For *dog,* a child said /d/—dog; for hat, the child said /h/—hat. When Terri and I reviewed her notes, we observed that this boy consistently heard and isolated the first sound, but not the medial and final sounds. If Terri modeled separating and saying each sound, the child was successful, indicating that he could hear the sound with the teacher's support. I suggested that Terri use squares made from red, green, and blue colored construction paper. One square to represent the sound each letter makes (Elkonin 1963, 1964, as cited in Lewkowicz 1980). First, Terri printed the word on an index card, said the word, and told the child there were three different sounds, one to match each letter. Then she modeled how to use the cards and the letters in the word. Using the colored squares helped the child focus on one sound at a time, associating each phoneme with a different color. You can use different colored chips, pennies, dimes, and nickels, and so on. The purpose is to have a different color or object for each sound.

So much of evaluation is embedded in the actual event unfolding between the teacher and child. Here, the teacher immediately intervenes to scaffold the learning. Knowledge of early literacy development is crucial for making beneficial, on-the-spot decisions. For example, Titus, a first grader who spent a year in Terri Auckland's Literacy Links kindergarten, during writing workshop, draws a picture of himself swimming. Then he puts a title on his paper, writing the letter *s* backwards, and the letter *u* for *w.* "Something's wrong," he tells me (Figure 9–3).

"Let's stretch the sounds," I suggest. "You did that so well earlier today," I add, wanting to build his confidence in separating and listening to the opening sounds. I start the stretching process.

Titus jumps in saying, "I got it." Quickly, he writes his story on the bottom and spells *swim* correctly. When I ask Titus if he wants to revise his title, he shakes his head and places his writing on the shelf for students who will share. I let it go and move on to another child. Research on writing process indicates that young children are not keen on revising (Calkins 1994). Knowing this, I did not push Titus who was ready to choose a free reading book. Instead, I celebrated his ability to hear the sounds and spell *swim* correctly the second time he used it.

**Figure 9–3.** Titus writes about swimming.

## Keeping Assessment Records

I recommend that teachers organize a literacy folder for each child. Before school opens, label a file folder with each child's name. Store these in a cabinet or plastic crate. Having important information that documents each child's progress in one place enables you to quickly locate all pertinent data and review it. Collect dated representative pieces from the beginning, middle, and end of each marking period. When a marking period ends, clip or staple assessments together, and place them in the back of the folder.

Included in the folders are the first piece of writing a child completes, called a *baseline piece*. It's the writing that I use to evaluate progress by comparing it to samples of later work. A baseline piece can be the first journal entry or the first piece of independent writing a child completes. Folders can also contain selected journal entries and pieces of independent writing, assessments that measure concepts about print, book knowledge, upper- and lowercase alphabet letters as well as the sounds each make, word study notebooks, artwork, spelling inventories, checklists of pretend play and emergent spelling and writing behaviors, and observational notes.

Review children's folders bimonthly to adjust instruction and plan beneficial scaffolding. You can refer to these folders to plan parent-teacher conferences, to pair children, and to monitor children's progress in developing emergent literacy.

### Interpreting a Range of Assessments

It's helpful, for some teachers, to jot down their thoughts on a form that organizes the process of moving from assessment, to evaluation and interpretation, and finally, to planning possible interventions. Figure 9–4 can guide you through this process and also provide you with documentation to share with parents and administrators and to refer to later in the year.

The following are some guidelines to help you through the evaluation process. Use these ideas as a starting point or let them spark ways you can adapt what I do to your teaching style.

*Review Your Assessment Folder* Reread observational notes, sample journal entries, checklists, screenings, writing samples, and any other assessments you've gathered. Set priorities and choose one issue that you think will benefit the child's progress at this time.

*Determine the Focus* Narrow the issue to a smaller focus. For example, the issue might be concepts about print that includes several elements. Focusing the issue might mean you will work on concept of words and spaces. For phonemic awareness issues, you might focus on rhyming words, hearing initial consonant sounds and blends, or segmenting the sounds in words. Young children cannot attend to several

# Evaluate, Interpret, Plan, Teach

Name _____ Date _____

Focus of evaluation:

Key points from assessments:

List any questions data raised and try to address these:

Note two to three possible interventions. Circle the one you will try first.

Additional Comments:

**Figure 9–4.** Evaluate, Interpret, Plan, Teach Assessment Form

© 2003 by Laura Robb from *Literacy Links*. Portsmouth, NH: Heinemann.

tough issues. Help them progress by pinpointing exactly what to work on over a few days or weeks.

*Note Key Points That Relate to the Focus*   Jot down issues that relate to the focus you've established. For example, when I decided to help a child track print, I note:

- ❏   Tracks first word accurately.
- ❏   Talks very fast—has memorized the text.
- ❏   Sweeps from right back to left at the end of a line.
- ❏   Writes in lists or scatters print.

*Raise Questions*   Questions can help you brainstorm ways to move a child from one place to another. I ask:

- ❏   Is directionality the first issue to address here?
- ❏   Should I use pages from a big book or a poem on a chart?
- ❏   Should we practice together on sentence strips the child dictated?

*Propose Possible Interventions*   Try to list more than one way to intervene, for if the first doesn't work, you've already thought through other choices. Often, I have to abandon a choice and discover that my second idea for scaffolding was much better. Here are the interventions I developed for helping the child learn to track print:

- ❏   Work on directionality, using big books, interactive writing or strips sentences the child dictated.
- ❏   Next, help child transfer to own writing.
- ❏   Practice tracking print with own writing.
- ❏   Practice tracking print with a short nursery rhyme.

Note how raising questions led me to the heart of this child's problem and enabled me to break down, into digestible bits, the process to develop the ability to match words and speech. My observational notes enabled me to identify this child's need. Completing the form enabled me to find the real issue and scaffold learning.

Taking observational notes when children play in literacy centers, read independently, write stories, and interact during recess provides you with valuable data that can inform instructional decisions.

### The Importance of Taking Observational Notes

The notes you take paint a more complete picture of how each child you teach learns and interacts with peers and adults. Regie Routman makes a point that I wholeheartedly support. Routman asserts that good observation is a key element in evaluation (1991). Moreover, teachers' ability to observe and interpret what they see is only as good as their theoretical knowledge base. Therefore, becoming an expert observer means that teachers must also become lifelong learners. Ongoing learning means studying your students and also increasing your knowledge base about how children learn by reading professional books and articles. Weekly or bimonthly, join colleagues to discuss students, ideas, articles or sections of books, and classroom practices (Robb 2000b).

If you're a novice at taking observational notes, start small. Reserve five to ten minutes twice a week to one student at a time. Once you gain comfort and confidence, do more.

### Some Tips for Taking Observational Notes

1. Use sticky notes. Prepare these in advance by placing the child's name, date, and the situation at the top of the note.
2. Carry sticky notes and a pencil at all times. I use a clipboard and place the notes on sheets of paper. Threaded through the hole of the board's large clip is a heavy cord or braided strands of wool. This allows me to wear the clipboard as if it were a pocketbook. It's always available. This system has eliminated my absentmindedly putting down the clipboard and feeling frustrated and annoyed when I can't recall where it is.
3. Tell students what you are doing so they don't think you are writing bad things about them. To empathize with students' feelings, I urge you to recall your emotions and inner thoughts when an administrator continually writes while observing you teach.
4. Start by observing one child in one specific situation, such as play centers or writing workshop. Next, observe and take notes on the same child in two or three different learning situations. Gathering data from varied situations gives you a more accurate picture of the child. For example, during writing workshop, kindergartner Carlton concentrates on drawing, then trying to stretch words to hear sounds. This week, however, during independent reading, Carlton whizzes through a book, then tries to chat with a friend. If these are repetitive observations, then it's appropriate to confer with a child. "I notice you are really into writing and that's great," I tell Carlton. "Can you tell me why you are chatting during silent, independent reading?"

Carlton's reply is honest, "I don't like those." [He points to the books in the basket children chose from this week.] The solution is simple; I ask Carlton what kinds of books he'd like to read. "About trucks and airplanes and cars," he explains. After school, I find several titles in the library and

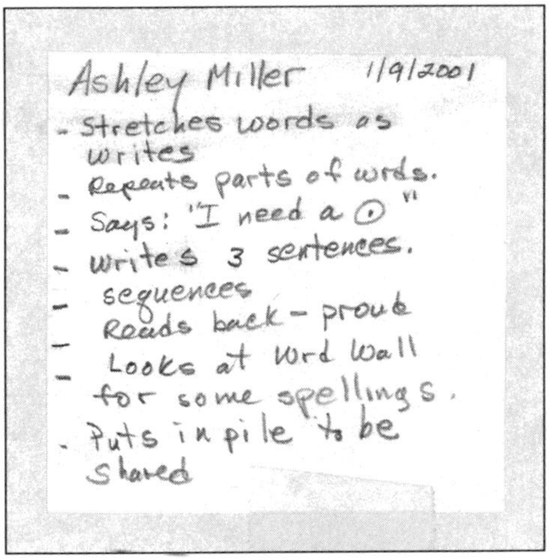

Ashley Miller 1/9/2001
- Stretches words as writes
- Repeats parts of words.
- Says: "I need a ⊙"
- writes 3 sentences.
- sequences
- Reads back – proud
- Looks at Word Wall for some spellings.
- Puts in pile to be shared

**Figure 9–5.** Observational notes for Ashley

place these in the independent reading basket. I've learned to always ask a child about a behavior that concerns me, then try to involve the child in finding a suitable solution. Often, the solution is quite easy. Most of the time, the children are totally candid.

5. Note what you see and hear when students work independently. Read students' written work and note what you learn.
6. Don't editorialize; simply write as objectively as you can. Use shorthand as you write what you see, as in my sample notes (Figure 9–5).
7. Decide what aspects of your observations you will share with a child. Encourage students to help you solve the problem.
8. Store notes in the child's literacy folder.

### *Some Guidelines for Reflecting on Independent Writing*

Throughout the year, continue to review many pieces of writing so you can understand where each child is regarding spelling and story structure. To help you pinpoint needs, set priorities, and develop helpful interventions, consider supporting your reflections by using forms that document progress or lack of progress. Knowing what to look for as you listen to children share their writing, as well as having a checklist of guidelines that help you compare pieces of writing, permits you to take valuable observational notes and plan ways to scaffold learning.

*Taking Notes When Children Share Their Writing* During writing workshop, when children sit in the author's chair and share a piece, you can complete the form in Figure 9–6. Staple the completed form to the back of the writing. Teachers agree that these notes are helpful because they can recall what happened on a specific date.

Name _____     Date _____

_____ Free choice topic.

_____ Assigned topic.

_____ Story has a title.

_____ Story has a beginning, middle, and end.

_____ Story's ending grows out of the beginning and middle.

_____ Child willingly talks about the piece.

_____ Print moves from left to right.

_____ Pictures match what the child says.

_____ Story has a main character with a problem.

_____ Record what the child said here:

**Other Comments:**

**Figure 9–6.** Writing Workshop Checklist for Author's Chair

Teachers' comments offer insights into children's process and attitudes toward writing—insights you might not be able to gain if you only look at children's writing. Here are some comments teachers made.

- ❏ "Copies words from word walls—these don't connect to picture."—Lisa Tusing
- ❏ "Writes and reads message from right to left."—Danielle Waters
- ❏ "She said much more than she wrote. Writing: 'I will' followed by strings of random letters. Shared story: 'I will go to the pumpkin patch next time because I was sick. I didn't go 'cause I was sick, sick, sick.'"—Terri Auckland
- ❏ "Points to and says what's in the picture. Does not tell a story about it."—Nancy Reedy
- ❏ "Asked me to hold writing and tracked print while he read."—Sharon Garber

*A Checklist for Evaluating Children's Writing*   At the end of each marking period, and at the end of the year, you can use my suggestions to compare pieces of writing to children's baseline piece. It's helpful to collect samples over three to four consecutive weeks by saving two samples each week, then reviewing them. Samples can come from the children's journals and/or independent writing. I recommend that you complete your first formal evaluation after the first six weeks of school, then at the end of each marking period.

The list in Figure 9–7 focuses your attention on three areas: spelling and word use, the written message, and directionality. Used in conjunction with the checklist that monitors the child when he or she tells about a piece in the author's chair, you

Name_____    Date _____

Observations                                Dates observed

**Spelling and Word Use**

Pictures only.                              _____ _____ _____

Random strings of letters only.            _____ _____ _____

Random strings of numbers only.            _____ _____ _____

Random strings of numbers and letters.     _____ _____ _____

A word that is recognizable.               _____ _____ _____

Two or more recognizable words.            _____ _____ _____

A simple sentence; no punctuation.         _____ _____ _____

A simple sentence with punctuation.        _____ _____ _____

Two or more related sentences; no punctuation.   _____ _____ _____

Two or more related sentences with punctuation.  _____ _____ _____

An entire paragraph; no punctuation.       _____ _____ _____

An entire paragraph with punctuation.      _____ _____ _____

**Written Message**

Knows that writing sends a message. Can be
   scribble, letters, words, sentences, and so on.
   Indicate which.                         _____ _____ _____

Uses letters to convey a message.          _____ _____ _____

Uses initial and final consonants to spell words.   _____ _____ _____

Uses punctuation.                          _____ _____ _____

Uses punctuation correctly.                _____ _____ _____

Uses writing from the room to spell words. _____ _____ _____

**Figure 9–7.** Checklist for Evaluating Children's Writing

Uses a pattern to start sentences: I like, I will,
I play, and so on. _____ _____ _____

Uses a pattern from stories: Once upon a time,
In the beginning, and so forth. _____ _____ _____

Message cannot be read by another reader. _____ _____ _____

Message can be read by another reader. _____ _____ _____

Finds own topics. _____ _____ _____

### Directionality

No discernible pattern. _____ _____ _____

Reverses directionality: right to left and back to right. _____ _____ _____

Part of directional pattern: _____ _____ _____

    Starts at the left. _____ _____ _____

    Moves left to right. _____ _____ _____

    Returns to left and moves right. _____ _____ _____

Correct directionality of print. _____ _____ _____

Correct directionality and words consistently spaced. _____ _____ _____

Continuous text with correct directionality and
word spacing. _____ _____ _____

**List Observed Strengths and Date**

**List Possible Interventions and Date**

**Figure 9–7.** *continued*

© 2003 by Laura Robb from *Literacy Links*. Portsmouth, NH: Heinemann.

can gain a clearer image of progress and specific needs. For both checklists to more effectively support evaluation, use each one on the same pieces of writing.

When you closely monitor children's writing, you gain countless opportunities to help them progress by building on what they can presently accomplish. Moreover, what children learn during shared reading, writing, and play experiences should eventually be reflected in their independent writing. If this does not occur, then meet frequently with the child and scaffold learning during writing workshop and your language arts block. Your list of possible interventions, based on what the child can presently do, will enable you to provide the scaffolding that can gently nudge each child forward and develop emergent literacy.

Concepts about print, book knowledge, and alphabet screening tests along with the checklists in this book provide you with a list of emergent literacy behaviors children need to be successful in first grade and beyond. Use these to support the unique needs of each child, knowing that responding to individuals, not delivering a program, is what enables children to improve and progress.

A the end of the first year of the Literacy Links program, all of us continually wondered if the improvements in students that we observed would occur in the second year.

## The Second Year of Literacy Links

Often, success can make you more nervous than failure. That's exactly how Literacy Links teachers and I felt during the second year of the program. The pressure to replicate first year results was great. Anxious and unproductive thoughts bombarded our minds during preparation meetings and the first two months of school: *Were results a fluke? Could we help this group move forward? Would the program end because of our failures? Would these children respond to family storybook reading as much as last year's group?* Finally, we agreed to a few minutes of venting and sharing doubts at a meeting, recognizing that our focus should be the children. And that's what saved us—concentrating on the children and continually assessing their progress so that we could plan supportive instruction.

### Second Year PALS Scores and Student Assessments at Robinson Elementary School

Terri Auckland and Lisa Tusing, Literacy Links kindergarten teachers at Robinson Elementary School, initiated word play and picture sorting earlier in the second year. Both believed that this accounted for fall testing scores that were better than first year fall scores. In May, when we received the second year results of the PALS, they matched the evaluations and recommendations that Terri and Lisa made.

Take Samantha Clark, a student in Terri Auckland's class. Her fall score of 24 (Figure 9–8) was the second lowest in the class. Her first piece of writing

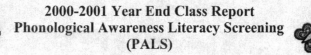

# 2000-2001 Year End Class Report
# Phonological Awareness Literacy Screening
# (PALS)

**May 15, 2001**

**Teacher:** Terry Auckland

**Students Screened Both Fall and Spring:** 10

**Grade:** Kindergarten
**School:** W. W. Robinson Elem.
**District:** Shenandoah County Public Schools

This report is divided into five sections,
   (1) Students who met or exceeded PALS criteria in Fall 2000 and Spring 2001
   (2) Students who were below criteria in Fall 2000 and above criteria in Spring 2001
   (3) Students who were below criteria in Fall 2000 and Spring 2001
   (4) Students who were above criteria in Fall 2000 and below criteria in Spring 2001
   (5) Students for whom Fall 2000 and/or Spring 2001 scores were not available.
Please scroll through your report and call the PALS office if you have any questions.

| Students who met or exceeded PALS criteria in Fall and Spring: 6 (60%) | | Sum Score | Rhyme | Beg Sound | ABC Lower | Letter Sound | Spelling |
|---|---|---|---|---|---|---|---|
| **Benchmark Range** | Spring | 74 | 9-10 | 9-10 | 24-26 | 20-23 | 12-17 |
| | Fall | 28 | 5-8 | 5-8 | 12-20 | 4-11 | 2-7 |
| Kelsey Barbero | Spring | 90 | 10 | 10 | 25 | 26 | 19 |
| | Fall | 39 | 8 | 9 | 11* | 7 | 4 |
| Darrian Dysart | Spring | 89 | 10 | 10 | 24 | 26 | 19 |
| | Fall | 34 | 6 | 6 | 13 | 5 | 4 |
| Tyler Polk | Spring | 92 | 10 | 10 | 26 | 26 | 20 |
| | Fall | 33 | 5 | 2* | 11* | 10 | 5 |
| Hayden Ramage | Spring | 89 | 10 | 10 | 26 | 25 | 18 |
| | Fall | 33 | 8 | 5 | 13 | 7 | 0* |
| Kali Tamkin | Spring | 92 | 10 | 10 | 26 | 26 | 20 |
| | Fall | 66 | 5 | 9 | 23 | 16 | 13 |
| Denzel Warr | Spring | 92 | 10 | 10 | 26 | 26 | 20 |
| | Fall | 50 | 6 | 8 | 16 | 14 | 6 |

**Figure 9–8.** PALS results with Samantha's fall summed score

| Students who were below criteria in Fall and above criteria in Spring: 3 (30%) | | Sum Score | Rhyme | Beg Sound | ABC Lower | Letter Sound | Spelling |
|---|---|---|---|---|---|---|---|
| **Benchmark Range** | **Spring** | 74 | 9-10 | 9-10 | 24-26 | 20-23 | 12-17 |
| | **Fall** | 28 | 5-8 | 5-8 | 12-20 | 4-11 | 2-7 |
| Wade Barb | Spring | 88 | 10 | 10 | 25 | 25 | 18 |
| | Fall | *25** | *3** | *3** | 16 | *3** | *0** |
| Samantha Clark | Spring | 88 | 9 | 10 | 26 | 25 | 18 |
| | Fall | *24** | *4** | 8 | *8** | *2** | 2 |
| Shana Rauch | Spring | 89 | 10 | 10 | 25 | 25 | 19 |
| | Fall | *24** | 8 | 5 | *8** | *2** | *1** |

| Students who were below criteria in Fall and Spring: 1 (10%) | | Sum Score | Rhyme | Beg Sound | ABC Lower | Letter Sound | Spelling |
|---|---|---|---|---|---|---|---|
| **Benchmark Range** | **Spring** | 74 | 9-10 | 9-10 | 24-26 | 20-23 | 12-17 |
| | **Fall** | 28 | 5-8 | 5-8 | 12-20 | 4-11 | 2-7 |
| William Waybright | Spring | *60** | 9 | 9 | *20** | *15** | *7** |
| | Fall | *5** | *2** | *1** | *2** | *0** | *0** |

| Students who were above criteria in Fall and below criteria in Spring: 0 |
|---|
| (none) |

| Students for whom Fall and/or Spring scores were not available: 0 |
|---|
| (none) |

Scores used to create summed scores: Rhyme, Beg Sound, ABC Lower, Letter Sound, Spelling

| Key: | At or above benchmark | *Below* * *benchmark* |
|---|---|---|

**Figure 9–8.** *continued*

**Figure 9–9.** An early piece of Samantha's writing

(Figure 9–9) compared to a piece completed on April 30 (Figure 9–10) reflects Samantha's literacy growth. Her first piece was scribbling with no message or organized picture. At the end of April, Samantha draws a detailed picture of Kali in her house. She uses lines to help her space words, and her message is readable, with the exception of *rod* for writing, and her spelling demonstrates phonemic awareness. Samantha places a period at the end of her message and can spell several words correctly. Other assessments reveal that Samantha has solid book knowledge; she's developed all the concepts of print, knows her alphabet, and engages in imaginative play with classmates, especially Kali. Her spring PALS testing scores mirror the growth Samantha's writing and other assessments illustrate: Her total score of 88 is four points below a perfect score. Samantha moves onto first grade. However, Samantha's PALS scores do not reveal her terrific progress in other areas of emergent literacy such as writing and concepts about print.

PALS scores of the children in Lisa Tusing's class also reveal great progress (Figure 9–11). Out of twenty children in both classes, three did not meet the benchmark. These children as well as eight others would move into Melissa Foltz's transition first-grade class. All entered heterogeneous second-grade classes after their year with Melissa.

One key thought that I hope will linger and cause school districts to amend their views of mandated testing is that high-stakes tests can only provide limited information

**Figure 9–10.** In May, Samantha's writing shows much progress.

about a child. Virginia's PALS Screening focuses on phonological awareness and tests children's ability to rhyme, hear beginning sounds, spell, and identify upper- and lowercase alphabet letters. Phonological awareness is only one small aspect of emergent literacy. To construct a more complete image of a child's progress, it is crucial to use and reflect on a wide range of assessments and observational notes.

### Winchester Test Scores and Students' Assessments

One cool October morning, Nancy Lee called me into her office at Quarles Elementary School and handed me a sheet that compared the testing of second graders in Winchester's five elementary schools (Figure 9–12). The second graders represented in these results had the benefit of family storybook reading in kindergarten and first grade. Those who needed extra bolstering in first grade visited a reading tutor three times a week for twenty minutes. Until this moment, the standardized testing scores of Quarles were always lower than other Winchester Elementary school scores. Quarles' population included a large number of ESL children and children from families living in poverty. In all language arts areas tested, second graders at Quarles Elementary School, were well above the benchmark of 50th percentile. "I have to believe," Nancy said, "that the emergent

# PALS-K

Return scores via the Internet at http://curry.edschool.virginia.edu/go/pals

**FALL 2000 CLASS SUMMARY SHEET**

Benchmarks are shown below each section head.

Teacher (First and Last): Lisa Tusing    Assess. Date 10/23/00

School: W. Robinson

School Division: Shenandoah Co.

Grade: ☑ Full-day Kindergarten  ☐ AM Kindergarten  ☐ PM Kindergarten

| Name (First and Last) | Birthdate | ID# | Gender | Ethnicity* | Services* | SEC I A. Group Rhyme | SEC I B. Group Beg. Sound | SEC I C. Ind. Rhyme★ | SEC I D. Ind. Beg. Sound★ | SEC II ABC Lower (12-20) | SEC III A. Letter Sounds (4-11) | SEC III B. Spelling (2-7) | SEC IV Preprimer | SEC IV Primer | SEC IV First Grade | SEC V Pointing (1-2) | SEC V Word I.D. (1-3) | Summed Score (Benchmark 28) |
|---|---|---|---|---|---|---|---|---|---|---|---|---|---|---|---|---|---|---|
| 1. Cynthia Barb | / / | 0895 | M | C | 2 | 10 | 3 | 3 | 3 | 3 | 2 | 0 | | | | 3 | 3 | 18 |
| 2. Jacob Breton | / / | 1010 | F | C | 2 | 9 | 9 | | | 4 | 2 | 0 | | | | 1 | 0 | 22 |
| 3. Richard Leal | / / | 0941 | M | C | 2 | 4 | 4 | 1 | 4 | 8 | 2 | | | | | 4 | 1 | 15 |
| 4. Alexander Litts | / / | 1018 | M | C | 5 | 10 | 4 | | 10 | 2 | 2 | 8 | | | | 2 | 6 | 24 |
| 5. Savannah Ludwig | / / | 0945 | M | C | 5 | 10 | 6 | | | 25 | 17 | | | | | 4 | 6 | 68 |
| 6. Tiffany Malone | / / | 0949 | M | C | 5 | 7 | 2 | 7 | 7 | 15 | 13 | 4 | | | | 3 | 5 | 46 |
| 7. Thomas Marte | / / | 0952 | M | C | 2 | 10 | 10 | | | 22 | 18 | 7 | | | | 4 | 5 | 67 |
| 8. Shawn Miller | / / | 0069 | M | C | 2 | 1 | | | | | | | | | | | | |
| 9. Brianna Rogers | / / | 0928 | M | C | 2 | 10 | 7 | | | 7 | 6 | 2 | | | | 2 | 1 | 33 |
| 10. Jody Wilcox | / / | 1005 | M | C | 3 | 3 | 6 | 4 | | 9 | 9 | 0 | | | | 2 | 1 | 36 |
| 11. Carlton Pietsch | / / | | M | C | | | | | | | | | | | | | | |
| 12. | / / | | M  F | | | | | | | | | | | | | | | |
| 13. | / / | | M  F | | | | | | | | | | | | | | | |
| 14. | / / | | M  F | | | | | | | | | | | | | | | |
| 15. | / / | | M  F | | | | | | | | | | | | | | | |
| 16. | / / | | M  F | | | | | | | | | | | | | | | |
| 17. | / / | | M  F | | | | | | | | | | | | | | | |
| 18. | / / | | M  F | | | | | | | | | | | | | | | |
| 19. | / / | | M  F | | | | | | | | | | | | | | | |
| 20. | / / | | M  F | | | | | | | | | | | | | | | |
| 21. | / / | | M  F | | | | | | | | | | | | | | | |
| 22. | / / | | M  F | | | | | | | | | | | | | | | |
| 23. | / / | | M  F | | | | | | | | | | | | | | | |
| 24. | / / | | M  F | | | | | | | | | | | | | | | |
| 25. | / / | | M  F | | | | | | | | | | | | | | | |

*See Teacher's Manual for codes.

★If given, use ind. score (not group) in summed score.

Sum only unshaded areas.

**Figure 9–11.** PALS scores of Lisa Tusing's class record progress

# PALS-K

SPRING 2001 CLASS SUMMARY SHEET

Return scores via the Internet at http://curry.edschool.virginia.edu/go/pals

Benchmarks are shown below each section head.

Teacher (First and Last): _Lisa Tusing_   Spring Assess. Date _5/5/01_

School: _____

School Division: _____

Grade: ☐ Full-day Kindergarten   ☐ AM Kindergarten   ☐ PM Kindergarten

| Name (First and Last) | Gender | SECTION I — A. Group Rhyme | B. Group Beg. Sound | C. Ind. Rhyme★ | D. Ind. Beg. Sound★ | SEC II ABC Lower (24-26) | SEC III A. Letter Sounds (20-23) | B. Spelling (12-?) | SECTION IV Preprimer | Primer | First Grade | SEC V Pointing (3-4) | Word I.D. (4-8) | Summed Score (Benchmark 74) |
|---|---|---|---|---|---|---|---|---|---|---|---|---|---|---|
| 1. Cindy Barb | M (F) | 10 | 10 | 7 | 8 | 26 25 | 25 | 18 | 30 | | | 4 | 8 | 89 |
| 2. Jacob Beaton | (M) F | 10 | 7 | 0 | 8 | 19 10 | 10 | 4 | 20 | 0 | | 4 | 1 | 56 |
| 3. Richard Lear | (M) F | 10 | 10 | | | 26 20 | 20 | 18 | 19 | 3 | | 4 | 8 | 90 |
| 4. Alex Litts | (M) F | 10 | 10 | | | 26 26 | 26 | 20 | 17 | 0 | | 4 | 8 | 92 |
| 5. Savannah Ludwig | M (F) | 10 | 10 | | | 26 20 | 20 | 19 | 9 | 9 | | 4 | 7 | 91 |
| 6. Tiffany Malone | M (F) | 10 | 10 | | | 26 26 | 26 | 18 | 10 | 9 | | 4 | 7 | 88 |
| 7. Thomas Martz | (M) F | 10 | 10 | | | 26 26 | 26 | 18 | 20 | 3 | | 4 | 8 | 92 |
| 8. Carlton Pietsch | (M) F | 9 | 9 | 3 | | 26 | 2 0 | 2 0 | 0 | | | 4 | 3 | |
| 9. Mark Ratcliffe | (M) F | 10 | 10 | | | 26 26 | 26 | 18 | 3 | 0 | | 4 | 8 | 90 |
| 10. Brianna Rogers | M (F) | 10 | 10 | | | 26 26 | 26 | 19 | 15 | 2 | | 4 | 8 | 91 |
| 11. Jody Wilcox II | (M) F | 10 | 10 | | | 26 26 | 26 | 19 | 0 | 0 | | 4 | 7 | 91 |
| 12. Miguel Argueta | M F | 6 | 8 | 6 | 10 | 18 | 6 | 6 | 0 | 0 | | 4 | 2 | 46 |
| 13. | M F | | | | | | | | | | | | | |
| 14. | M F | | | | | | | | | | | | | |
| 15. | M F | | | | | | | | | | | | | |
| 16. | M F | | | | | | | | | | | | | |
| 17. | M F | | | | | | | | | | | | | |
| 18. | M F | | | | | | | | | | | | | |
| 19. | M F | | | | | | | | | | | | | |
| 20. | M F | | | | | | | | | | | | | |
| 21. | M F | | | | | | | | | | | | | |
| 22. | M F | | | | | | | | | | | | | |
| 23. | M F | | | | | | | | | | | | | |
| 24. | M F | | | | | | | | | | | | | |
| 25. | M F | | | | | | | | | | | | | |

Figure 9–11. continued

266

# WINCHESTER PUBLIC SCHOOLS
## GRADE 2: FALL 2000 SAT-9 COMPARISON
## PERCENT OF STUDENTS AT OR ABOVE THE 50TH PERCENTILE

| SCHOOL | TOTAL READING | WORD STUDY | WORD READING | READING COMP | TOTAL MATH | PROBLEM SOLVING | PRO-CEDURES | LAN-GUAGE | ENVI RONMENT | LISTEN ING | BASIC BATTERY | COMPLETE BATTERY |
|---|---|---|---|---|---|---|---|---|---|---|---|---|
| **WPS** | | | | | | | | | | | | |
| FALL 00 | 60 | 52 | 63 | 64 | 62 | 59 | 61 | 44 | 57 | 52 | 58 | 57 |
| **FDES** | | | | | | | | | | | | |
| FALL 00 | 73 | 73 | 74 | 72 | 74 | 74 | 64 | 64 | 77 | 73 | 71 | 75 |
| **QES** | | | | | | | | | | | | |
| FALL 00 | 69 | 61 | 69 | 66 | 72 | 69 | 72 | 51 | 61 | 54 | 70 | 69 |
| **JKES** | | | | | | | | | | | | |
| FALL 00 | 57 | 42 | 64 | 68 | 64 | 55 | 66 | 34 | 58 | 57 | 55 | 51 |
| **VACD** | | | | | | | | | | | | |
| FALL 00 | 45 | 38 | 52 | 56 | 44 | 44 | 46 | 31 | 41 | 36 | 42 | 41 |

JVL 11/22/2000

Figure 9–12. Comparison of test results of second graders in Winchester's five elementary schools

267

| Child | Fall | Spring |
|---|---|---|
| Channing | 17 | 88 |
| Holly | 32 | 75 |
| Uvaldo | 19 | 84 |
| Timea | 28 | 85 |
| Megan | 13 | 68 |

**Figure 9–13.** Comparison of Results on the PALS Screening Test

literacy gained from a balanced read-aloud program and writing workshop in kindergarten and first grade had something to do with this change in test scores."

Of the five children I worked with in Deena Baker's class at Virginia Avenue Elementary School, all but one met the PALS benchmark score of 72. Megan made gains during the year and fell short of the benchmark score of 72. Individual PALS scores coincided with what Deena observed: Megan is unable to hear beginning sounds, match sounds and alphabet letters, and recognize twenty-four of the

**Figure 9–14.** Timea's writing in September

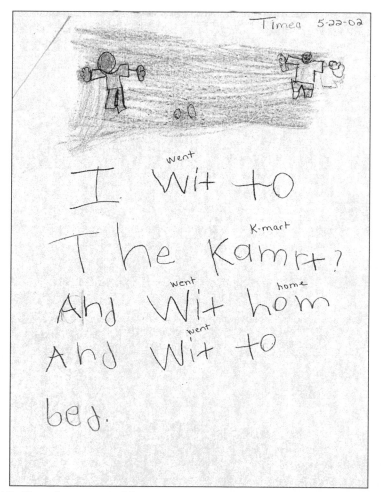

twenty-six lowercase letters. Even though Megan had developed book knowledge and concepts about print, Deena's evaluation of Megan's performance assessments indicated that she did not have the emergent literacy needed for success in first grade.

Figure 9–13 is a comparison of the five children's fall and spring summed scores on the PALS Screening Test.

A comparison of this group's baseline piece of writing completed on September 5, 2001, with their last piece of writing, completed on May 22, 2002, shows growth that neither the PALS alone nor assessments such as alphabet and book knowledge can reveal. The directions from the teacher are simply, "Write a story." No teacher assistance is given.

In September, Timea's writing has her name, a picture that lacks specific details, and a dictated message that the teacher recorded (Figure 9–14). In May, Timea's drawing matches her story and the figures are detailed (Figure 9–15). She

**Figure 9–15.** Timea's writing in May

divides her message into two sentences that can be read by me and Deena. Though Timea incorrectly uses a question mark, her writing shows that she has absorbed punctuation and is experimenting with its use in her writing. She starts each sentence with an uppercase letter, and spells seven words correctly. Invented spellings reveal good phonemic awareness and Timea's ability to hear vowels in the middle of a word. Directionality and spacing of words are excellent. Timea even indented "to mark a paragraph." Using a range of assessments, especially student's writing, enables teachers to determine each child's progress and decide the best placement for the following year.

## Literacy Links: Implications for Teaching and Learning

Rigid recipes, such as scripted programs, and one-size-fits-all programs that the government sanctions—programs that categorize all human beings under one heading and place them into an environment that Lois Lowery called "sameness" in *The Giver* (1993), fail to recognize the uniqueness of each individual child. The emphasis that state and federal politicians have placed on high-stakes testing has resulted in parents and school administrators looking for a program that fixes students' learning in a short amount of time.

The pressure to gain state accreditation in Virginia has caused several elementary schools to adopt a rigid tutorial plan to help children who arrive at school in the preemergent or preliterate stage score high on the PALS test at the close of the year (Figure 9–16). This tutorial divides learning into small time bites. The tutorial uses simple caption books or ones with a patterned text that teachers use for guided reading. Children in the preliterate stage memorize a text before they have developed a knowledge of story structure, book knowledge, concepts about print, and so on. One tutor using this format that changes weekly observed that the process produces great anxiety and frustration between tutor and children. So why this ritualized attempt at stuffing knowledge into children when they aren't ready to receive it?

The goal of high-stakes testing is that schools reach benchmark scores in two to three years. What's not considered is the population schools serve. For example, a school where 30 percent of the children are ESL and more than 60 percent of the children are on free breakfast and lunch because their families live in poverty, has a population that doesn't score high on standardized tests. Over one year, such a school might improve their reading and math test scores from a summed average of 15 percent to a summed average of 35 percent. Even though scores have more than doubled, indicating that there is progress, this school will be designated a failing school.

A large county in Florida removed its entire secondary education and reading administrative staff—more than one dozen men and women and offered them

Student: _____ Tutor: _____ Date: _____ Lesson #@@

| Preliterate Reader Plan | Activity/Book | Time | Outcome/Comment |
|---|---|---|---|
| *Rereading* | Read book from previous lesson | 5 min. | — Child can read material quickly and correctly |
| *Word Study* | **Letter Formation**<br>• Letter: l  Say: top, down<br>(Review formation of other letters in ABC book) | 1 min. | — Child held pencil correctly<br>— Child said formation while writing |
| | **Word/Letter to Fluency**<br>• @@: "is" 5 mediums (floor, chair, air, marker, crayon, paint brush, pencil, back, magnetic letters, playdough, sandpaper) | 3 min. | — Child completed task with ease or comment: |
| | **Phonics**<br>• @@: Name It "l" (font sort) | 2 min. | — Child completed sort with ease or comment: |
| | **Letter/Sound Associations**<br>• Using abc cards ask beginning sound for cat, goat, raccoon, valentine | 1 min. | — List incorrect associations: |
| *Writing* | Ask:  What is a color you like?<br>Write: | 10 min. | — Child formed letters correctly<br>— Space between words<br>— Child read text back |
| *New Reading* | Title: @@ | 5 min. | |

Figure 9–16. Tutorial plan to help at-risk children score high on PALS test

271

lower-level positions. The reason? The superintendent was hired and given a large salary to raise test scores. When some schools failed, to save his position, the superintendent demoted a dedicated staff. Here are the statistics that caused these actions:

❏   Out of eighty elementary schools, three failed state tests.
❏   Out of twenty-three high schools, four failed state tests.
❏   All twenty-nine middle schools passed state tests.

The high schools that failed were in high poverty areas with a large migrant worker population. The number of schools that passed far outnumbered those that failed. Hiring a superintendent to raise test scores is not the way to improve teaching and raise students' achievement.

Instead of pouring millions of dollars into creating more tests and scripted programs whose sole purpose is to raise schools' scores on one annual test, schools need to address issues that affect teachers and teaching, students and learning.

## Raising the Level of Teaching

Richard Allington (2002) writes that recent studies show that "Good teachers, effective teachers, matter much more than particular curriculum materials, pedagogical approaches, or 'proven programs'"(740). Studies completed by Allington and Johnston (2001), Linda Darling-Hammond (1999), and Duffey (1997) all make it quite clear that ongoing professional study and outstanding preservice training can create effective, highly skilled teachers who continually update and enlarge their knowledge of how children learn.

To accomplish this, schools need to invest in building level professional study programs that meet teachers' diverse backgrounds and experience (Robb 2000b). Teachers need to organize support groups, have weekly conversations on teaching (Routman 2002), and study professional articles and books together. Administrators need to make time for teachers to learn and continue to grow as professionals as well as join study groups so they can support their faculty and students.

Schools that make ongoing professional study a top priority enable teachers to continually gain the background knowledge and reflect on educational theory and practice. Ongoing professional study creates effective teachers who have the theoretical background to be responsive decision-makers and meet the diverse needs of the students they teach.

## Raising the Level of Students' Learning

There are many states in this country that have classrooms packed with forty to forty-seven students. In a county in Florida, where I was brought in to train teachers to

272

organize students for small group instruction and one-on-one reading and writing conferences, teachers wondered how it was possible to bring these practices to a class with that many children. It's not possible, especially when classes also have a large percentage of at-risk learners. In such classes most teachers struggle to maintain control as they teach the entire group, rather than individuals.

Literacy Links programs demonstrated that small classes and/or working with small groups of children does enable children to progress. The resounding conclusion for me is that the best way to help those children who lack emergent literacy is to give them the time to experience the hours of family storybook reading they missed.

Reading aloud should begin at birth. Communities and schools can develop programs that show expecting mothers and fathers how to read interactively with a child as well as the importance of reading aloud for their child's future success in school. Requiring middle and high school students to give community service by reading aloud at day care centers and in schools teaches these students the read-aloud process and builds strong bonds between young and old. When the concept of "a community of readers and learners" bursts beyond the walls of a classroom and spills over into community life, children can arrive at school having heard more than the one thousand hours of stories that Adams suggests they need to succeed. I believe that children living in poverty must have the benefits of exemplary preschool programs that also educate parents and adults and are funded by state and federal governments. In a learning environment that encourages literacy development, these children will gather the family storybook reading experiences and conversations with adults, and enlarge their background knowledge, before entering kindergarten.

## Closing Reflections

As far back as the early 1960s, a landmark study called the *High/Scope Perry Preschool Study* clearly established the "human and financial value of high-quality preschool education" (Schweinhart 2002, 7). In 1975, Lawrence J. Schweinhart joined the team that evaluated the study and wrote about it in the June 2002 issue of Phi Delta Kappa International's *Newsletter*. The Perry Preschool Study looked at the effects of the program on the children after they completed preschool, at age 10, at age 15, at age 19, and at age 27. The research team is presently collecting data on participants at age 39 through 41. The summary of findings is quite remarkable.

❑ Adults in the program were four times more likely to earn $2,000 or more per month than those who did not participate in the program.
❑ High school degrees and GED certification were earned by 71 percent of those in the program, compared to 54 percent of those who did not participate.

❏ Analysis of data gathered about participants in the program who were 27 years old discovered that every tax dollar spent on the preschool program translated into these economic benefits: higher earnings, fewer special education services, less welfare assistance, and lower crime and punishment rates.

The message from this study is clear. Investing in very young children by creating outstanding preschool programs and helping all families build literate home environments can make a huge difference in children's lives. Words are empty and meaningless rhetoric until we transform them into positive actions. To build a nation of children who enter school having heard more than one thousand hours of stories means that the preschool and community programs we develop need to bring the finest books to children and their families. It also means that schools, parents, and communities must forge strong and lasting partnerships in order to care for and meet the learning and emotional needs of every child in a community. Then, perhaps, we can eradicate the harsh inequalities that exist between the poor and middle and upper classes.

# Appendix

Books About Phonemic Awareness

Twenty Top-notch Rhyming Books for Language Play

Twenty Top-notch Patterned and Repetitive Books

Twenty Top-notch Nonfiction Read-Alouds

Thirty Books Children Will Want to Hear Again and Again

Ten Top-notch Alphabet Books

Ten Top-notch Counting Books

Log of Storybooks Read Each Week

Twenty-five High-Frequency Words

Discussion Graph for *Noisy Nora* by Rosemary Wells

Take-Home Stories Form

Making Masking Devices

## Books About Phonemic Awareness

*A Basic Guide to Understanding, Assessing, and Teaching Phonological Awareness* by Joseph K. Torgesen & Patricia G. Mathes. 2000. Pro-Ed, 8700 Shoal Creek Boulevard, Austin, TX 778757-6897.

*Teaching Phonics, Phonemic Awareness, and Word Recognition* by Ashley Bishop and Suzanne Bishop. 1996. Teacher-created materials, 6421 Industry Way, Westminster, CA 92683.

*Teaching Phonics Today: A Primer for Educators* by Dorothy Strickland. 1998. Newark, DE: International Reading Association.

## *Books That Also Contain Linguistic Background Information*

*Phonemic Awareness in Young Children: A Classroom Curriculum* by Marilyn Jager Adams, Barbara R. Forman, Ingvar Lundberg, and Terri Beeler. 1998. Paul H. Brookes, PO Box 10624, Baltimore, MD 21285-0624.

*Road to the Code: A Phonological Awareness Program for Young Children* by Benita A. Blachman, Eileen Wynne Ball, Rochella Black, and Darlene M. Tangel. 2000. Paul H. Brookes, PO Box 10624, Baltimore, MD 21285-0624.

*Phonemic Awareness: Playing with Sounds to Strengthen Beginning Reading Skills* by Jo Fitzpatrick. 1997. Creative Teaching Press, PO Box 2723, Huntington Beach, CA 92647-0723.

*Phonemic Awareness Activities for Early Reading Success: Easy, Playful Activities That Prepare Children for Phonics Instruction* by Wiley Blevins. 1997. Scholastic, 524 Broadway, New York, NY 10012.

*Phonemic Awareness Songs and Rhymes* by Wiley Blevins. 1999. Scholastic, 524 Broadway, New York, NY 10012.

# Twenty Top-notch Rhyming Books for Language Play

*Baby Tamer* written and illustrated by Mark Teague. 1997. New York: Scholastic.

*Barn Dance!* by Bill Martin Jr. and John Archambault. 1996. Illus. by Ted Rand. New York: Henry Holt.

*A Beasty Story* by Bill Martin Jr. and Steven Kellogg. 1999. Illus. by Steven Kellogg. San Diego, CA: Harcourt.

*Big Bear Ball* by Joanne Ryer. 2002. Illus. by Steven Kellogg. New York: HarperCollins.

*Central Park Serenade* by Laura Godwin. 2002. Pictures by Barry Root. New York: HarperCollins.

*Down by the Cool of the Pool* by Tony Mitton. 2001. Pictures by Guy Parker Rees. New York: Orchard.

*Fix-It Duck* by Jez Alborough. 2001. New York: HarperCollins.

*Higgle Wiggle: Happy Rhymes* by Eve Merriam. 1994. Pictures by Hans Wilhelm. New York: Mulberry Books.

*Homes* poems by Carol Diggory Shields. 2001. Paintings by Sujetlan Juna Ković. New York: Handprint Books.

*A Hug Goes Around* by Laura Krauss Melmed. 2002. Illus. by Betsy Lewin. HarperCollins.

*If the Shoe Fits* by Gary Soto. 2002. Illus. by Terry Widener. New York: Terry Widener.

*Lizards, Frogs, and Polliwogs,* poems and paintings by Douglas Florian. 2001. San Diego, CA: Harcourt.

*Once Upon a Farm* by Marie Bradby. 2002. Illus. by Ted Rand. New York: Orchard Books.

*A Pinky Is a Baby Mouse and Other Baby Animal Names* by Pam Munoz Ryan. 1997. Illus. by Diane deGroat. New York: Hyperion.

*Moondogs* written and illustrated by Daniel Kirk. 1999. New York: Putnam.

*My World of Color* by Margaret Wise Brown. 2002. Pictures by Loretta Krupinski. New York: Hyperion.

*No Hickory, No Dickory, No Dock: Caribbean Nursery Rhymes.* Written and remembered by John Agard and Grace Nichols. 1995. Illus. by Cynthia Jabar. Cambridge, MA: Candlewick.

*Puffins Climb, Penguins Rhyme* written and illustrated by Bruce McMillan. 2001. New York: Harcourt.

*Riddle Rhymes* by Charles Ghigna. 1995. Illus. by Julia Gorton. New York: Hyperion.

*Summersaults,* poems and paintings by Douglas Florian. 2002. New York: Greenwillow.

# Twenty Top-notch Patterned and Repetitive Books

*A-Hunting We Will Go!* written and illus. by Steven Kellogg. 1998. New York: Morrow.

*BOO to a goose* by Mem Fox. 1996. Pictures by David Miller. New York: Puffin.

*Chili-Chili-Chin-Chin* written and illus. by Belle Yang. 1999. San Diego, CA: Harcourt.

*Does A Kangaroo Have A Mother Too?* written and illus. by Eric Carle. 2000. New York: HarperCollins.

*Hattie and the Fox* by Mem Fox. 1986. Illus. by Patricia Mullins. New York: Bradbury.

*The Important Book* by Margaret Wise Brown. 1949. Pictures by Leonard Weisgard. New York: HarperTrophy.

*Is Your Mama a Llama?* by Deborah Guarino. 1989. Illus. by Steven Kellogg. New York: Scholastic.

*New Cat* written and illus. by Yangsook Choi. 1999. New York: Farrar, Straus & Giroux.

*On the Day You Were Born* written and illus. by Debra Frasier. 1991. New York: Harcourt.

*We're Going on a Picnic* written and illus. by Pat Hutchins. 2002. New York: Greenwillow.

*One Lucky Girl* written and illus. by George Ella Lyon. 2000. New York: DK Publishing.

*Otis* written and illus. by Janie Bynum. 2000. San Diego, CA: Harcourt.

*A Pig Is Big* written and illus. by Douglas Florian. 2000. New York: Greenwillow.

*Rain* written and illus. by Manya Stojic. 2000. New York: Crown.

*The Seals on the Bus* by Lenny Hort. 2000. Illus. by G. Brian Karas. New York: Holt.

*Things That Are Most in the World* by Judi Barrett. 1998. Illus. by John Nickle. New York: Atheneum.

*Tick-Tock* written and illus. by Lena Anderson. 1998. New York: Farrar, Straus & Giroux.

*This Is the Sunflower* by Lola M. Schaefer. 2000. Pictures by Donald Crews. New York: Greenwillow.

*Tortillas and Lullabies/Tortillas y Cancioncitas* by Lynn Reiser. 1998. Illus. by Corazones Valientes. New York: Greenwillow.

*Willy the Dreamer* written and illus. by Anthony Browne. 1998. Cambridge, MA: Candlewick.

# Twenty Top-notch Nonfiction Read-Alouds

*About Reptiles: A Guide for Children* by Cathryn Sill. 1999. Illus. by John Sill. Atlanta, GA: Peachtree.

*Abraham Lincoln* by Amy L. Cohn and Suzy Schmidt. 2002. Pictures by David A. Johnson. New York: Scholastic.

*Butterflies in the Garden* written and illus. by Carol Lerner. 2002. New York: HarperCollins.

*Down, Down, Down, In The Ocean* by Sandra Markle. 1999. Illus. by Bob Marstall. New York: Walker & Company.

*Drip! Drop! How Water Gets To Your Tap* by Barbaras Seuling. 2000. Illus. by Nancy Tobin. New York: Holiday House.

*Everglades* by Jean Craighead George. 1995. Paintings by Wendell Minor. New York: HarperCollins.

*Exploring the Deep, Dark Sea* written and illus. by Gail Gibbons. 1999. Boston, MA: Little Brown.

*From Seed to Plant* written and illus. by Gail Gibbons. 1993. New York: Holiday House.

*Is This a House for Hermit Crab?* by Megan McDonald. 1990. Illus. by S. D. Schindler. New York: Orchard.

*Jody's Beans* by Malachy Doyle. 1999. Illus. by Judith Allibone. Cambridge, MA: Candlewick.

*Messages in the Mailbox: How to Write a Letter* written and illus. by Loreen Leedy. 1991. New York: Holiday House.

*Open Wide: Tooth School Inside* written and illus. by Laurie Keller. 2000. New York: Holt.

*Red-Eyed Tree Frog* by Joy Cowly. 1999. Photographs by Nic Bishop. New York: Scholastic.

*Seymour Simon's Book of Trains* by Seymour Simon. 2002. New York: HarperCollins.

*Snow Is Falling* by Franklyn M. Branley. 2000. Illus. by Holly Keller. Reissue (1986). New York: HarperCollins.

*Starfish* by Edith Thacher Hurd. 2000. Illus. by Robin Brickman. New York: HarperCollins.

*This is the Rain* by Lola M. Schaeffer. 2001. Illus. by Jan Wattenberg. New York: Greenwillow.

*A Tree is a Plant* by Clyde Robert Bulla. 2001. Illus. by Stacey Schuett. (Reissue, 1960). New York: HarperCollins.

*The True-Or-False Book of Horses* by Patricia Lauber. 2000. Illus. by Rosalyn Schanzer. New York: HarperCollins.

*What Do You Do When Something Wants to Eat You?* written and illustrated by Diane Hoyt-Goldsmith. 1997. Boston, MA: Houghton.

## Thirty Books Children Will Want to Hear Again and Again

*A Bargain for Frances* by Russell Hoban. 1970. Illus. by Lillian Hoban. New York: Harper.

*Amazing Grace* by Mary Hoffman. 1991. Illus. by Caroline Binch. New York: Dial.

*The Bravest Ever Bear* by Allan Ahlberg. 2000. Illus. by Paul Howard. Cambridge, MA: Candlewick.

*Buzz* by Janet S. Wong. 2000. Illus. by Margaret Chodos-Irvine. San Diego, CA: Harcourt.

*Caps For Sale: A Tale of a Peddler, Some Monkeys, and Their Monkey Business* told and illus. by Esphyr Slobodkina. 1968. New York: HarperCollins.

*Chrysanthemum* written and illus. by Kevin Henkes. 1991. New York: Greenwillow.

*Come A Tide* by George Ella Lyon. 1990. Pictures by Stephen Gammell. New York: Orchard.

*Daisy Comes Home* written and illus. by Jan Brett. 2002. New York: Putnam.

*Farmer Duck* by Martin Waddell. 1992. Illus. by Helen Oxenbury. Cambridge, MA: Candlewick.

*The Gingerbread Boy* retold and illus. by Richard Egielski. 1997. New York: HarperCollins.

*The Hatseller and the Monkeys* written and illus. by Baba Wague Diakite. 1999. New York: Scholastic.

*Hunter's Best Friend at School* by Laura Malone Elliott. 2002. Illus. by Lynn Munsinger. New York: HarperCollins.

*Juan Bobo Goes to Work* retold by Marisa Montes. 2000. Illus. by Joe Cepeda. New York: HarperCollins.

*3 Magic Balls* by Richard Egielski. 2000. New York: HarperCollins.

*McDuff Saves The Day* by Rosemary Wells. 2002. Illus. by Susan Jeffers. New York: Hyperion.

*Mud Is Cake* by Pam Munoz Ryan. 2002. Illus. by David McPhail. New York: Hyperion.

*Madeline* written and illus. by Ludwig Bemelmans. 1998. New York: Puffin.

*Matthew's Dream* written and illus. by Leo Lionni. 1991. New York: Knopf.

*Me Too!: Two Small Stories About Small Animals* written and illus. by Katya Arnold. 2000. New York: Holiday House.

*Officer Buckle and Gloria* written and illus. by Peggy Rathman. 1995. New York: Putnam.

*Out of the Ocean* written and illus. by Debra Frasier. 1998. San Diego, CA: Harcourt.

*A Place to Grow* by Soyung Pak. 2002. Illus. by Marcelino Truong. New York: Scholastic.

*Read-Aloud Rhymes for the Very Young* selected by Jack Prelutsky. 1986. Illus. by Marc Brown. New York: Knopf.

*Sometimes I'm BOMBALOO* by Rachel Vail. 2002. Illus. by Yumi Heo. New York: Scholastic.

*The Snow Bear* by Liliana Stafford. 2002. Illus. by Lambert Davis. New York: Scholastic.

*A Story for Bear* by Dennis Haseley. 2002. Illus. by Jim LaMarche. San Diego, CA: Harcourt.

*The Story of Chopsticks* by Ying Cnang Compestine. 2001. Illus. by YongSheng Yuan. New York: Holiday House.

*Sweet, Sweet Memory* by Jacqueline Woodson. 2000. Illus. by Floyd Cooper. New York: Hyperion.

*Tumble Me Tumbily* by Karen Baiker. 2002. Illus. by David Bennett. New York: Handprint.

*When I Am Old and With You* by Angela J. Johnson. 1990. Pictures by David Soman. New York: Orchard.

# Ten Top-notch Alphabet Books

*Alphabestiary: Animal Poems from A to Z* collected by Jane Yolen. 1995. Illus. by Allan Eitzen. Honesdale, PA: Boyds Mills.

*A Was Once an Apple Pie* by Edward Lear. 1997. Illus. by Julie Lacome. Cambridge, MA: Candlewick.

*B is for Baby: An Alphabet of Verses* by Myra Cohn Livingston. 1996. Photographs by Steel Stillman. New York: McElderry/Simon & Schuster.

*The Baseball Counting Book* by Barbara McGrath. 1999. Illus. by Brian Shaw. Watertown, MA: Charlesbridge.

*Chicka Chicka Boom Boom* by Bill Martin Jr. and John Archambault. 1989. Illus. by Lois Ehlert. New York: Simon & Schuster.

*Girls A to Z* by Eve Bunting. 2002. Illus. by Suzanne Bloom. Honesdale, PA: Boyds Mill Press.

*Matthew A.B.C.* written and illus. by Peter Catalanotto. 2002. New York: Atheneum.

*My Beastie Book of A B C* written and illustrated. by David Frampton. 2002. New York. HarperCollins.

*V for Vanishing: An Alphabet of Endangered Animals* written and illus. by Patricia Mullins. 1993. New York: HarperCollins.

*The Z Was Zapped* written and illus. by Chris Van Allsburg. 1987. Boston, MA: Houghton.

## Ten Top-notch Counting Books

*A Creepy Countdown* by Charlotte Huck. 1998. Pictures by Jos. A. Smith. New York: Greenwillow.

*Dancing in the Moon: Counting Rhymes* written and illus. by Fritz Eichenberg. 1975. San Diego, CA: Harcourt.

*Moja Means One: Swahili Counting Book* by Muriel Feelings. 1971. Illus. by Tom Feelings. New York: Dial.

*1 2 3 Pop!* written and illus. by Rachel Isadora. 2000. New York: Viking.

*1 Is One* by Tasha Tudor. 2000. (Reissue 1956, Oxford) New York: Simon & Schuster.

*Over in the Meadow* written and illus. by Ezra Jack Keats. 1999. (Reissue 1971, Four Winds) New York: Viking.

*Ten Go Tango* by Arthur Dorros. 2000. Pictures by Emily Arnold McCully. New York: HarperCollins.

*Ten Red Apples* written and illus. by Pat Hutchins. 2000. New York: Greenwillow.

*Ten Sly Piranhas: A Counting Story in Reverse* by William Wise. 1993. Pictures by Victoria Chess.

*Zin! Zin! Zin! A Violin* by Lloyd Moss. 1995. Illus. by Marjorie Priceman. New York: Simon & Schuster.

# Log of Storybooks Read Each Week

Week of _____

**Title and Author**                        **Number of Times**

**Monday:**

_____

_____

_____

_____

**Tuesday:**

_____

_____

_____

_____

**Wednesday:**

_____

_____

_____

_____

**Thursday:**

_____

_____

_____

_____

**Friday:**

_____

_____

_____

_____

## Twenty-five Easy High-Frequency Words

These words occur frequently in oral and written language. Place the words on a word wall and encourage children to use them during writing workshop. Help children learn these high-frequency words by adding a noun, adjective, or verb to each one so they can associate meaning with each word. For example, *a truck, she runs, is big,* and so on. Add these words, when appropriate, to labels in your room, such as *my desk, the computer, paper and pencils.*

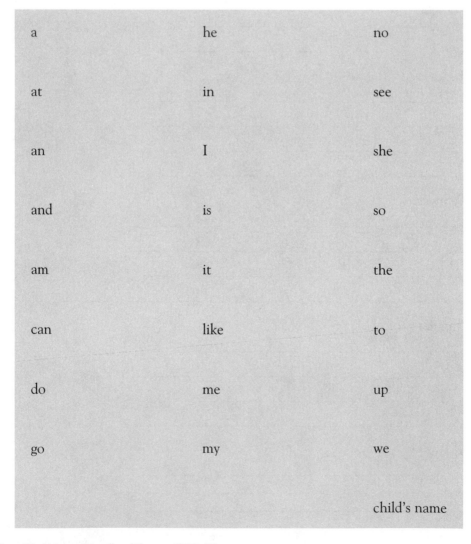

| a   | he   | no          |
| at  | in   | see         |
| an  | I    | she         |
| and | is   | so          |
| am  | it   | the         |
| can | like | to          |
| do  | me   | up          |
| go  | my   | we          |
|     |      | child's name |

From *Word Matters,* Pinnell and Fountas (1998, 89)

## Discussion Graph for *Noisy Nora* by Rosemary Wells

|  | Nora | Father | Kate | Jack | Mother |
|---|---|---|---|---|---|
| **Worried** |  |  |  |  |  |
| **Angry** |  |  |  |  |  |
| **Impatient** |  |  |  |  |  |
| **Jealous** |  |  |  |  |  |
| **Sad** |  |  |  |  |  |
| **Mean** |  |  |  |  |  |
| **Spiteful** |  |  |  |  |  |
| **Naughty** |  |  |  |  |  |

## Take-Home Stories Form

- ❏ Open the envelope. Inside you'll find a library book and a recordkeeping form.
- ❏ Read the book to your child. Any family member can do this.
- ❏ Reread the book often.
- ❏ Encourage your child to use the pictures to retell the story after a family member has read the book aloud to the child several times.
- ❏ Write the title and author on the record sheet. Ask your child to comment on the book and record your child's words under "Comments."
- ❏ Put the book and the completed form in the envelope. Have your child return the book and exchange it for a new one.

**1. Date**                          **Title**

———————

**Comments**

———————————————————————

———————————————————————

———————————————————————

**2. Date**                          **Title**

———————

**Comments**

———————————————————————

———————————————————————

———————————————————————

# Making Masking Devices

I recommend making enough of each size so that each child in your class has his or own masking devices. Store these in children's cubbies.

**Materials:** file folders, ruler, pencil, clear tape, scissors

### Directions

1.  From folded part of file folder, use a ruler to measure 4¼ inches and draw a line.
2.  Cut along the line.
3.  Mark off, with a ruler, 2¼ inches from each open edge.
4.  Mark off, with a ruler, 1¼ inches from folded edge and long open edge. This will create a long rectangle that measures 5¾ inches by ⅝ of an inch.
5.  Cut the rectangle out.
6.  Make a slider, by cutting a piece of the remaining file folder that measures 3½ × 10⅛.
7.  Tape together the side opposite the folded side and the shorter, left opening.
8.  Place slider in short opening and use it to uncover one letter, several letters, words, or an entire sentence.
9.  Make other masking devices that have wider or narrower open rectangles so children can use them with different type sizes.

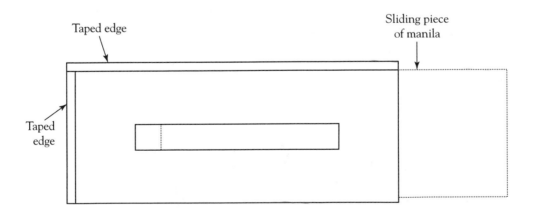

Taped edge

Sliding piece of manila

Taped edge

# Bibliography

## Professional Books and Journals

Adams, M. J. 1990. *Beginning to Read: Thinking and Learning About Print.* Cambridge, MA: MIT Press.

Allington, R. 2002. "What I've Learned About Effective Reading Instruction: From a Decade of Studying Exemplary Elementary Classroom Teachers." *Phi Delta Kappan* 83: 740–47.

Allington, R., and P. Johnston. 2001. "What Do We Know About Effective Fourth Grade Teachers and Their Classrooms?" In *Learning to Teach Reading: Setting the Research Agenda*, edited by C. Roller. Newark, DE: International Reading Association.

Artley, A. S. 1996. "Controversial Issues Relating to Word Perception." *The Reading Teacher* 50 (1): 10–13.

Ashton-Warner, S. 1963. *Teacher.* New York: Simon & Schuster.

Barrentine, S. J. 1996. "Storytime Plus Dialogue Equals Interactive Read Alouds." In *Lively Discussion: Fostering Engaged Reading*, edited by L. B. Gambrell and J. F. Almasi. Newark, DE: International Reading Association.

Bear, D. R., M. Invernizzi, S. Templeton, and F. Johnston. [1996] 2000. *Words Their Way: Word Study for Phonics, Vocabulary, and Spelling Instruction.* Upper Saddle River, NJ: Merrill.

Beck, I. L., M. G. McKeown, R. L. Hamilton, and L. Kucan. 1997. *Questioning the Author: An Approach for Enhancing Student Engagement with Text.* Newark, DE: International Reading Association.

Bembry, K. L., H. R. Jordan, E. Gomez, M. Anderson, and R. L. Mendro. 1998. Policy Implications of Long-Term Teacher Effects on Student Achievement. Paper presented at the American Educational Research Association.

Bruner, J. 1985. *Child's Talk: Learning to Use Language.* New York: W. W. Norton.

Burgess, K. A., K. A. Lundgren, J. W. Lloyd, and R. C. Pianta. 2001. Preschool Teachers' Self-Reported Beliefs and Practices About Literacy Instruction. University of Virginia. CIERA Report #2-012.

Burns, S. M., P. Griffin, and C. E. Snow, eds. 1999. *Starting Out Right: A Guide to Promoting Children's Reading Success.* National Research Council. Washington, DC: National Academy Press.

Calkins, L. M. [1986] 1994. *The Art of Teaching Writing* (New Ed.). Portsmouth, NH: Heinemann.

Calkins, L. M., with S. Harwayne. 1991. *Living Between the Lines*. Portsmouth, NH: Heinemann.

Cambourne, B. 1988. *The Whole Story: Natural Learning and the Acquisition of Literacy in the Classroom*. Auckland, NZ: Ashton, Scholastic.

Campbell, R. 2001. *Read-Alouds with Young Children*. Newark, DE: International Reading Association.

Casbergue, R. M. 1998. "How Do We Foster Young Children's Writing Development?" In *Children Achieving: Best Practices in Early Literacy*, edited by S. B. Neuman and K. A. Roskos. Newark, DE: International Reading Association.

Cazden, C. 1983. "Adult Assistance to Language Development: Scaffolds, Models, and Direct Instruction." In *Developing Literacy: Young Children's Use of Language*, edited by R. P. Parker and F. A. Davis. Newark, DE: International Reading Association.

Chomsky, C. 1971. "Write First, Read Later." *Childhood Education*, 47, 296–99.

Chomsky, N. 1968. *Language and Mind*. New York: Harcourt, Brace, Jovanovich.

Clay, M. M. [1979] 2000. *Concepts About Print: What Have Children Learned About the Way We Print Language?* Portsmouth, NH: Heinemann.

———. 1998. *By Different Paths to Common Outcomes*. Portsmouth, NH: Heinemann.

———. 1991. *Becoming Literate: The Construction of Inner Control*. Portsmouth, NH: Heinemann.

———. 1986. *The Early Detection of Reading Difficulties, with Recovery Procedures*. 3rd ed. Portsmouth, NH: Heinemann.

———. 1985. *Reading: The Patterning of Complex Behavior*. Portsmouth, NH: Heinemann.

Clymer, T. [1963] 1996. "The Utility of Phonic Generalizations in the Primary Grades." *The Reading Teacher* 50: 182–97.

Coles, R. 1989. *The Call of Stories: Teaching and the Moral Imagination*. Boston: Houghton Mifflin.

Cullinan, B. E. [1992] 2000. *Read to Me: Raising Kids Who Love to Read*. New York: Scholastic.

Cunningham, P. M. [1995] 2000. *Phonics They Use: Words for Reading and Writing*. 2nd and 3rd eds. New York: HarperCollins.

Cunningham, P. M., and R. L. Allington. 1999. *Classrooms That Work: They Can All Read and Write*. 2nd ed. New York: Longman.

Cunningham, P. M., and J. W. Cunningham. 2002. "What We Know About How to Teach Phonics." In *What Research Has to Say About Reading Instruction*, edited by A. E. Farstrup and S. J. Samuels. Newark, DE: International Reading Association.

Cunningham, P. M., D. P. Hall, and M. Defoe. 1998. "Nonability Grouped, Multilevel Instruction: Light Years Later." *The Reading Teacher* 51: 652–64.

Cunningham, P. M., S. A. Moore, J. W. Cunningham, and D. W. Moore. 1989. *Reading in Elementary Classrooms: Strategies and Observations*. New York: Longman.

Dahl, K. L., P. L. Scharer, L. L. Lawson, and P. R. Grogan. 2001. *Rethinking Phonics: Making the Best Teaching Decisions*. Portsmouth, NH: Heinemann.

Darling-Hammond, L. 1999. *Teaching Quality and Student Achievement: A Review of State Policy Evidence*. Seattle, WA: Center of Teaching Policy, University of Washington.

Delpit, L. D. 1986. "Skills and Other Dilemmas of a Progressive Black Educator." *The Harvard Review* 56 (4): 379–85.

Donovan, C. A., and L. B. Smolkin. 2002. "Considering Genre, Content, and Visual Features in the Selection of Trade Books for Science Instruction." *The Reading Teacher* 55 (6): 502–20.

Duffey, G. G. 1997. "Powerful Models or Poserful Teachers? An Argument for Teacher-as-Entrepeneur." In *Instructional Models of Reading*, edited by S. Stah and D. Hayes. Mahwah, NJ: Erlbaum.

Duffy, R. 1994. "It's Just Like Talking to Each Other: Written Conversation with Five-Year-Old Children." In *Keeping in Touch: Using Interactive Writing with Young Children*. Portsmouth, NH: Heinemann.

Duke, N. K. 1999. The Scarcity of Informational Texts in First Grade. Michigan State University CIERA Report #1-007.

Dyson, A. H. 1990. "Weaving Possibilities: Rethinking Metaphors for Early Literacy Development." *The Reading Teacher* 44 (3): 202–13.

———. 1987. "Individual Differences in Beginning Composing: An Orchestral Vision of Learning to Compose." *Written Communication* 4: 411–42.

———. 1983. "The Role of Oral Language in Early Writing Processes." *Research in the Teaching of English* 17: 1–30.

———. 1982. "The Emergence of Visible Language: Interrelationships Between Drawing and Early Writing." *Visible Language* 6: 360–81.

Ehrenreich, B. 2001. *Nickel and Dimed: On (Not) Getting By in America*. New York: Metropolitan Books.

Ehri, L. C., S. R. Nunes, D. M. Willows, B. V. Schuster, and Z. Yaghoub-Zadeh. 2001. "Phonemic Awareness Instruction Helps Children Learn to Read: Evidence from the National Reading Panel's Meta-analysis." *Reading Research Quarterly* 36(5): 250–87.

Elkonin, D. B. 1973. "Methods of Teaching Reading: USSR." In *Comparative Reading: Cross-National Studies of Behavior and Processes in Reading and Writing*, edited by J. Downing. New York: Macmillan.

Ericson, L., and M. F. Juliebo. 1998. *The Phonological Awareness Handbook for Kindergarten and Primary Teachers*. Newark, DE: International Reading Association.

Fiderer, A. 1998. *35 Rubrics and Checklists to Assess Reading and Writing: Time-Saving Reproducible Forms for Meaningful Assessment*. New York: Scholastic.

Fielding, L. G., and C. M. Roller. 1998. "Theory Becomes Practice at the Point of Intersection." *Primary Voices K–6* 7(1): 2–8.

Fisher, B. 1998. *Joyful Learning in Kindergarten*. Rev. ed. Portsmouth, NH: Heinemann.

———. 1991. "Getting Started with Writing." *Teaching K–8* (August/September): 49–51.

Fisher, B., and E. F. Medvic. 2000. *Perspectives on Shared Reading: Planning and Practice*. Portsmouth, NH: Heinemann.

Flippo, R. F. 1999. *What Do the Experts Say? Helping Children Learn to Read.* Portsmouth, NH: Heinemann.

Fountas, I. C., and G. S. Pinnell. 1998. *Word Matters: Teaching Phonics and Spelling in the Reading/Writing Classroom.* Portsmouth, NH: Heinemann.

———. 1997. *Guided Reading: Good First Teaching for All Children.* Portsmouth, NH: Heinemann.

Fox, M. 2001. *Reading Magic: Why Reading Aloud to Our Children Will Change Their Lives Forever.* San Diego, CA: Harcourt.

Gallagher, P., and G. Norton. 2000. *A Jumpstart to Literacy: Using Written Conversation to Help Developing Readers and Writers.* Portsmouth, NH: Heinemann.

Gambrell, L. B. 1996. "What Research Reveals About Discussion." In *Lively Discussion: Fostering Engaged Reading,* edited by L. B. Gambrell and J. F. Almasi. Newark, DE: International Reading Association.

Gesell, A., and F. Ilg. 1949. *Child Development: An Introduction to Human Growth.* New York: Harper and Brothers.

Gillet, J. W., and C. Temple. 2000. *Understanding Reading Problems: Assessment and Instruction.* 5th ed. New York: Longman.

Goodman, Y. 1981. "Test Review; Concepts About Print Test." *The Reading Teacher* 34, 445–48.

———. 1978. "Kidwatching: An Alternative to Testing." *National Elementary Principal* 57: 41–45.

Graves, D. 1983. *Writing: Teachers and Children at Work.* Portsmouth, NH: Heinemann.

Hall, N. 1991. "Play and the Emergence of Literacy." In *Play and Early Literacy Development,* edited by J. Christie. Albany, NY: State University of New York Press.

Hall, N., and A. Robinson. 1994. *Keeping in Touch: Using Interactive Writing with Young Children.* Portsmouth, NH: Heinemann.

Halliday, M. A. K. 1975. *Learning How to Mean: Explorations in the Development of Language.* New York: Elsevier North-Holland.

Hannon, P. 1998. "How Can We Foster Children's Early Literacy Development Through Parent Involvement?" In *Children Achieving: Best Practices in Early Literacy,* edited by S. B. Newuman and K. A. Roskos. Newark, DE: International Reading Association.

Harvey, S., and A. Gouevis. 2000. *Strategies That Work: Teaching Comprehension to Enhance Understanding.* York, ME: Stenhouse.

Heath, S. B. 1983. *Ways with Words. Language, Life, and Work in Communities, and Classrooms.* Cambridge, MA: Cambridge University Press.

Heath, S. B., and L. Mangiola. 1991. *Children of Promise: Literate Activity in Linguistically and Culturally Diverse Classrooms.* Washington, DC: National Education Association.

Henderson, E. 1985. *Teaching Spelling.* Boston: Houghton Mifflin.

Hill, B. C., and C. Ruptic. 1994. *Practical Aspects of Authentic Assessment: Putting the Pieces Together.* Norwood, MA: Christopher-Gordon.

Holdaway, D. 1979. *The Foundations of Literacy.* Portsmouth, NH: Heinemann.

Huck, C. S. 1992. "Literature and Literacy." *Language Arts* 69: 520–25.

International Reading Association (IRA) and National Association for the Education of Young People (NAEYP). 1998. "Learning to Read and Write: Developmentally Appropriate Practices for Young Children." *The Reading Teacher* 52: 193–213.

Johnston, P. H. 1992. *Constructive Evaluation of Literate Activity*. New York: Longman.

Keene, E. O., and S. Zimmerman. 1997. *Mosaic of Thought*. Portsmouth, NH: Heinemann.

Lewkowica, N. 1980. "Phonemic Awareness Training: What to Teach and How to Teach It." *Journal of Educational Psychology* 72: 686–700.

Lundberg, I., J. Frost, and O-P. Petersen. 1988. "Effects of an Extensive Program for Stimulating Phonological Awareness in Preschool Children." *Reading Research Quarterly* 23: 264–84.

Lyon, G. E. 1994. "Gifts, Not Stars." In *Whole Language, Whole Learners: Creating a Literature-Centered Curriculum* edited by L. Robb. New York: Morrow.

Mason, J. M., C. L. Peterman, and B. M. Kerr. 1986. "Reading to Kindergarten Children." In *Emerging Literacy: Young Children Learn to Read and Write*, edited by D. S. Strickland and L. M. Morrow. Newark, DE: International Reading Association.

McCarrier, A., G. S. Pinnell, and I. C. Fountas. 2000. *Interactive Writing: How Language and Literacy Come Together, K–2*. Portsmouth, NH: Heinemann.

McGee, L. M. 1998. "How Do We Teach Literature to Young Children?" In *Children Achieving: Best Practices in Early Literacy*, edited by S. B. Neuman and K. A. Roskos. Newark, DE: International Reading Association.

Moustafa, M. 1997. *Beyond Traditional Phonics: Research Discoveries and Reading Instruction*. Portsmouth, NH: Heinemann.

Murray, D. 1984. *Write to Learn*. New York: Holt, Rinehart and Winston.

National Assessment of Educational Progress (NAEP). 1999. *NAEP 1998 Reading Report Card for the Nation and the States* [Online]. Available at http://www.ed.gov/NCES/NEAP.

National Reading Panel. 2000a. Teaching Children to Read: An Evidence-based Assessment of the Scientific Research Literature on Reading and Its Implications for Reading Instruction. National Institute of Health Pub. No. 00-4769. Washington, DC: National Institute of Child Health and Human Development.

National Reading Panel. 2000b. Teaching Children to Read: An Evidence-based Assessment of the Scientific Research Literature on Reading and Its Implications for Reading Instruction: Reports of the Subgroups. National Institute of Health Pub. No. 00-4754. Washington, DC: National Institute of Child Health and Human Development.

Neuman, S. B. 1998. "How Can We Enable All Children to Achieve?" In *Children Achieving: Best Practices in Early Literacy*, edited by S. B. Neuman and K. A. Roskos. Newark, DE: International Reading Association.

Neuman, S. B., and S. Bredekamp. 2002. "Becoming a Reader: A Developmentally Appropriate Approach." In *Beginning Reading and Writing*, edited by D. S. Strickland and L. M. Morrow. Newark, DE: International Reading Association.

Neuman, S. B., and D. Delano. 2001. "Books Aloud: A Campaign to 'Put Books in Children's Hands.'" *The Reading Teacher* 54(6): 550–57.

Neuman, S. B., D. C. Delano, A. N. Greco, and P. Shue. 2001. *Access for All: Closing the Book Gap for Children in Early Education.* Newark, DE: International Reading Association.

Ohanian, S. 1999. *One Size Fits Few.* Portsmouth, NH: Heinemann.

Opitz, M. F. 2000. *Rhymes and Reasons: Literature and Language Play for Phonological Awareness.* Portsmouth, NH: Heinemann.

Owocki, G. 1998. "Facilitating Literacy Through Play and Other Child-Center Experiences." In *Facilitating Preschool Literacy,* edited by R. Campbell. Newark, DE: International Reading Association.

Owocki, G. 1999. *Literacy Through Play.* Portsmouth, NH: Heinemann.

Payne, C. D., and M. B. Schulman. 2000. *Guided Reading: Making It Work.* New York: Scholastic.

Pearson, P. D. 1996. "Reclaiming the Center." In *The First R: Every Child's Right to Read,* edited by M. E. Graves, P. van den Broek, and B. M. Taylor. New York: Teachers College Press and Newark, DE: International Reading Association.

Pearson, P. D., and L. Fielding. 1991. "Comprehension Instruction." In *Handbook of Reading Research,* edited by M. Kamil, R. Barr, P. Mosenthal, and P. D. Pearson, vol. 2, pp. 815–60. New York: Longman.

Pearson, P. D., L. R. Roehler, J. A. Dole, and G. G. Duffy. 1992. "Developing Expertise in Reading Comprehension." In *What Research Has to Say About Reading Instruction,* 2nd ed., edited by J. Samuels and A. Farstrup. Newark, DE: International Reading Association.

Pellegrini, A. D., and L. Galda. 2000. "Children's Pretend Play and Literacy." In *Beginning Reading and Writing,* edited by D. S. Strickland and L. M. Morrow. Newark, DE: International Reading Association.

Perlmutter, J., and L. Burrell. 2001. *The First Weeks of School: Laying a Quality Foundation.* Portsmouth, NH: Heinemann.

Pflaum, S. W. 1986. *The Development of Language and Literacy in Young Children.* 3rd ed. Columbus, OH: Charles E. Merrill.

Piaget, J. 1977. *The Development of Thought: Equilibrium of Cognitive Structures.* New York: Viking.

Pianta, R. C., K. M. La Paro, C. Payne, M. J. Cox, and R. Bradley. 2002. "The Relation of Kindergarten Classroom Environment to Teacher, Family, and School Characteristics and Child Outcomes." *The Elementary School Journal* 102(3): 225–38.

Pinker, S. 1994. *The Language Instinct: How the Mind Creates Language.* New York: Morrow.

Pressley, M., R. Wharton-McDonald, R. L. Allington, C. C. Block, L. Morrow, D. Tracey, K. Baker, G. Brooks, J. Cronin, E. Nelson, and D. Wood. 2001. "A Study of Effective First-Grade Reading Instruction." *Scientific Studies of Reading* 5(1): 35–58.

Ratcliff, N. J. 2001/2002. "Using Authentic Assessment to Document the Emerging Literacy Skills of Young Children." *Childhood Education* 78(2): 66–69.

Richgels, D. J. 2002. "Informational Texts in Kindergarten." *The Reading Teacher* 55(6): 586–95.

———. 2001. "Phonemic Awareness." *The Reading Teacher* 55: 274–78.

Robb, L. 2002. "The Myth of Learn to Read/Read to Learn." *Instructor* (May/June): 23–25.

———. 2001. *35 Must-Have Assessment and Record-Keeping Forms for Reading.* New York: Scholastic.

———. 2000a. "Developing Emergent Literacy Skills." *Early Childhood News* 12(6): 34–40.

———. 2000b. *Redefining Staff Development: A Collaborative Model for Teachers and Administrators.* Portsmouth, NH: Heinemann.

———. 2000c. *Teaching Reading in Middle School: A Strategic Approach to Teaching Reading That Improves Comprehension and Thinking.* New York: Scholastic.

———. 1993. "Reading and Writing with At-Risk Students." *The New Advocate* 610: 25–40.

Routman, R. 2002. "Teacher Talk." *Education Leadership* 59(6): 32–35.

———. 2000. *Conversations: Strategies for Teaching, Learning, and Evaluating.* Portsmouth, NH: Heinemann.

———. 1991. *Invitations: Changing as Teachers and Learners, K–12.* Portsmouth, NH: Heinemann.

Santman, D. 2002. "Teaching to the Test? Test Preparation in the Reading Workshop." *Language Arts* 79(3): 203–11.

Schickedanz, J. A. 1998. "What Is Developmentally Appropriate Practice in Early Literacy? Considering the Alphabet." In *Children Achieving: Best Practices in Early Literacy,* edited by S. B. Neuman and K. A. Roskos. Newark, DE: International Reading Association.

Schulman, M. G., and C. D. Payne. 2000. *Guided Reading: Making It Work.* New York: Scholastic.

Schweinhart, L. J. 2002. "How the High/Scope Perry Preschool Study Grew: A Researcher's Tale." *Phi Delta Kappa International Newsletter* 40(3): 7–9.

Shunk, D. H., and B. J. Zimmerman. 1997. "Developing Self-Efficacious Readers and Writers: The Role of Social and Self-Regulatory Processes." In *Reading Engagement: Motivating Readers Through Integrated Instruction,* edited by J. T. Guthrie and A. Wigfield. Newark, DE: International Reading Association.

Slaughter, J. P. 1993. *Beyond Storybooks: Young Children and the Shared Book Experience.* Newark, DE: International Reading Association.

Smith, F. 1988. *Joining the Literacy Club.* Portsmouth, NH: Heinemann.

Smolkin, L. B., and C. A. Donovan. 2001. "The Contexts of Comprehension: The Information Book Read-Aloud, Comprehension Acquisitions, and Comprehension Instruction in a First-Grade Classroom." *The Elementary School Journal* 102(2): 97–122.

Snow, C., S. Burns, and P. Griffin, eds. 1998. *Preventing Reading Difficulties in Young Children.* Washington, DC: National Academy Press.

Snowball, D., and F. Bolton. 1999. *Spelling K–8: Planning and Teaching.* York, ME: Stenhouse.

Strickland, D. S. 1998. *Teaching Phonics Today: A Primer for Educators.* Newark, DE: International Reading Association.

———. 1989. "A Model for Change: Framework for an Emergent Literacy Curriculum." In *Emerging Literacy: Young Children Learn to Read and Write,* edited by D. S. Strickland and L. M. Morrow. Newark, DE: International Reading Association.

Sulzby, E., and W. Teale. 1991. "Emergent Literacy." In *Handbook of Reading Research*, edited by M. L. Kamil, P. B. Mosenthal, P. D. Pearson, and R. Barr, vol. 2, pp. 727–57. New York: Longman.

Taylor, D., and D. S. Strickland. 1986. *Family Storybook Reading*. Portsmouth, NH: Heinemann.

Teale, W. H., and E. Sulzby. 1989. "Emergent Literacy: New Perspectives." In *Emerging Literacy: Young Children Learn to Read and Write*, edited by D. S. Strickland and L. M. Morrow. Newark, DE: International Reading Association.

Turner, J. C. 1997. "Starting Right: Strategies for Engaging Young Literacy Learners." In *Reading Engagement: Motivating Readers Through Integrated Instruction*, edited by J. T. Guthrie and A. Wigfield. Newark, DE: International Reading Association.

Vardell, S. 1998. "Using Read-Alouds to Explore the Layers of Nonfiction." In *Making Facts Come Alive: Choosing Quality Nonfiction Literature, K–8*, edited by R. A. Bamford and J. V. Kristo. Norwood, MA: Christopher-Gordon.

Vygotsky, L. S. 1978. *Mind in Society*. Edited and translated by M. Cole, V. John-Steiner, S. Scribner, and E. Souberman. Cambridge, MA: MIT Press.

———. 1962. *Thought and Language*. Cambridge, MA: MIT Press.

Warner, S. A. [1963] 1986. *Teacher*. New York: Simon and Schuster.

Wells, G. 1986. *The Meaning Makers: Children Learning Language and Using Language to Learn*. Portsmouth, NH: Heinemann.

Wigfield, A. 1997. "Children's Motivations for Reading and Reading Engagement." In *Reading Engagement: Motivating Readers Through Integrated Instruction*, edited by J. T. Guthrie and A. Wigfield. Newark, DE: International Reading Association.

Wilhelm, J. 2003. *Action Strategies for Deepening Comprehension: Role-Plays, Text Structure Tableaux, Talking Statues, and Other Enactment Techniques That Engage Students with Text*. New York: Scholastic.

———. 2000. *Improving Comprehension with Think-Aloud Strategies: Modeling What Good Readers Do*. New York: Scholastic.

———. 1997. *"You Gotta Be the Book": Teaching Engaged and Reflective Reading with Adolescents*. Urbana, IL and New York: National Council of Teachers of English and Teachers College Press.

Yaden, D. B. Jr., and A. Tam. 2000. Enhancing Emergent Literacy in a Preschool Program Through Teacher-Researcher Collaboration. Ciera Report # 2-011, University of Michigan—Ann Arbor.

Yopp, H. K., and R. H. Yopp. 2000. "Supporting Phonemic Awareness Development in the Classroom." *The Reading Teacher* 54: 130–43.

## Children Books Cited

Baker, A. 1994. *White Rabbit's Color Book*. New York: Kingfisher Books.

Berger, M. 1994. *Life in a Coral Reef*. New York: Newbridge.

Blanco, A. 1992. *The Desert Mermaid*. Pictures by P. Revah. San Francisco, CA: Children's Book Press.

Bradley, K. B. 2001. *POP! A Book About Bubbles.* Illus. by M. Miller. New York: HarperCollins.

Branley, F. M. 2000. *The International Space Station.* Illus. by T. Kelley. New York: HarperCollins.

———. [1984] 1999. *Is There Life in Outer Space?* Illus. by E. Miller. New York: HarperCollins.

Brown, M. W. 1989. *Big Red Barn.* Pictures by F. Bond. New York: Harper & Row.

———. 1947. *Goodnight Moon.* Illus. by Clement Hurd. New York: Harper.

Carle, E. 1984. *The Very Busy Spider.* New York: Philomel.

———. 1981. *The Very Hungry Caterpillar.* New York: Philomel.

Catalanotto, P. 2002. *Matthew A.B.C.* New York: Atheneum.

Crews, D. 1998. *Night at the Fair.* New York: Greenwillow.

Degan, B. 2000. *Daddy Is a Doodlebug.* New York: HarperCollins.

Falwel, C. 1993. *Feast for 10.* New York: Clarion.

Flowler, A. 1993. *The Chicken or the Egg?* Chicago, IL: Children's Chicago Press.

Fox, M. 1989. *Night Noises.* Illus. by T. Denton. San Diego, CA: Harcourt, Brace, & Jovanovich.

———. 1988. *Koala Lou.* Illus. by P. Lofts. San Diego, CA: Harcourt, Brace, & Jovanovich.

Grossman, B. 1989. *Tommy at the Grocery Store.* Illus. by V. Chess. New York: Harper & Row.

Hogan, P. Z. 1979. *The Elephant.* Illus. by K. Craft. Milwaukee, WI: Raintree Children's Books.

Hutchins, P. 1992. *Silly Billy!* New York: Greenwillow.

———. 1983. *You'll Soon Grow Into Them, Titch.* New York: Mulberry Big Books.

Keats, E. J. 1971. *Over in the Meadow.* New York: Scholastic.

———. 1962. *The Snowy Day.* New York: Viking.

Kellogg, S. 2000. *The Missing Mitten Mystery.* New York: Dial.

———. 1985. *Chicken Little.* New York: Dial.

Kovalski, M. 1987. *The Wheels on the Bus.* Boston, MA: Joy Street/Little, Brown.

Kraus, R. 1987. *Come Out and Play, Little Mouse.* Illus. by J. Aruego and A. Dewey. New York: Greenwillow.

Kurtz, J., and C. Kurtz. 2002. *Water Hole Waiting.* Pictures by L. Christianson. New York: Greenwillow.

Lowry, L. 1993. *The Giver.* Boston: Houghton Mifflin.

Maynard, J. 1999. *I Know Where My Food Goes.* Cambridge, MA: Candlewick.

Medearis, A. S. 1991. *Dancing with the Indians.* Illus. by S. Byrd. New York: Holiday House.

Mitton, T. 2001. *Down by the Cool of the Pool.* Pictures by G. Parker-Rees. New York: Orchard.

Most, B. 1990. *The Cow That Went Oink.* New York: Harcourt, Brace, & Jovanovich.

Olaleye, I. O. 2000. *In the Rainfield, Who Is the Greatest?* Illus. by A. Grifalcone. New York: Blue Sky.

Pinkney, B. 2000. *Cosmos and the Robot*. New York: Greenwillow.

Pinkney, S. L. 2002. *A Rainbow All Around Me*. Photographs by M. C. Pinkney. New York: HarperCollins.

Radcliffe, T. 1997. *Bashi, Elephant Baby*. Illus. by J. Butler. New York: Puffin.

Rockwell, A. 2001. *Bugs Are Insects*. Illus. by S. Jenkins. New York: HarperCollins.

Rylant, C. 2001. *Scarecrow*. Illus. by L. Stringer. San Diego, CA: Voyager.

Shields, C. D. 2002. *Food Fight!* Pictures by D. Gay-Kassel. New York: Handprint.

Showers, P. [1985] 2001. *What Happens to a Hamburger?* Illus. by E. Miller. New York: HarperCollins.

Simon, S. 2000. *Seymour Simon's Book of Trucks*. New York: HarperCollins.

Weiss, N. 1989. *Where Does the Brown Bear Go?* New York: Viking.

Wells, R. 2001. *McDuff Goes to School*. Illus. by S. Jeffers. New York: Hyperion.

Wells, R. 1973. *Noisy Nora*. New York: Scholastic.

Williams, V. 1983. *Something Special For Me*. New York: Greenwillow.

Wood, A. 1991. *Silly Sally*. New York: Harcourt, Brace, & Jovanovich.

Wood, D. 1990. *The Little Mouse, the Red Ripe Strawberry, and the Big Hungry Bear*. New York: Child's Play.

Woodson, J. 2001. *The Other Side*. Illus. by E. B. Lewis. New York: Putnam.

# Index